Talking About the U.S.A.

Talking About the U.S.A.:

An Active Introduction
to American Culture

Janet Giannotti

Suzanne Mele Szwarcewicz

Prentice Hall Regents
Upper Saddle River, New Jersey 07458

Library of Congress Cataloging-in-Publication Data

Giannotti, Janet.
    Talking about the U.S.A. : an active introduction to American culture /
Janet Giannotti,   Suzanne Mele Szwarcewicz.
      p.   cm.
    ISBN 0-205-15962-1
     1. Readers--United States. 2. United States--Civilization--Problems, exercises, etc.
   3. English language--Textbooks for foreign speakers.   I. Szwarcewicz, Suzanne Mele.
  II. Title.
   PE1127.H5G53   1995   95-21001
   428.6'4--dc20   CIP

Vice President/Editorial Director: *Arley Gray*
Manager of Development Services: *Louisa Hellegers*
Development Editor: *Gino Mastascusa*
Director of Production and Manufacturing: *Aliza Greenblatt*
Executive Managing Editor: *Dominick Mosco*
Editorial/Production Supervision and Design: *Paula Williams, Dit Mosco*
Art Director: *Merle Krumper*
Cover Art and Design: *Paul Polara*
Illustrator: *Don Martinetti*
Manufacturing Manager: *Ray Keating*

Printed in the United States of America
10 9 8 7 6 5 4 3 2 1

ISBN 0-205-15962-1

Prentice-Hall International (UK) Limited, *London*
Prentice-Hall of Australia Pty. Limited, *Sydney*
Prentice-Hall Canada Inc., *Toronto*
Prentice-Hall Hispanoamericana, S.A., *Mexico*
Prentice-Hall of India Private Limited, *New Delhi*
Prentice-Hall of Japan, Inc., *Tokyo*
Simon & Schuster Asia Pte. Ltd., *Singapore*
Editora Prentice-Hall do Brasil, Ltda., *Rio de Janeiro*

CONTENTS

SONGS

Unit 1

Meet the U.S.A.:
An Introduction to
American Geography

CHAPTER ONE

THIS LAND

The United States contains a wide variety of geographic features. In this chapter you will learn the names and locations of some of the most important ones, and you will listen to a song that tells about the country's geographic features.

SHOW WHAT YOU KNOW

Look at the map on page 3.

What countries do you see?
What oceans are there?
Can you say the name of any of the mountains, lakes, rivers, or cities marked on the map?

Tell your classmates about what parts of the United States you have visited.

FOCUS ON CONTENT: GEOGRAPHIC FEATURES

In this section you will hear a short lecture about U.S. geography. You will learn about the borders of the country and some geographic features such as rivers, lakes, and mountains. You will also learn about some cities and states.

Vocabulary 📼

The following words are important in the lecture. Listen to the cassette and complete the sentences with words from the box.

range	census	center	located
population `	border	major	flows

1. The _____ of the United States is about 250 million.
2. Kansas is in the _____, or middle, of the United States.
3. The line between two countries is the _____.
4. In a _____, the government counts the people in a country.
5. A mountain _____ is a group of mountains, such as the Rockies.
6. The Mississippi River system is a _____, important river system.
7. The Great Lakes are _____ on the border with Canada.
8. The Missouri River _____ into the Mississippi.

Listen and Write 📼

Listen to the lecture as many times as you need to in order to fill in the blanks on and around the map on this page. Use the information in the box.

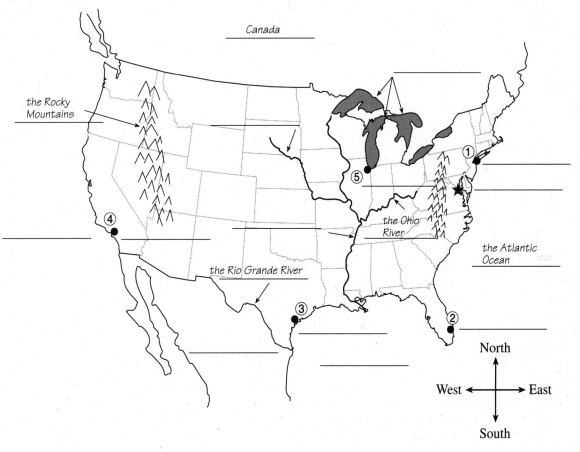

Canada

the Rocky
Mountains

the Ohio
River

the Rio Grande River

the Atlantic
Ocean

North

West ←——→ East

South

Alaska	Hawaii	New York
the Appalachian Mountains	Houston	the Ohio River
the Atlantic Ocean	Los Angeles	the Pacific Ocean
Canada	Mexico	the Rio Grande River
Chicago	Miami	the Rocky Mountains
the Great Lakes	the Mississippi River	the United States of America
the Gulf of Mexico	the Missouri River	Washington, D.C.

Full name of the country: _____

Number of states: _____

Two states you can't see here: _____

_____

Population: _____

Listen and Choose 📼

Listen to the questions on the cassette and circle the letter of the best answer.

1. a. the Pacific Ocean
    b. the Atlantic Ocean
    c. the Arctic Ocean

2. a. Lake Michigan
    b. Great Salt Lake
    c. Lake Ontario

3. a. the Ohio River
    b. the Missouri River
    c. the Colorado River

4. a. the Appalachian Mountains
    b. the Adirondack Mountains
    c. the Rocky Mountains

5. a. fifty
    b. forty-eight
    c. fifty-two

6. a. Alaska
    b. Hawaii
    c. Texas

7. a. in the Atlantic Ocean
    b. near Canada
    c. in the Pacific Ocean

8. a. 249,000,000
    b. 249,000,000,000
    c. 29,000,000

Read and Decide

Read each statement and decide if it is true or false. Write T *or* F *on the line.*

1. _____ Canada is to the south of the United States.
2. _____ The Appalachian Mountains are in the West.
3. _____ The Great Lakes are on the border between the United States and Canada.
4. _____ The Rocky Mountains are higher than the Appalachian Mountains.
5. _____ There are seven Great Lakes.
6. _____ Alaska and Hawaii are the two newest states.
7. _____ The Rio Grande River forms part of the border between the United States and Canada.
8. _____ Washington, D.C. is in Maryland.
9. _____ The Missouri River flows into the Mississippi River.
10. _____ The United States government conducted a census in 1990.

Talk About This!

Which of the following geographic features described in the lecture have you seen? Which other features have you seen? Circle items and fill in names below and then share your answers with your classmates.

I have seen . . .   I saw it when I visited . . .

Rivers	Mountains	Lakes	Oceans, Other Water
the Mississippi River	the Appalachian Mountains	the Great Lakes	the Atlantic Ocean
the Ohio River	the Rocky Mountains	Lake Michigan	the Pacific Ocean
the Rio Grande River	Cadillac Mountain	Lake Erie	the Gulf of Mexico
the Missouri River	Mount Ranier	Great Salt Lake	the _____
the _____	_____	_____	

FOCUS ON SKILLS: USING *THE* AND *BE/DO*

In this section you will practice using *the* and work with *be* and *do*.

When you talk about geographic place names, sometimes you use *the,* and sometimes you don't.

Use *the*	Don't use *the*
Countries with Union, United, or Republic in the name, or plural country names. Example: *the* United States	All other country names, names of cities, and states. Example: Canada
Groups of mountains or lakes (plurals). Example: *the* Rocky Mountains	Single mountains or lakes. Example: Cadillac Mountain
Bodies of water other than lakes (rivers, oceans, etc.). Example: *the* Mississippi River	Lakes. Example: Lake Michigan

Practice

Write the *or X in the blanks.*

1. _____ United States is bordered on the north by _____ Canada, and on the south by _____ Mexico and _____ Gulf of Mexico.
2. _____ Mount McKinley, in _____ Alaska, is the tallest mountain in _____ United States.
3. _____ Appalachian Mountains are lower than _____ Rocky Mountains.
4. _____ United States is bordered on the east by _____ Atlantic Ocean and on the west by _____ Pacific Ocean.
5. _____ In the middle of the country, you can find _____ Mississippi River, _____ Missouri River, and _____ Ohio River.
6. _____ Dominican Republic and _____ Haiti are to the southeast of Florida.
7. _____ Finger Lakes are in _____ New York State.
8. _____ Lake Michigan and _____ Lake Ontario are two of _____ Great Lakes.
9. _____ Shenandoah Mountains are in _____ Virginia.
10. _____ Potomac River flows through _____ Washington, D.C.

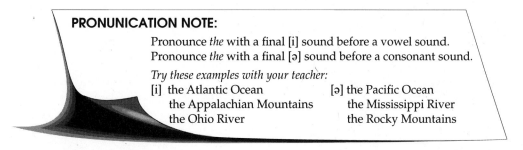

PRONUNICATION NOTE:

Pronounce *the* with a final [i] sound before a vowel sound.
Pronounce *the* with a final [ə] sound before a consonant sound.

Try these examples with your teacher:

[i] the Atlantic Ocean   [ə] the Pacific Ocean
    the Appalachian Mountains   the Mississippi River
    the Ohio River   the Rocky Mountains

Speak, Listen, and Choose

In this exercise, you and a partner will take turns asking and answering questions about U.S. geography. Look back at your notes on page 3 if you can't remember an answer. Circle the letter of the best answer and fill in the word the *if necessary. When you finish, check your answers with your teacher.*

Follow this example:

Student A asks first: What country is to the
                             north of the U.S.A.?

Student B responds: Canada
    and circles *a*.

Student B then asks: What ocean is to the west of
                           the United States?

Student A answers: *The* Pacific Ocean.
    and circles *b*, **filling**
    in *the*.

Student A: *Look here and cover the right side of this page. You start by asking the first question.*

1. What country is to the north of the U.S.?

2. a. _____ Atlantic Ocean
   (b.) _The_ Pacific Ocean
3. What body of water is to the south?

4. a. _____ Great Lakes
   b. _____ Rio Grande River
5. Which river flows into the Mississippi?

6. a. _____ Appalachians
   b. _____ Rockies
7. Which is the largest state?

8. a. _____ Hawaii
   b. _____ California
9. Where is Hawaii?

10. a. _____ Washington, D.C.
    b. _____ New York City

Student B: *Look here and cover the left side of this page.*

1. (a.) _____ Canada
   b. _____ Mexico
2. What ocean is to the west of the United States?

3. a. _____ Gulf of Mexico
   b. _____ Pacific Ocean
4. What is on the border between the U.S.A. and Canada?

5. a. _____ Colorado River
   b. _____ Missouri River
6. Which mountain range is in the East?

7. a. _____ Texas
   b. _____ Alaska
8. Which state is the newest?

9. a. in _____ Pacific Ocean
   b. in _____ Atlantic Ocean
10. What is the capital of the United States?

Talk About This!

In this activity, you are going to share the names of important geographical features in your country with your classmates. Fill in the chart on page 7 with examples from your country or near your country.

After you have filled in examples from your country, get together with a partner and share your information. Fill in the information about your partner's country.

When your chart is complete, share what you learned with your classmates.

FEATURE	THE U.S.A.	YOUR COUNTRY	YOUR PARTNER'S COUNTRY
Full name of the country	the United States of America		
An ocean or a sea	the Atlantic Ocean		
A river	the Mississippi River		
A lake	Lake Michigan		
A mountain chain	the Rocky Mountains		
A mountain	Mount Rainier		
The capital city	Washington, D.C.		
Another city	Los Angeles		

Present Tense Sentence Combinations

You can use forms of *be* and *do* in the present tense to describe geographic features.

be	do
Use *is/isn't* and *are/aren't* before nouns, adjectives, and prepositional phrases.	Use *doesn't/don't* before verbs in negative statements.
Puerto Rico *isn't* a state. (**N**) Rhode Island *is* very small. (**ADJ**) New York *is* in the Northeast. (**PREP. PHRASE**)	Hawaii *doesn't* have a border with any other states. (**V**)

Work with your classmates to combine the following into sentences about the geography of the United States. Check your answers with your teacher.

Example: Mexico isn't to the north of the U.S.A.

The Great Lakes		important cities.
Alaska and Hawaii		in the Pacific Ocean.
The Pacific Ocean		have large populations.
Canada		the two newest states.
Alaska	is	very high.
Mexico	isn't	in the West.
Wyoming and Montana	are	have much commercial traffic.
Hawaii	aren't	share a border with any other state.
The Atlantic Ocean	don't	to the east of the U.S.A.
Texas	doesn't	the largest state.
The Rocky Mountains		include Great Salt Lake.
The Potomac River		to the north of the U.S.A.
New York and Los Angeles		on the border with Canada.
The Appalachian Mountains		
Portland and Springfield		

ong

"This Land Is Your Land" *Words and music by Woody Guthrie*

Woody Guthrie was one of the great folk singers and songwriters of the twentieth century in the United States. **"This Land Is Your Land"** is about the beautiful geographic features of the United States.

Listen and Write

Listen to the song and fill in the missing words below:

Chorus: This land is your land, this land is my land,
From California to the New York island,
From the redwood forest to the Gulf Stream waters;
This land was made for you and me.

1.   As I was _____ that ribbon of highway,
I saw above me that endless skyway;
I saw _____ me that golden valley;
This land was made for you and me.

Chorus: This land is your land, this land is my land,
From _____ to the New York island,
From the redwood forest to the Gulf Stream waters;
This land was _____ for you and me.

2.   I've roamed and rambled, and I _____ my footsteps
To the sparkling sands of her diamond deserts;
And all around me a _____ was sounding;
This land was made for you and me.

Chorus: This land is your _____, this land is my land,
From California to the New York island,
From the redwood forest to the Gulf Stream _____;
This land was made for you and me.

3.   When the sun came _____, and I was strolling,
And the wheat fields waving and the dust clouds rolling,
As the fog was lifting, a voice was chanting:
This _____ was made for you and me.

Chorus: This land is your land, this land is my land,
From California to the New York _____,
From the redwood forest to the Gulf Stream waters;
This land was _____ for you and me.

Talk About the Song

1. Study the vocabulary.

Find a word in	that means	and write it here:
the Chorus	a type of tree	_____
Verse 1	low place between two mountains	_____
Verse 2	walked without purpose	_____ and _____
Verse 2	shining	_____
Verse 2	dry areas	_____
Verse 3	walking without purpose	_____

2. What are some geographic features that Woody Guthrie mentions in the song? What parts of the country are those geographical features in?

8   Talking About the U.S.A.

PUT IT TOGETHER

Find Someone Who . . .

Find out where your classmates' homes are in their countries. Use questions beginning with Do you live . . . *to find someone who says* yes *for each of the items on the left. Then write the person's name in the space.*
Example: *Do you live in the capital of your country?*

Find someone who lives . . .

near the Atlantic Ocean.

in the capital of his/her country.

near a large mountain range. (Which one?)

near the Pacific Ocean.

near an important river. (Which one?)

in the largest city in his/her country.

near a lake.

on an island.

Write that person's name here:

_____

_____

_____

_____

_____

_____

_____

_____

Cloze 🔲

Read the following information about the United States. Fill in as many words as you can remember. After you have filled in as much as you can, listen to the lecture on the cassette again as many times as necessary to fill in all the blanks.

The country in the center of this map is _____ United States of America. It is located on the continent of _____ America. Let's look at the borders of the country first. The United States has borders with just _____ other countries. The country to the north of the United States is _____. Mexico is to the _____.

Many important bodies of water are located in and around the United States. The Atlantic Ocean is to the _____ of the United States, and the _____ Ocean is to the west. To the south, next to Mexico, is the Gulf of Mexico. The largest group of _____ in the world is located on the border between the United States and Canada, in the eastern half of the country. These are called the _____ Lakes, and there are five of them: Michigan, Erie, Superior, Huron, and Ontario. In the southwestern part of the United States is the Rio Grande River. It forms part of the _____ with Mexico. The most important _____ in the country, the Mississippi River, flows through the _____ of the country, from near the Great Lakes to the Gulf of Mexico. It is part of a large river system including the _____ River, which flows in from the west, and the Ohio River, which flows in from the _____.

While the center of the United States is quite flat, there are _____ mountain ranges in the West and in the _____. In the West are the _____ Mountains. They are a younger, higher range with many sharp, snow-capped peaks. The Appalachian _____ are in the East. They are an older, lower range, and they look rounded and very green.

The United States is divided into _____ states. Forty-eight states are on the map here. The two _____ states, Alaska and Hawaii, are separated from these forty-eight. Alaska, the _____ state, is to the northwest, bordering on Canada. Hawaii is a group of islands in the _____ Ocean, to the southwest of the continental United States.

Some of the important cities in the United States are marked on the map. Look for the star. The star represents Washington, D.C., the _____ of the United States. Washington, D.C. is a federal district, located _____ the states of Maryland and Virginia in the middle of the east Coast. Other important cities are represented on the map by circles. They include New York, in the Northeast, _____, in the Southeast, Houston in Texas near the Gulf of Mexico, Los Angeles on the West Coast, in California and _____ in the North, on Lake Michigan, one of the Great Lakes.

The government of the United States counts the population every ten years in a _____. According to the 1990 census, the _____ of the United States is about 249,000,000.

The United States is divided into fifty states. In this chapter you will learn how to pronounce the names of the states, and you will learn the locations of many of them.

SHOW WHAT YOU KNOW

Look at the map of the United States below, and answer these questions with your classmates.

Find the state where you are living and studying now.
Identify as many other states as you can.
Can you see
California?
Texas?
Florida?
Hawaii?

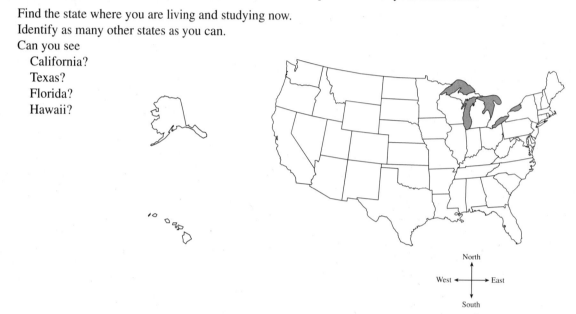

North
West ← → East
South

FOCUS ON SKILLS: PRONOUNCING STATE NAMES

In this section you will learn how to pronounce the names of the states. You will also learn about the origins of some of the names.

Pronunciation 📼

Study the information in the box. Then practice the pronunciation of the names below while listening to the cassette.

When a vowel is unstressed, the pronunciation is [ə], as in *but*.				
Alabama	Alaska	Arizona	California	Colorado
Connecticut	Delaware	Florida	Georgia	Montana
Nebraska	Nevada	Oklahoma	Oregon	Texas

The final *nia* sound is pronounced like "nya."			
California	Pennsylvania	Virginia	West Virginia

The sounds *z, s,* and *ss* are pronounced like [z] in these state names:			
Arizona	Louisiana	Missouri	New Jersey

Stress occurs on different syllables in different words. Notice the stress placement in these state names:				
Idaho	Iowa	Ohio	Tennessee	Vermont

Warning! You don't always pronounce the way you spell. Here are some tricky ones.	
Arkansas: pronounce *sas* like "saw"	Illinois: has no final [s]
Rhode Island: there is no [s] in Island [ailënd]	Connecticut: there is no [k] before the first [t]

Listen and repeat

Alabama	Indiana	Nebraska	South Carolina
Alaska	Iowa	Nevada	South Dakota
Arizona	Kansas	New Hampshire	Tennessee
Arkansas	Kentucky	New Jersey	Texas
California	Louisiana	New Mexico	Utah
Colorado	Maine	New York	Vermont
Connecticut	Maryland	North Carolina	Virginia
Delaware	Massachusetts	North Dakota	Washington
Florida	Michigan	Ohio	West Virginia
Georgia	Minnesota	Oklahoma	Wisconsin
Hawaii	Missouri	Oregon	Wyoming
Idaho	Mississippi	Pennsylvania	
Illinois	Montana	Rhode Island	

Matching

Many state names come from American Indian languages. Others come from Spanish, British English, and French.

Work with your classmates to match the state names with their origins. Write the letter of each answer on the line. Check your answers with your teacher.

1. Mississippi _____ a. means "flowery"—from Spanish.
2. Virginia _____ b. means "great water" (*mici gama*) in Chippewa, an American Indian language.
3. Florida _____ c. was named for Queen Henrietta *Maria* of England.
4. Michigan _____ d. means "great river" (*mici zibi*) in Chippewa, an American Indian language.
5. Maryland _____ e. means "big hill"—from Algonquian, an American Indian language.
6. Massachusetts _____ f. was named for the "*virgin*" queen, Elizabeth I of England.

Look at the state names below and try to guess whether they come from British English, Spanish, French, or an American Indian language. Work with your classmates to write the names in the appropriate spaces in the chart. Check your answers with your teacher.

Colorado	New Hampshire	Montana	Louisiana	Tennessee	New Jersey
Vermont	Connecticut	Washington	Nevada	Georgia	Wyoming

British English	Spanish	French	American Indian
_____	_____	_____	_____
_____	_____	_____	_____
_____	_____	_____	_____
_____	_____	_____	_____

Talk About This!

Is your country divided into states or provinces? Tell your classmates about your country.

FOCUS ON CONTENT: STATE LOCATIONS

In this section you will learn the locations of the states.

Look at the map below and study these examples.

California is to the west of Nevada.
Idaho is to the east of Washington and Oregon.

Listen and Decide 📼

Look at the locations of the western states on the map, and listen to the statements on the cassette. Circle TRUE *or* FALSE.

1.	TRUE	FALSE		6.	TRUE	FALSE
2.	TRUE	FALSE		7.	TRUE	FALSE
3.	TRUE	FALSE		8.	TRUE	FALSE
4.	TRUE	FALSE		9.	TRUE	FALSE
5.	TRUE	FALSE		10.	TRUE	FALSE

Listen and Write 📼

Now listen to the cassette to learn the locations of these western and southern states. Write the names of the states on the map.

Montana	Wyoming	Colorado	New Mexico	Texas
Oklahoma	Arkansas	Louisiana	Mississippi	Alabama

Speak, Listen, and Change

When you describe locations, the prepositional phrase can go at the beginning or the end of the sentence. Study the word order. Each pair of sentences has the same meaning.

Washington is to the north of Oregon.
To the north of Oregon is Washington.

Arizona is to the south of Utah.
To the south of Utah is Arizona.

You and a partner will practice describing the locations of the states in two different ways.
Your partner will read a sentence with the prepositional phrase in one place. You should respond by changing the order. Some words are written in to help you.

Follow this example:

Student A says:	Montana is to the north of Wyoming.
Student B responds:	To the north of Wyoming is Montana.
Student B then says:	Nevada is to the west of Utah.
Student A says:	To the west of Utah is Nevada.

Student A: *Look here and cover the right side of the page. You start by reading the first sentence aloud.*

1. Montana is to the north of Wyoming.
2. To the _____ of _____ is _____.
3. Colorado is to the east of Utah.
4. To the _____ of _____ is _____.
5. New Mexico is to the south of Colorado.
6. To the _____ of _____ is _____.
7. Oklahoma is to the north of Texas.
8. To the _____ of _____ is _____.
9. Nevada is to the east of California.
10. To the _____ of _____ is _____.
11. Wyoming is to the south of Montana.
12. To the _____ of _____ is _____.

Student B: *Look here and cover the left side of the page.*

1. To the _____ of _____ is _____.
2. Nevada is to the west of Utah.
3. To the _____ of _____ is _____.
4. Arizona is to the west of New Mexico.
5. To the _____ of _____ is _____.
6. Colorado is to the south of Wyoming.
7. To the _____ of _____ is _____.
8. Louisiana is to the east of Texas.
9. To the _____ of _____ is _____.
10. Colorado is the north of New Mexico.
11. To the _____ of _____ is _____.
12. Oregon is to the south of Washington.

Speak, Listen, and Decide

You and a partner will take turns reading statements about the locations of some western and southern states and deciding if they are TRUE or FALSE. Refer to the map on page 12 if you can't remember the locations. When you finish the exercise, check your answers with your teacher.

Follow this example:

Student A reads: Washington is to the north of Oregon.
Student B responds: That's true.
  and circles TRUE.
Student B reads: Nevada is to the east of Utah.
Student A responds: That's false.
  and circles FALSE.

Student A: *Look here and cover the right side of the page.*

1. Washington is to the north of Oregon.
2. TRUE   FALSE
3. Arizona is to the south of Utah.
4. TRUE   FALSE
5. Texas is to the north of Oklahoma.
6. TRUE   FALSE
7. To the west of Idaho is Wyoming.
8. TRUE   FALSE
9. Mississippi is to the east of Louisiana.
10. TRUE   FALSE
11. To the east of Nevada is California.
12. TRUE   FALSE

Student B: *Look here and cover the left side of the page.*

1. TRUE   FALSE
2. Nevada is to the east of Utah.
3. TRUE   FALSE
4. Alabama is to the east of Mississippi.
5. TRUE   FALSE
6. To the south of California is Oregon.
7. TRUE   FALSE
8. Arkansas is to the north of Louisiana.
9. TRUE   FALSE
10. New Mexico is east of Arizona.
11. TRUE   FALSE
12. To the west of Oklahoma is Arkansas.

Speak, Listen, and Write

In this activity you and a partner will take turns describing the location of the states you have on your map. Both maps have the states that are written in italics, and each map has more states that you will describe. Student A will describe his/her map first; then student B will talk. Write the name of the state your partner describes in the correct space. When you finish, check your answers by looking at your partner's map.

Follow this example:

Student A asks: Do you see Missouri?
Student B responds: Yes.

Student A then says: Iowa is to the north of Missouri.
Student B writes *Iowa* in the space to the north of Missouri.

Student A: *Look at this map and cover the other map.*

Student B: *Look at this map and cover the other map.*

FOCUS ON SKILLS: PRONOUNCING LETTERS IN ABBREVIATIONS

In this section you will learn about postal abbreviations for the states while you practice saying the letters of the English alphabet.

Each state has a postal abbreviation of two letters that you should use when you address an envelope.

For example:

The abbreviation for Massachusetts is MA.
The abbreviation for Maine is ME.
The abbreviation for Michigan is MI.

If you want information about Massachusetts, write a letter to the tourism office and address your envelope like this:

Massachusetts Office of Travel & Tourism
100 Cambridge Street, 13th Floor
Boston, MA 02202

FACTS NOTE:
Use *Postal Abbreviations* and *ZIP Codes* on all your letters. You don't have to memorize them. Ask someone at the post office to help you find the abbreviation and ZIP code you need.

PRONUNCIATION

Practice the pronunciation of the names of the letters in the English alphabet. Repeat after your teacher and practice with your classmates.

VOWELS:	a	e	i	o	u			
CONSONANTS:	b	v		p	f	c	z	s
	d	t		g	j	h	k	q
	l	r		m	n	w	x	y

Speak, Listen, and Write

In this exercise you will practice saying and writing the postal abbreviations for some of the states. You have half of the information, and your partner has the other half. Ask and answer questions so that you and your partner can complete the charts below. When you are finished, check your answers by comparing your chart with your partner's chart.

Follow this example:

Student A asks: What's the abbreviation for Arizona?
Student B responds: It's AZ.
Student A writes *AZ* in the space next to Arizona.

Student B then asks: What's the abbreviation for Connecticut?
Student A responds: It's CT.
Student B writes *CT* in the space next to Connecticut.

Student A: *Look at this chart and cover the other chart.*

Arizona		Kentucky	
Connecticut	CT	Louisiana	LA
Delaware		Montana	
Georgia	GA	Nebraska	NE
Hawaii		Nevada	
Idaho	ID	Pennsylvania	PA
Illinois		Vermont	
Iowa	IA	West Virginia	WV

Student B: *Look here and cover the other chart.*

Arizona	AZ	Kentucky	KY
Connecticut		Louisiana	
Delaware	DE	Montana	MT
Georgia		Nebraska	
Hawaii	HI	Nevada	NV
Idaho		Pennsylvania	
Illinois	IL	Vermont	VT
Iowa		West Virginia	

Find Your Partner

In this activity you will practice saying postal abbreviations and state names. Your teacher will prepare pairs of cards. Write the name of a state on one card and the postal abbreviation on the other, using the list below. Each member of the class receives one card (either a state or an abbreviation). Students stand up and move around, saying their state names and abbreviations, until each student finds his or her match and stands with that person. Repeat the game with more pairs.

Alabama	AL	Missouri	MO	Rhode Island	RI
Alaska	AK	New Hampshire	NH	South Carolina	SC
Arkansas	AR	New Jersey	NJ	South Dakota	SD
California	CA	New Mexico	NM	Tennessee	TN
Colorado	CO	New York	NY	Texas	TX
Florida	FL	North Carolina	NC	Utah	UT
Indiana	IN	North Dakota	ND	Virginia	VA
Kansas	KS	Ohio	OH	Washington	WA
Maryland	MD	Oklahoma	OK	Wisconsin	WI
Minnesota	MN	Oregon	OR	Wyoming	WY

PUT IT TOGETHER

Word Search Puzzle

Find the names of 20 states in the puzzle. They can be horizontal or vertical.

A	L	A	S	K	A	A	N	E	R	L	A	N	V
L	R	L	R	A	R	R	K	E	I	K	T	O	E
A	S	N	C	S	B	I	A	M	F	S	E	S	R
B	L	T	I	T	A	Z	N	T	L	S	L	P	M
A	V	S	O	N	R	O	S	E	O	H	I	O	O
M	I	Y	W	L	I	N	A	O	R	E	G	O	N
A	R	K	A	N	S	A	S	R	I	H	N	R	T
I	G	E	D	L	E	H	A	I	D	A	H	O	W
N	I	N	E	B	R	A	S	K	A	W	T	N	Y
D	N	T	N	E	M	G	L	T	S	A	E	E	O
I	I	U	F	A	A	I	A	E	R	I	X	V	M
A	A	C	A	L	I	F	O	R	N	I	A	A	I
N	A	K	E	T	N	J	T	W	I	V	S	D	N
A	X	Y	N	L	E	G	E	O	R	G	I	A	G

Hangman

Play Hangman with state names. One person draws a gallows on the blackboard and writes blanks near it equal to the number of letters in a state name. Guess the name of the state by asking for letters. Ask "Is there a/an _____?" If your guess is correct, the letter will be written in the blank. If your guess is wrong, part of the "man" will be hanged. Play until you draw a head, a body, two arms, and two legs.

Map Race

Work in groups. Use the information in this chapter to fill in the names of all 50 states on this map. Check your answers with your teacher. The first group to fill in the whole map correctly is the winner.

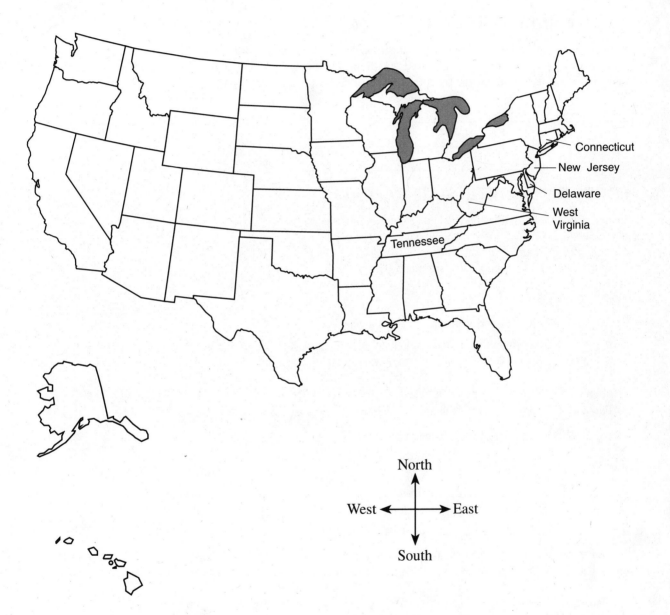

Connecticut

New Jersey

Delaware

West Virginia

Tennessee

North

West ◄———► East

South

CHAPTER THREE

CITIES BIG AND SMALL

There are many cities in the United States, including world-famous cities such as New York and Los Angeles and smaller, but still important cities. In this chapter you will learn about state capitals and large, important cities. You will practice saying the time when you study about the time zones of the United States.

SHOW WHAT YOU KNOW

A city can be important for many reasons. It can be the capital of a state or the country. It can be important for business or industry. Or it can be a tourist destination. Work with your classmates to list twelve important cities in the United States. Why do you think the cities you chose are important?

_____   _____   _____   _____

_____   _____   _____   _____

_____   _____   _____   _____

FOCUS ON CONTENT: STATE CAPITALS

In this section you will learn about state capitals and their populations. Each state in the United States has a capital city. The capital city is the center of the government of that state.

Look for a star (★) on a map if you are looking for a capital.

Look and Write

Sometimes, but not often, the state capital is also the largest city in the state.

Each city in this box is not only a state capital, but also the largest city in its state. Use a map of the United States and work in groups to write the names of the capital cities next to the states below.

| Columbia | Denver | Salt Lake City | Des Moines | Phoenix | Little Rock |
| Atlanta | Honolulu | Oklahoma City | Indianapolis | Providence | Boston |

1. _____, Hawaii   7. _____, Utah

2. _____, Indiana   8. _____, Arkansas

3. _____, Georgia   9. _____, Iowa

4. _____, Arizona   10. _____, Massachusetts

5. _____, Oklahoma   11. _____, Rhode Island

6. _____, Colorado   12. _____, South Carolina

Very often the state capital is not the largest or most important city in the state. The cities in this box are smaller cities that are capitals. Continue working in groups to write the name of the city next to the state.

| Tallahassee | Albany | Annapolis | Sacramento |
| Harrisburg | Springfield | Austin | Olympia |

1. _____, New York   5. _____, Illinois

2. _____, California   6. _____, Pennsylvania

3. _____, Texas   7. _____, Maryland

4. _____, Florida   8. _____, Washington

Pronunciation 📼

Practice the pronunciation of these numbers while listening to the cassette.

100	one hundred
202	two hundred two
340	three hundred forty
415	four hundred fifteen
765	seven hundred sixty-five
5,963	five thousand nine hundred sixty-three
7,210	seven thousand two hundred ten
9,406	nine thousand four hundred six
68,600	sixty-eight thousand six hundred
54,017	fifty-four thousand seventeen
92,333	ninety-two thousand three hundred thirty-three
165,080	one hundred sixty-five thousand eighty
952,478	nine hundred fifty two thousand four hundred seventy-eight
1,500,000	one million five hundred thousand

Speak, Listen, and Write

Study these sentences:

Juneau is the capital of *Alaska*. Its population is *26,751*.
Montgomery is the capital of *Alabama*. Its population is *187,543*.

In this exercise you will practice saying and writing the populations for some state capitals. You have half of the information and your partner has the other half. Work back and forth so that you and your partner can complete your charts. When you have finished, check your answers by looking at your partner's chart.

Follow this example:

Student A says: Tell me about Dover.
Student B responds: Dover is the capital of Delaware. Its population is 27,630.
Student A fills in *Delaware* and *27,630*.

Student B then says: Tell me about Boise.
Student A responds: Boise is the capital of Idaho. Its population is 125,551.
Student B fills in *Idaho* and *125,551*.

Student A: *Look at this chart and cover the other chart.*

CAPITAL	STATE	POPULATION
Dover		
Boise (boi-zi)	Idaho	125,551
Topeka (tə-pi-kə)		
Augusta	Maine	21,325
Helena		
Columbus	Ohio	565,032
Nashville		
Cheyenne (šai-æn)	Wyoming	50,008
Lincoln		
Carson City	Nevada	40,443
Trenton		
Raleigh (ra-li)	North Carolina	212,050
Santa Fe (sæn-tə-fei)		
Bismarck	North Dakota	49,272

Student B: *Look at this chart and cover the other chart.*

CAPITAL	STATE	POPULATION
Dover	Delaware	27,630
Boise (boi-zi)		
Topeka (tə-pi-kə)	Kansas	119,883
Augusta		
Helena	Montana	24,609
Columbus		
Nashville	Tennessee	488,374
Cheyenne (šai-æn)		
Lincoln	Nebraska	191,972
Carson City		
Trenton	New Jersey	88,675
Raleigh (ra-li)		
Santa Fe (sæn-tə fei)	New Mexico	56,537
Bismarck		

Talk About This!

The capital of California is Sacramento, but the most important city in California is Los Angeles. The capital of the United States is Washington, D.C. but at the time that was chosen, New York, Philadelphia, and Boston were the most important cities in the country.

Why do you think people choose to put capitals in smaller, less important cities? Why do you think Washington, D.C. was chosen to be the capital of the original 13 states?

What is the capital of your country? Of your province or state? Is the capital also the most important city? Can you think of an example of a country in which the capital isn't the most important city?

Work with your classmates to decide on advantages and disadvantages of having the capital in a small city or a large city.

Small, Less Important City

Advantages:

_____   _____

Disadvantages:

_____   _____

Large, Important City

Advantages:

_____   _____

Disadvantages:

_____   _____

FOCUS ON CONTENT: OTHER LARGE CITIES

In this section you will learn about the ten largest metropolitan areas and other large cities in the United States.

Listen and Write 📼

Here is a list of the 10 largest metropolitan areas in the United States. Listen to the cassette and fill in their populations. Then, look at the map below and work with your classmates and your teacher to write the number of the metropolitan area in the correct circle.

1. New York City, including northern New Jersey and Long Island: _____
2. Los Angeles, California, including Riverside and Orange County: _____
3. Chicago, Illinois, including Gary, Indiana, and Kenosha, Wisconsin: _____
4. Washington, D.C. and Baltimore, Maryland: _____
5. San Francisco, California, including Oakland and San Jose: _____
6. Philadelphia, Pennsylvania, including Wilmington, Delaware, and Atlantic City, New Jersey: _____
7. Boston, Massachusetts, including Brockton, Massachusetts, and Nashua, New Hampshire: _____
8. Detroit, Michigan, including Ann Arbor and Flint: _____
9. Dallas and Fort Worth, Texas: _____
10. Houston and Galveston, Texas: _____

Matching

Look at the cities in the box. Work with your classmates to match the city with the state. Write the name of the city in the correct state on the map.

Seattle	San Diego	Phoenix	New Orleans	San Antonio
Denver	Atlanta	Memphis	Minneapolis	Baltimore
Albuquerque	Las Vegas	Pittsburgh	Milwaukee	Miami

Talk About This!

1. What is the population of your country? _____

   What is the population of your city or the capital of your country? _____

   Compare the populations from your country with your classmates and with the populations above.

2. Where do more people live in your country: in rural areas and small towns, or in urban areas and large cities? There are advantages and disadvantages to both. Work with a small group to fill in your ideas below. When you finish, share what your group decided with the class.

Living in Rural Areas /Small Towns:	
Advantages:	Disadvantages:
_____	_____
_____	_____
_____	_____

Living in Urban Areas /Large Cities:	
Advantages:	Disadvantages:
_____	_____
_____	_____
_____	_____

FACTS NOTE:

Many people in the United States live in large metropolitan areas. A metropolitan area can include one or more cities and each city's suburbs. There are 40 metropolitan areas in the United States with populations of at least 1,000,000 people; 51% of the population of the United States lives in these 40 metropolitan areas.

Concentration

Play Concentration to help you memorize the locations of the cities in the United States. Here is how to play: Get packets of 12 index cards, or cut paper into 12 equal pieces. Write the city–state combinations below on the cards, a city on one card and a state on another. Mix up the cards. Put them face down on a table or on the floor. Play in groups of 3 or 4. Take turns turning up two cards. Try to match the city and the state. If you don't make a match, turn the cards back over. If you make a match, you keep the cards and have another turn.

CAPITALS	10 LARGEST CITIES	OTHER CITIES
Phoenix, Arizona	Chicago, Illinois	Miami, Florida
Denver, Colorado	Dallas, Texas	Tucson, Arizona
Atlanta, Georgia	Detroit, Michigan	San Diego, California
Albany, New York	Philadelphia, Pennsylvania	Memphis, Tennessee
Madison, Wisconsin	San Francisco, California	St. Louis, Missouri
Hartford, Connecticut	Boston, Massachusetts	Las Vegas, Nevada

Continue playing with more sets of six cities and states.

FOCUS ON CONTENT: TIME ZONES

In this section you will learn about the time zones in the continental United States. You will practice saying the time while remembering the locations of the cities you learned about in this chapter.

Listen and Write

There are four time zones in the continental United States. Listen to the cassette and fill in the time zones and times on this map:

Eastern

Time

4:00

> **FACTS NOTE:**
> From October to April, the time is called Standard Time. From April to October, the time is one hour later and is called Daylight Savings Time.

Listen and Choose

Look at the map above. Listen to the statements and questions on the cassette. Circle the letter of the best answer and write the time.

1. a. It's 3 hours later.
    b. It's 3 hours earlier.
    c. It's 4 hours earlier.
    Time in San Francisco, California: _____

2. a. It's 2 hours later.
    b. It's 2 hours earlier.
    c. It's 3 hours earlier.
    Time in Houston, Texas: _____

3. a. Central Time
    b. Mountain Time
    c. Pacific Time

4. a. It's 1 hour later.
    b. It's 1 hour earlier.
    c. It's the same time.
    Time in Philadelphia, Pennsylvania: _____

5. a. It's 1 hour later.
    b. It's 1 hour earlier.
    c. It's the same time.
    Time in Phoenix, Arizona: _____

6. a. Eastern Time
    b. Mountain Time
    c. Pacific Time

7. a. It's 1 hour later.
    b. It's 1 hour earlier.
    c. It's the same time.
    Time in Denver, Colorado: _____

8. a. It's 3 hours earlier.
    b. It's 3 hours later.
    c. It's 4 hours later.
    Time in Atlantic City, New Jersey: _____

9. a. It's 1 hour earlier.
    b. It's 1 hour later.
    c. It's the same time.
    Time in Oklahoma City, Oklahoma: _____

10. a. It's 1 hour later.
    b. It's 2 hours later.
    c. It's the same time.
    Time in Toledo, Ohio: _____

Speak, Listen, and Decide

Study the different forms of saying the time in English:

| eight oh five | four fifteen | nine thirty | seven forty-five | two fifty |
| five past eight | quarter past four | half past nine | quarter to eight | ten to three |

In this exercise, you and a partner are going to practice saying what time it is in different parts of the country. Tell the time you see on your clock and ask for the time where your partner is. When your partner asks, fill in the time on your clock and say the time you wrote. When you finish the exercise, uncover the other side of the page and check your answers.

Follow the example in this short telephone conversation:

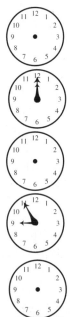

Student A: *Look here and cover the right side of this page.*

1. Phoenix, Arizona

2. Las Vegas, Nevada

3. Richmond, Virginia

4. Albuquerque, New Mexico

5. San Diego, California

Student B: *Look here and cover the left side of this page.*

1. Minneapolis, Minnesota

2. Detroit, Michigan

3. New Orleans, Louisiana

4. Pittsburgh, Pennsylvania

5. Houston, Texas

PUT IT TOGETHER

Circulation

In this activity you will have the chance to speak with 9 different members of your class.

First, write the name of a different classmate on each line to the left of the questions. Then, stand up, go to your classmates whose names you have written, and ask the questions next to their names. Write short answers. When you finish, share what you learned with your classmates.

_____	What are two important cities in your country?
_____	What is the capital of your country?
_____	What cities have you visited in the United States?
_____	What is the most important city in your country?
_____	What is the largest city in your country?
_____	What is the population of your country?
_____	What is the population of your city?
_____	What time is it in your city right now?
_____	What time is it in the capital of your country right now?

Crossword Puzzle

CITIES AND STATES

ACROSS:

1. _____, Georgia
4. _____, Colorado
6. Trenton, __ __ (abbreviation)
8. San Francisco/____, California
9. Philadelphia, __ __
11. Capital of California
13. Capital of Maine
14. Bismarck, __ __
15. _____, Florida

DOWN:

1. _____, Maryland
2. ___,__, California
3. Largest U.S. city
4. Washington, __. __.
5. Providence, _____
7. _____, Texas
10. ____, Massachusetts
12. _____, Texas
16. Kansas City, __ __

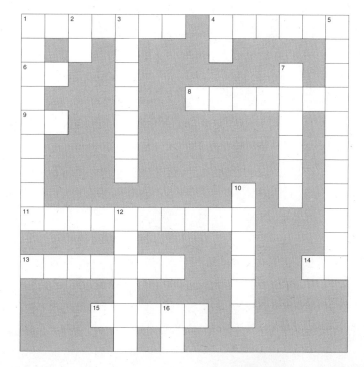

CHAPTER FOUR

REGIONS, RESOURCES, AND PRODUCTS

The fifty states in the United States can be divided into nine general regions, plus Alaska and Hawaii, which are separate. Regions are made up of groups of similar states. In this chapter you will learn about the regions as well as resources and products from the regions and individual states.

SHOW WHAT YOU KNOW

Below is a map of the United States divided into nine regions. Alaska and Hawaii are at the bottom of the map. Work with your classmates to match the names of the regions with the spaces on the map. Write the name of the region on the top line next to the number. When you finish, check your answers with your teacher.

The Regions

Alaska	the Mountain Region
the Appalachian Highlands	New England
Hawaii	the Pacific Coast
the Heartland	the Southeast
the Great Lakes Region	the Southwest
the Mid-Atlantic Region	

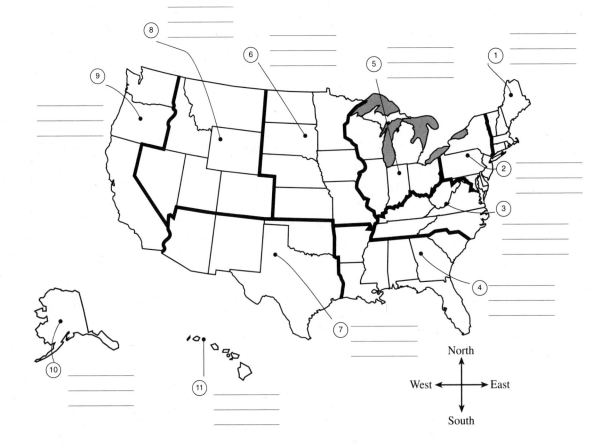

What states are in each region? Compare this map with the map on page 19 to find out.

FOCUS ON CONTENT: THE REGIONS OF THE UNITED STATES

In this section you will learn more about the regions of the United States. You will learn some characteristics of each region, including a little of what the region looks like, what the weather is like, what resources are found there, and what products or business are important to the region.

Listen and Write 🔲

In this exercise you will hear descriptions of the regions of the United States. Look at the words in the box below and ask your teacher about any words you don't understand. Then listen to the descriptions of the regions on the cassette. Write the words from the box on the lines below the region names on the map on page 28.

cactus	maple trees	pine forests	sheep
lobsters	financial center	dairy products	mining
cod fish	coal mines	sugar cane	cotton
peanuts	wheat	palm trees	corn
oats	cattle	pineapples	oil

Listen and Choose 🔲

Listen to the questions on the cassette and circle the letters of the best answers. Look back at the map on page 28 if you can't remember the information.

1. a. maple trees
   b. coal mines and horse farms
   c. cotton and peanuts

2. a. in Hawaii
   b. in the Mountain Region
   c. in New England

3. a. in the Southeast
   b. in the Southwest
   c. in Alaska

4. a. in the Great Lakes Region
   b. in the Heartland
   c. in New England

5. a. the Great Lakes Region
   b. New England
   c. the Pacific Coast

6. a. It's cold and snowy.
   b. It's hot and dry.
   c. It's cool and rainy.

7. a. in the Southeast
   b. in the Southwest
   c. in the Heartland

8. a. in New England
   b. in the Mid-Atlantic Region
   c. in the Mountain Region

9. a. the Mid-Atlantic Region
   b. the Mountain Region
   c. the Great Lakes Region

10. a. because of the fruit trees there
    b. because of the wheat, oats, and corn grown there
    c. because of the cattle and sheep there

Speak, Listen, and Decide

You and your partner will take turns reading statements about the regions of the United States and deciding if they are TRUE *or* FALSE. *Refer to the map on page 28 if you are not sure of an answer. When you finish the exercise, check your answers with your teacher.*

Follow this example:

Student A reads: There are green mountains in New England.

Student B reads: That's true.
  and circles TRUE.

Student B reads: There is coal in the Appalachian Highlands.

Student A responds: That's true.
  and circles TRUE.

Student A: *Look here and cover the right side of the page.*

1. There are green mountains in New England.
2. TRUE   FALSE
3. There are pine forests in the Southwest.
4. TRUE   FALSE
5. There are dairy farms in Alaska.
6. TRUE   FALSE
7. There is oil in the Mid-Atlantic states.
8. TRUE   FALSE
9. There are fruit trees in Alaska.
10. TRUE   FALSE
11. There are palm trees in New England.
12. TRUE   FALSE
13. There are historic places in the Mid-Atlantic Region.
14. TRUE   FALSE
15. There are cotton farms in New England.
16. TRUE   FALSE

Student B: *Look here and cover the left side of the page.*

1. TRUE   FALSE
2. There is coal in the Appalachian Highlands.
3. TRUE   FALSE
4. There are large cities in the Mid-Atlantic Region.
5. TRUE   FALSE
6. There is a lot of wheat in New England.
7. TRUE   FALSE
8. There is a lot of mining in the Mountain Region.
9. TRUE   FALSE
10. There is oil in the Southwest.
11. TRUE   FALSE
12. There are pineapples in Hawaii.
13. TRUE   FALSE
14. There are horse farms in the Appalachian Highlands.
15. TRUE   FALSE
16. There is a lot of corn in Hawaii.

Talk About This!

Many countries are divided into regions. Regions can be distinguished by different weather or different geographical features, or by business, industry, or resources. In this activity you will tell your classmates about two regions in your country. Fill in the chart below, following the examples from the United States. Try to think about what makes one region different from the other.

After you have filled in the chart, get together with a partner and share your information. Fill in the information about your partner's country. When your chart is complete, share what you learned with your classmates.

CATEGORY	THE UNITED STATES		YOUR COUNTRY		YOUR PARTNER'S COUNTRY	
Region	New England	the Southwest				
Weather	cold, snowy, winters	hot, dry				
The Land	green mountains	deserts				
Resources, Products, Business	cod fish, lobsters	cattle, oil				

FOCUS ON CONTENT: RESOURCES AND PRODUCTS

In this section you will learn about resources and products in the United States. You will learn the names of many resources and products, and you will learn where the resources are located and which states produce which products.

Vocabulary

Here are the names of many resources and products that you will talk about in this section. Write the names of the resources and products from the list in the appropriate place in the chart below. If you don't understand some of the words, ask your teacher or use a dictionary.

airplanes	copper	hogs	paper	steel
apples	corn	horses	peaches	sugar cane
blueberries	cotton	iron ore	peanuts	textiles
cattle	cranberries	lead	pineapples	tobacco
cheese	dairy cows	lumber	potatoes	wheat
chemicals	electronic equipment	maple syrup	rice	whiskey
chickens	glass	motor vehicles	sheep	wool
cigarettes and cigars	gold	oranges	silver	zinc
coal				

AGRICULTURE		MINING	AGRICULTURAL PRODUCTS	MANUFACTURED GOODS
Crops	Farm Animals	coal	cheese	airplanes
apples	cattle			
blueberries				

Listen and Write 📼

Listen to the cassette and write the name of the product or resource on the correct state.

Speak, Listen, and Change

You can use the passive voice to describe locations of resources and products. In the passive voice, the resource or product is the subject of the sentence.

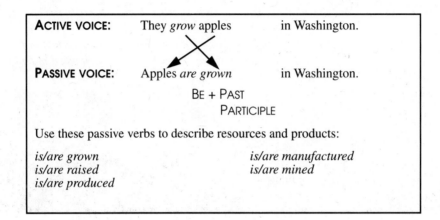

Use these passive verbs to describe resources and products:

is/are grown   *is/are manufactured*
is/are raised   *is/are mined*
is/are produced

In this exercise you and a partner will practice describing resources and products in two different ways, using active voice and passive voice. Your partner will read a sentence in active voice. You should respond by changing it to passive voice. Some words are written in to help you.

Follow this example:

GRAMMAR NOTE:
Use *is* with non-count nouns (rice, copper, corn, lumber, whiskey). Use *are* with plural count nouns (apples, hogs, horses, cigarettes).

Student A says:	They grow apples in Washington.
Student B responds:	Apples are grown in Washington.
Student B then says:	They raise hogs in Iowa.
Student A responds:	Hogs are raised in Iowa.

Student A: *Look here and cover the right side of the page.*

1. They grow apples in Washington.
2. Hogs _____ _____ in Iowa.
3. They produce cheese in Wisconsin.
4. Copper _____ _____ in Arizona.
5. They raise horses in Kentucky.
6. Corn ____ _____ in Nebraska.
7. They grow pineapples in Hawaii.
8. Textiles _____ _____ in South Carolina.
9. They grow cranberries in Massachusetts.
10. Silver _____ _____ in Idaho.

Student B: *Look here and cover the left side of the page.*

1. Apples _____ _____ in Washington.
2. They raise hogs in Iowa.
3. Cheese _____ _____ in Wisconsin.
4. They mine copper in Arizona.
5. Horses _____ _____ in Kentucky.
6. They grow corn in Nebraska.
7. Pineapples _____ _____ in Hawaii.
8. They produce textiles in South Carolina.
9. Cranberries _____ _____ in Massachusetts.
10. They mine silver in Idaho.

Speak, Listen, and Connect

In this exercise you and a partner will practice describing the locations of some resources and products in passive voice. Use the verbs at the top of each section for the words in that section. You have half of the information, and your partner has the other half. Work back and forth until both charts are complete. When you finish, check your answers by comparing your chart with your partner's chart.

Follow this example:

Student A says: Peanuts are grown in Georgia.
Student B connects the words *peanuts* and *Georgia*.

Student A then says: Tell me about cotton.
Student B responds: Cotton is grown in Texas.
Student A connects the words *cotton* and *Texas*.

Student A: *Look at this chart and cover the other chart.*

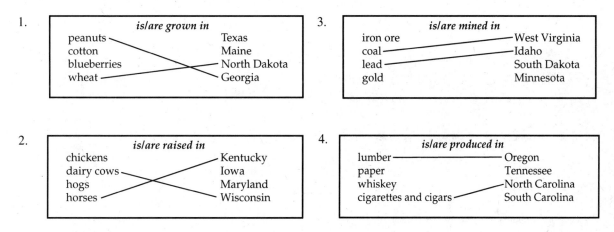

Student B: *Look at this chart and cover the other chart.*

Speak, Listen, and Write

In this activity you and a partner will take turns describing the locations of the resources and products written on your map. Student A should describe all of the resources and products on his/her map first while student B writes. Then student B speaks while student A writes. When you finish, check your answers by looking at your partner's map.

Follow this example:

Student A says: Airplanes are manufactured in Washington.
Student B writes *airplanes* on the state of Washington.

Student B then says: Potatoes are grown in Idaho.
Student A writes *potatoes* on the state of Idaho.

Student A: *Look at this map and cover the map on page 35.*

Student B: *Look at this map and cover the other map.*

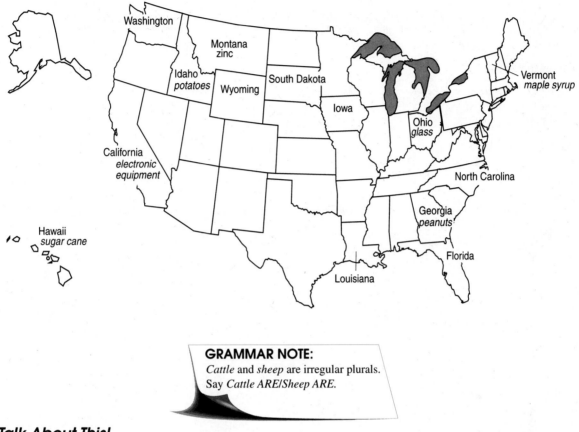

GRAMMAR NOTE:
Cattle and *sheep* are irregular plurals.
Say *Cattle ARE/Sheep ARE.*

Talk About This!

You have learned a lot about resources and products in the United States. What resources and products does your country have? Is your country famous for any of its resources or products?

In this activity, you will share information about your country with your classmates. Fill in the following chart with examples of resources or products from your country. Try to fill in at least one example for each category. You might want to bring in samples of products from your country if you have some.

After you have filled in examples from your country, get together with a partner and share your information. Fill in the information about your partner's country.

When your chart is complete, share what you learned with your classmates.

CATEGORY	THE UNITED STATES	YOUR COUNTRY	YOUR PARTNER'S COUNTRY
Agriculture (crops and farm animals)	corn, wheat, fruit, tobacco, chickens, cattle, hogs		
Mining	coal, iron		
Agricultural Products	lumber, cheese, cigarettes		
Manufactured Goods	electronic equipment, airplanes, chemicals, cars		

PUT IT TOGETHER

Speak, Listen, and Choose

In this exercise you and a partner are going to take turns asking and answering questions about the information in this chapter. Look back through the chapter if you can't remember an answer. Circle the letter of the best answer and say the answer. When you finish, check your answers with the teacher.

Follow this example:

Student A asks first: What region is Chicago in?
Student B responds: The Great Lakes Region.
    and circles *a*.

Student B then asks: Where is Miami?
Student A responds: In the Southeast.
    and circles *b*.

Student A: *Look here and cover the right side of the page.*

1. What region is Chicago in?

2.   a.   in the Southwest
      b.   in the Southeast
3. Is New York in the Mid-Atlantic?

4.   a.   the Mountain Region
      b.   New England
5. Where is California?

6.   a.   the Heartland
      b.   the Southwest
7. Where can you see maple trees?

8.   a.   the Mountain Region
      b.   the Mid-Atlantic Region

9. Where can you see natural pine forests?

10.   a.   yes
      b.   no
11. In which region is fishing a major industry?

12.   a.   in the Pacific Coast Region
      b.   in the Southeast
13. Where do they manufacture airplanes?

(continued on next page)

Student B: *Look here and cover the left side of the page.*

1.   a.   the Great Lakes Region
      b.   the Mountain Region
2. Where is Miami?

3.   a.   yes
      b.   no
4. What is the smallest region?

5.   a.   in the Southeast
      b.   in the Pacific Coast Region
6. What region is Texas in?

7.   a.   in the Southwest
      b.   in New England
8. What region is the financial center of the nation?

9.   a.   in the Southwest
      b.   in the Southeast
10. Are there palm trees in Hawaii?

11.   a.   the Mountain Region
      b.   Alaska
12. Where do they grow apples?

13.   a.   in the Mid-Atlantic Region
      b.   in the Pacific Coast Region

(continued on next page)

14.   a.   in North Carolina
        b.   Maine
15.   Where is cheese produced?

16.   a.   in Hawaii
        b.   in Kentucky
17.   Where is iron mined?

18.   a.   in Arizona
        b.   in Ohio
19.   Where do they grow oranges?

20.   a.   in Tennessee
        b.   in New York
21.   Where are sheep raised?

22.   a.   in Arizona
        b.   in Oregon

14.   Where is tobacco grown?

15.   a.   in Wisconsin
        b.   in Louisiana
16.   Where do they raise horses?

17.   a.   in Minnesota
        b.   in Florida
18.   Where is glass manufactured?

19.   a.   in New Hampshire
        b.   in Florida
20.   Where is whiskey produced?

21.   a.   in Wyoming
        b.   in South Carolina
22.   Where is copper mined?

Concentration

Play Concentration to help you remember the products and resources of different states and regions. Follow the directions in Chapter 3, on page 24. Write a state or region on one card, and write a product or resource on another, until you have 6 pairs.

Tic Tac Toe

Play Tic Tac Toe with your classmates. Your teacher will draw a big tic-tac-toe grid on the blackboard and fill in each square with the name of a resource or product.

Divide the class into two teams—X and O. X goes first. One student chooses a word from the grid and makes a passive voice statement telling where that product or resource is produced, raised, or grown. If the statement is correct, the teacher erases the word and writes an X, and the other team has a chance. If the statement is incorrect, the teacher doesn't write an X, and the other team has a chance. If the other team makes a correct statement, the teacher erases the word and writes an O. The purpose of the game is to get three Xs or three Os in a row.

oranges	**X**	horses
airplanes	cheese	silver
tobacco	pineapples	**O**

ON YOUR OWN MEET THE U.S.A.: AN INTRODUCTION TO AMERICAN GEOGRAPHY

Here are some activities related to geography for you to do on your own, with a small group, or with your whole class.

1. Interview an American who has lived in one state for many years. Ask that person about his/her home town and other cities, good places to visit, important ethnic and/or religious groups living in the state, and what makes that state special or different from others. Prepare a 5-minute talk to report to the class on what you learn, or invite your friend to class and interview him/her while your classmates listen.

2. Prepare a poster describing a state or geographic region. Write or call state tourism offices for a free information packet. You can find addresses in *The World Almanac*, or ask a librarian. You can also sometimes get information from travel agencies. Cut pictures out of the free packet and paste them on poster board to make a travel poster. Be sure to show geographic features, cities, resources, and products. Fill in around the pictures with information including population, capital and other cities, and information on the economy and history. Put your poster on the wall of the classroom and prepare a 5-minute speech to present the information.

3. Prepare a poster describing your country. Follow the directions in question 2 above. Try to get free tourist information from your embassy, or an office of your country's tourist bureau, or a travel agent. Prepare a 5-minute speech to present the poster to your classmates.

4. Have a food fair in class. First, make a list of all the states. Then think of a food product for as many states as you can. For example, blueberries are grown in Maine, chickens are raised in Maryland. Then assign one food to each member of the class or group. Bring the food, or a dish prepared using that food, to class to share. Label it with the ingredients and the name of the state. Before you eat, tell your classmates what you know about the food you brought.

5. Have an international food fair. Bring dishes from your country and be prepared to explain the ingredients to your classmates.

6. Review Chapter One: This Land. Prepare a 5-minute presentation about the geographical features of your country for your classmates. Use an encyclopedia from the reference section of the library to find information.

7. Plan a trip to a local natural history museum. Learn about the natural features of the part of the United States where you are studying. After your trip, report back to your class on what you learned.

8. Are you studying in a smaller city or town? Plan a Saturday trip to the closest large city. When you return, discuss how the large city compares with cities in your country.

Unit **2**

Looking Back: Two Hundred Years of American History

CHAPTER FIVE

1776: THE BIRTH OF A NATION

The United States became an independent country in the eighteenth century. In this chapter you will learn about the Revolutionary War and how the United States won its independence. You will also hear a song that was popular during the Revolutionary War period.

SHOW WHAT YOU KNOW

In the next section you will hear a lecture about the Revolutionary War and other events connected with American independence. The following questions will be answered in the lecture. How much of the information do you already know?

1. Before independence, there were British colonies in America. Where were they? How many were there? What states did they become?

    _____ already know_____ don't know

2. What was a major cause of the Revolutionary War between the American colonies and Great Britain?

    _____ already know_____ don't know

3. In what year did the United States declare independence from Great Britain?

    _____ already know_____ don't know

4. Who was the first president of the United States?

    _____ already know_____ don't know

FOCUS ON CONTENT: THE AMERICAN REVOLUTION

In this section you will hear a short lecture about the Revolutionary War. You will learn about the events leading up to the war, some facts about the war, and about the formation of the United States after the war.

Vocabulary 🔲

The following words are important in the lecture. Listen to the cassette and complete the sentences with words from the box.

colony	protest	tax	federal
independent	harbor	colonists	battle

1. A _____ is one fight in a war.
2. People often _____ when they think the government is unfair.
3. Gibraltar is a _____ of Great Britain.
4. Ships can sail into a _____ to unload cargo.
5. The _____ government is in Washington, D.C.
6. People who live in a colony are called _____ .
7. The United States became an _____ country after the Revolutionary War with Britain.
8. A _____ is money paid to the government.

Listen and Write 📼

Listen to the lecture as many times as necessary in order to fill in the blanks below. First, complete the list of the thirteen British colonies by writing in the missing names. Then complete the time line with dates from the lecture. Review the information after you finish writing.

The British Colonies in North America:

New Hampshire, Massachusetts, _____ _____, Connecticut,

_____ _____, New Jersey, Pennsylvania, _____,

Maryland, _____, North Carolina, South Carolina, and _____.

Time Line

1765	The Stamp Act, the first British tax in the colonies.
1773	The Boston Tea Party, one of the first major protests against Britain.
_____	The Continental Congress met in Philadelphia.
_____	The Revolutionary War started with the Battle of Lexington and Concord, in Massachusetts.
_____	The Declaration of Independence was signed in Philadelphia by the members of the Continental Congress.
_____	The Revolutionary War ended with the Battle of Yorktown, in Virginia.
_____	The Articles of Confederation made a weak federal government.
_____	The Constitution of the United States made a strong federal government.
_____	George Washington became the first president.

Listen and Choose 📼

Listen to the questions on your cassette and circle the letter of the best answer.

1. a. 13
   b. 30
   c. 33

2. a. a battle in the Revolutionary War
   b. a rebellion
   c. a tax

3. a. because they were poor
   b. because they already had a lot of taxes
   c. because they didn't have a vote in the British government

4. a. in Philadelphia
   b. in Washington, D.C.
   c. in New York

5. a. in Philadelphia
   b. in Massachusetts
   c. in Virginia

6. a. the Constitution of the United States
   b. the Articles of Confederation
   c. the Declaration of Independence

7. a. in Philadelphia
   b. in Massachusetts
   c. In Virginia

8. a. in 1776
   b. in 1789
   c. in 1781

Read and Decide

Read each statement and decide if it is true or false. Write T *or* F *on the line. If a statement is false, change it to make it true.*

1. _____ Maryland was one of the original 13 colonies.
2. _____ Britain began to tax the colonists in 1765.
3. _____ The Boston Tea Party was a protest against British taxes.
4. _____ The Continental Congress met in Boston.
5. _____ The Continental Congress met in 1765.
6. _____ The Revolutionary War started in 1775 in Virginia.
7. _____ The Declaration of Independence was signed in 1776.
8. _____ The Revolutionary War lasted ten years.
9. _____ At first, the United States had a weak federal government.
10. _____ The Constitution of the United States calls for a weak federal government.

Put these events in the history of the United States in the correct order.

_____ The Revolutionary War started with the Battle of Lexington and Concord.

_____ The Constitution of the United States was written and accepted by the people; George Washington became the first president.

_____ The Colonists protested British taxes in the Boston Tea Party.

_____ The Revolutionary War ended with the Battle of Yorktown.

_____ The Continental Congress met in Philadelphia for the first time.

_____ The Declaration of Independence was written and signed.

___1___ Britain charged the colonists a tax in the Stamp Act.

_____ The Articles of Confederation set up a weak federal government.

Speak, Listen, and Connect

You can talk about many past events using the past of the verb *be.*

Singular	*was*	Massachusetts *was* one of the thirteen colonies.
Plural	*were*	The thirteen colonies *were* on the east coast of North America.

In this exercise you and a partner are going to review the information in the lecture by reading statements about the events in the lecture using the past tense of the verb *be.* You have half of the information, and your partner has the other half. Work back and forth, following the lines to make statements with *was* or *were,* and drawing lines to connect the parts when your partner speaks. When you finish, check your answers by looking at your partner's chart.

Follow this example:

Student A says: Maryland *was* one of the thirteen colonies.
Student B draws a line.

Student B then says: The Stamp Act *was* a tax on newspapers and other papers.
Student A draws a line.

Student A: *Look here and cover the other chart.*

Maryland	a town in Virginia
The Stamp Act	the country's first president, elected in 1789
The Continental Congress	the first battle of the Revolutionary War
Georgia	a tax on newspapers and other papers
The Boston Tea Party	in Philadelphia during the Revolutionary War
Lexington and Concord	one of the thirteen colonies
The Battle of Lexington and Concord	signed in Philadelphia by the members of the Continental Congress on July 4, 1776
The Declaration of Independence	weak under the Articles of Confederation
Yorktown	one of the thirteen colonies
The Battle of Yorktown	towns near Boston
The United States government	the last battle in the Revolutionary War
George Washington	a protest against tax on tea

Student B: *Look here and cover the other chart.*

Maryland	a town in Virginia
The Stamp Act	the country's first president, elected in 1789
The Continental Congress	the first battle of the Revolutionary War
Georgia	a tax on newspapers and other papers
The Boston Tea Party	in Philadelphia during the Revolutionary War
Lexington and Concord	one of the thirteen colonies
The Battle of Lexington and Concord	signed in Philadelphia by the members of the Continental Congress on July 4, 1776
The Declaration of Independence	weak under the articles of confederation
Yorktown	one of the thirteen colonies
The Battle of Yorktown	towns near Boston
The United States government	the last battle in the Revolutionary War
George Washington	a protest against tax on tea

Talk About This!

1. Is your country older than the United States? Has your country ever received independence from another country? Tell your classmates about your country's history.

2. In this activity, you will share information about your country with your classmates. Fill in the chart with examples from your country's history. Try to fill in one example for each category.

    After you have filled in examples from your country, get together with a partner and share your information. Tell your partner about your country and fill in the information about your partner's country. You can use this pattern when you speak:

    A famous person in my country's history was _____ .
    He/she was famous because _____ .

CATEGORY	THE UNITED STATES	YOUR COUNTRY	YOUR PARTNER'S COUNTRY
Person	Thomas Jefferson Why: He wrote the Declaration of Independence.	_____ Why:	_____ Why:
Group of People	The Continental Congress Why: They governed the colonies during the Revolutionary War.	_____ Why:	_____ Why:
City	Philadelphia Why: The Continental Congress met there.	_____ Why:	_____ Why:
Town/Small Place	Yorktown Why: The last battle of the Revolutionary War was there.	_____ Why:	_____ Why:
Event	The Stamp Act Why: It started the protest against Britain.	_____ Why:	_____ Why:
Document	The Constitution Why: It established a strong federal government.	_____ Why:	_____ Why:

FOCUS ON SKILLS: SAYING YEARS AND ORDINAL NUMBERS

In this section you will practice saying years and ordinal numbers while you talk about the American Revolution and the first ten presidents of the United States.

Pronunciation

Pronounce names of years correctly by learning the rules about the pronunciation of teens and tens. Study the information in the box, then practice the pronunciation of the years with your teacher and your classmates.

TEENS		TENS	
Put the stress on the last syllable and pronounce the *t* clearly.		Put the stress on the first syllable and pronounce the *t* like [d].	
Thir TEEN	Fif TEEN	THIR ty	FIF ty

1760	Seven TEEN SIX ty	1770	1800	1775	1798
1780	Seven TEEN EIGHT y	1790	1762	1787	1801

Speak, Listen, and Answer

You can talk about the duration of past events with questions with *how long* and answers with *from . . . to.*

How long was George Washington president?	From 1789 to 1796.
How long were the Articles of Confederation in effect?	From 1781 to 1789.

In this exercise you and a partner are going to take turns asking questions with how long + be *and making answers with* from . . . to. *Make a question with the cues, and write the years that you hear. Then listen to your partner's question and answer it by reading the dates in parentheses. When you finish, check that you wrote the correct dates by looking at your partner's side of the page.*

Follow this example:

Student A asks: How long was the Revolutionary War?
Student B answers: From 1775 to 1781.

Student B then asks: How long was Thomas Jefferson president?
Student A answers: From 1801 to 1809.

Student A: *Look here and cover the right side of the page.*

1. the Revolutionary War? _____
2. (1801–1809)
3. the Articles of Confederation in effect? _____
4. (1765 –1766)
5. the federal government weak? _____
6. (1797–1801)
7. George Washington's presidency? _____
8. (1775–1781)
9. Thomas Jefferson's presidency? _____
10. (1789–1797)

Student B: *Look here and cover the left side of the page.*

1. (1775– 1781)
2. Thomas Jefferson president? _____
3. (1781–1789)
4. the Stamp Act in effect? _____
5. (1781–1789)
6. John Adams president? _____
7. (1789–1797)
8. the Revolutionary War? _____
9. (1801–1809)
10. George Washington president? _____

Fill In

You can use ordinal numbers to talk about the order of the first ten presidents.

Study the ordinal numbers:

1st—first	4th—fourth	7th—seventh
2nd—second	5th—fifth	8th—eighth
3rd—third	6th—sixth	9th—ninth
		10th—tenth

SKILLS NOTE:
Always use *the* before ordinal numbers.
He was *the* first president.

Here is a list of the first ten presidents of the United States, in the order in which they served. Fill in the blanks with the correct ordinal numbers. Write the abbreviations in the parentheses.

1. George Washington was the _first_ (1st) president of the United States.
2. John Adams was the _____ (____) president of the United States.
3. Thomas Jefferson was the _____ (____) president of the United States.
4. James Madison was the _____ (____) president of the United States
5. James Monroe was the _____ (____) president of the United States.
6. John Quincy Adams was the _____ (____) president of the United States.
7. Andrew Jackson was the _____ (____) president of the United States.
8. Martin VanBuren was the _____ (____) president of the United States.
9. William Henry Harrison was the _____ (____) president of the United States.
10. John Tyler was the _____ (____) president of the United States.

Concentration

Play Concentration to help you learn about the first ten presidents of the United States. Here is how to play: Take twenty index cards. Write the ordinal numbers *first* to *tenth* on ten cards. Then write the names of the first ten presidents on the other ten cards. Mix up the cards. Put them face down on a table or on the floor. Play in groups of three or four. Take turns turning up two cards. Try to match the president with the ordinal number. If you don't make a match, turn the cards back over. If you make a match, you keep the cards and have another turn.

Speak, Listen, and Decide

In this exercise, you and a partner are going to practice saying ordinal numbers while you talk about the first ten presidents of the United States. Ask a question beginning with "Which president was . . . ?" and write the ordinal number from the answer that your partner gives. Then listen to your partner's question and make a long answer by looking at the list above. When you finish, check your answers with your teacher.

Follow this example:

Student A asks:	Which president was George Washington?
Student B answers:	He was the first president.
Student A writes *1st*.	
Student B then asks:	Which president was Martin VanBuren?
Student A answers:	He was the eighth president.
Student B writes *8th*.	

Student A: *Look here and cover the right side of the page.*

1. George Washington __1st__
2. _____
3. William Henry Harrison _____
4. _____
5. James Madison _____
6. _____
7. John Adams _____
8. _____
9. Andrew Jackson _____
10. _____

Student B: *Look here and cover the left side of the page.*

1. _____
2. Martin VanBuren __8th__
3. _____
4. John Quincy Adams _____
5. _____
6. John Tyler _____
7. _____
8. Thomas Jefferson _____
9. _____
10. James Monroe _____

Talk About This!

The first ten presidents had very common English names. In English, we often use nicknames for common names.

Draw lines to match the nicknames that might have been used for some of the first ten presidents.

John	Tom, Tommy
Thomas	Andy, Drew
James	Jack, Johnny
Andrew	Hank
Martin	Jim, Jimmy
William	Marty
Henry	Bill, Billy

Women also use nicknames. Match these women's names with their nicknames.

Elizabeth	Sue, Suzy
Susan	Terry
Rebecca	Beth, Liz, Betsy
Catherine	Peggy, Meg, Maggie
Margaret	Becky
Mary	Cathy, Katie
Theresa	Molly, Polly

Do you use nicknames in your country? If you do, what are some common names and their nicknames in your language? Make a note below, and share the nicknames from your country with your classmates. Are there any language represented in your class that do not use nicknames?

Name: _____ Nickname: _____

Song

"The Rich Lady Over the Sea"
is an old folk song that tells the story of the Boston Tea Party, the protest in which colonists threw boxes of tea into Boston Harbor rather than pay the tax that Great Britain wanted to charge. It is a traditional song from the time of the Revolution, and the author is unknown. Another name for the song is "Revolutionary Tea."

Listen and Write

Listen to the song and fill in the missing words below. Check your answers with your teacher.

1. There was an old _____ lived over the sea,
2. And she was an _____ Queen.
3. Her daughter lived off in the new _____,
4. With an _____ of water between;
5. The old lady's pockets were full of _____,
6. But never contented was _____.
7. So she called on her daughter to pay her a _____
8. Of three pence a pound on her _____,
9. Of three pence a pound on her _____.

10. "Now mother, dear mother," the _____ replied,
11. "I'll not do the thing that you ask.
12. I'm willing to pay a fair _____ for the tea,
13. But _____ the three-penny tax."
14. "You shall," cried the _____, and reddened with rage,
15. "For you're my own daughter, you _____.
16. And sure 'tis quite proper the daughter should _____
17. Her mother a _____ on her tea,
18. Her mother a _____ on her tea."
19. And so the old _____ her servant called up

20. And packed off a shipment of tea;
21. And eager for three pence a _____, she put in
22. Enough for a large _____.
23. She ordered her servants to bring _____ the tax,
24. Declaring her _____ should obey,
25. For _____ as she was, and almost woman grown,
26. She'd half whip her life away,
27. She'd half whip her life away.

28. The tea was conveyed to her daughter's own _____,
29. All down by the ocean's side;
30. And the bouncing _____ poured out every pound
31. In the _____ and boiling tide;
32. And then she _____ out to the Island Queen,
33. "Oh, mother, dear mother," called she,
34. "Your _____ you may have when'tis steeped enough,
35. But _____ a tax from me,
36. But _____ a tax from me."

Talk About the Song

1. Study the vocabulary.

Find a word in line	that means	and write it here:
6	happy	_____
8, 9	a unit of money	_____
14	became red in the face	_____
14	anger	_____
16	correct, fair	_____
24	saying	_____
28	sent	_____
31	ocean	_____
34	brewed (for tea)	_____

2. "The Rich Lady Over the Sea" tells the story of the colonists' protest against a tax on tea. Many people and places in the song represent real people and places.

   Look at the people and places from the song and decide if they represent *Great Britain*, *the American Colonies*, *the Atlantic Ocean*, or *Boston Harbor*:

an old lady	an ocean of water	her child
the sea	the old lady	her daughter's own door/down by the ocean side
an Island Queen	her mother	the bouncing girl
her daughter	a large family	the dark and boiling tide

3. The song has two titles, "The Rich Lady Over the Sea" and "Revolutionary Tea." Which title do you like better? Why?

PUT IT TOGETHER

Tic Tac Toe

Play Tic Tac Toe with your classmates. Your teacher will draw a big tic-tac-toe grid on the blackboard and fill in each square with the name of a person, place, or event from this chapter.

Divide the class into two teams—X and O. X goes first. One student chooses a name or title from the grid and makes a statement to identify it. If the statement is correct, the teacher erases the word(s) in the grid and writes an X. Then the other team has a turn. The purpose of the game is to get three Xs or three Os in a row.

Cloze 🔲

Read the following information about the independence of the United States. Try to fill in the blanks with the correct word. After you have filled in as much as you can, listen to the lecture on the cassette again as many times as necessary to fill in all the blanks.

The people who lived in the colonies, the _____, were generally happy being part of Great _____ from the time the colonies were first settled in the 17th _____ until the middle of the 18th century. Then, in 1765, Britain decided to collect _____ from the colonists. They called the tax the "_____ Act." It was a tax on _____ and other papers. The colonists did not want to _____ the tax because they were not permitted to vote in British elections. They called it "taxation _____ representation." They did not want to pay a tax if they did not have a voice in the government. The colonists _____ the tax, and in 1766, the British stopped charging it.

After that, Britain tried to charge other taxes, but the colonists protested until the British removed all of the taxes except a tax on _____. The tax on tea led to a famous protest called the _____ Tea Party. The colonists did not want to pay tax on British tea which was arriving on ships in Boston _____. They went on the _____ and destroyed all of the tea by throwing it into the harbor.

When Britain tried to punish the Massachusetts _____ for the Boston Tea Party, colonists from other colonies came together to support them. They called themselves the _____ Congress. They met for the first time in _____ in 1774. The Continental Congress governed the country throughout the Revolutionary War.

The Revolutionary War _____ with the Battle of Lexington and Concord, in Massachusetts, on April 19, 1775. The Continental Congress chose George _____ to lead the Continental Army.

One year after the war started, the Continental Congress officially declared _____ from Great Britain. Thomas Jefferson wrote the _____ of Independence, and the members of the Continental Congress signed it in Philadelphia on _____ _____, 1776.

Revolutionary War battles were fought throughout the colonies and in the territory to the west of the colonies. The war lasted _____ years. It ended with the Battle of Yorktown, in _____, in 1781.

From 1781 to 1789, the country was governed under the Articles of Confederation. The Articles of Confederation set up a _____ federal government.

In 1789, the _____ of the United States went into effect. That gave the country a _____ federal government. In that year, George Washington was elected as the first _____ .

CHAPTER SIX

TERRITORIAL EXPANSION: MOVING WEST

After independence, the area of the United States included the original thirteen colonies and the territory west to the Mississippi. The country grew quickly between 1800 and 1850. Alaska and Hawaii were added later. In this chapter you will learn about how the United States expanded west of the Mississippi River, practice talking about years and populations, and learn about the California Gold Rush of 1849.

SHOW WHAT YOU KNOW

Countries frequently change borders. Why do borders change? Think of some examples of borders changing around the world today.

In the next section you will hear a lecture describing how the territory of the United States expanded west of the Mississippi River. Look at the map below. Use what you know about the states to write as many names from the box as you can on the map. The lecture in the next section will help you to fill in what you can't guess.

the Alaska Purchase	the Hawaii Annexation	the Oregon Country
East and West Florida	the Louisiana Purchase	the Red River Basin
the Gadsden Purchase	the Mexican Cession	the Texas Annexation

FACTS NOTE:
One square mile is equal to 2,590 square kilometers.

FOCUS ON CONTENT: TERRITORIAL EXPANSION

In this section you will hear a lecture about the expansion of the United States west of the Mississippi River during the nineteenth century.

Listen and Write 📼

This lecture will tell about the expansion of the United States, including names of territories added, the dates they were added, and the square miles of each. Listen to the lecture as many times as necessary in order to fill in the names, dates, and square miles on the map.

Listen and Choose 📼

Listen to the questions on the cassette and circle the letter of the best answer.

1. a. $11,000,000
    b. $822,000
    c. $18,000,000

2. a. in Florida
    b. in Great Britain
    c. in Minnesota and North Dakota

3. a. France
    b. Spain
    c. Great Britain

4. a. Florida
    b. Texas
    c. Oregon

5. a. They bought it from Mexico.
    b. They bought it from France.
    c. They won it in a war with Mexico.

6. a. They needed it for a railroad.
    b. They knew there was oil there.
    c. They knew there was gold there.

7. a. $586,000
    b. $7,000,000
    c. $7,000

8. a. kings and queens
    b. missionaries
    c. businessmen

Read and Decide

Read each statement and decide if it is true or false. Write T or F on the line. If a statement is false, change it to make it true.

1. _____ The Louisiana Purchase tripled the area of the United States.

2. _____ The United States and Spain almost went to war over Florida.

3. _____ Sam Houston was president of the Texas Republic.

4. _____ The United States and Spain owned the Oregon Country together before 1846.

5. _____ The Mexican War ended in 1846.

6. _____ Phoenix, Arizona, is located in the territory that was the Gadsden Purchase.

7. _____ Russia probably didn't know the value of Alaska's oil when they sold the land to the United States.

8. _____ Hawaii was a monarchy in the 1800s.

Read and Decide

The territories described in the lecture were acquired in four ways: by purchase, by peaceful treaty, after a war, and by request of the people in the territory. Look at the chart below and put a check in the correct column after the name of each territory. Look back at your notes or listen to the lecture again if you don't remember all of the information.

TERRITORY	PURCHASE	TREATY	WAR	REQUEST
the Alaska Purchase				
East and West Florida				
the Gadsden Purchase				
the Hawaii Annexation				
the Louisiana Purchase				
the Mexican Cession				
the Oregon Country				
the Red River Basin				
the Texas Annexation				

Talk About This!

Have the borders of your country changed over time? If they have, explain the changes to your classmates. Find out how the borders of some of your classmates' countries have changed over time. Talk to at least four classmates. Write the information here:

COUNTRY	BORDERS CHANGED?		WHY?
U.S.A.	(YES)	NO	Purchases, treaties, wars, and requests
	YES	NO	
	YES	NO	
	YES	NO	
	YES	NO	

FOCUS ON SKILLS: USING PAST VERBS, SAYING NUMBERS AND YEARS

In this section you will talk about how the territory and the population of the United States grew during the one hundred years after independence.

Regular Past Tense Verbs		
Rule 1: ____e + d	*Rule 2: ____y → i + ed*	*Rule 3:____ + ed*
decide—decided	occupy—occupied	own—owned
Irregular Past Tense Verbs		
pay—paid	come—came	grow—grew
have—had	become—became	

Speak, Listen, and Write

In this exercise, you and a partner are going to review information about the territorial expansion of the United States. Take turns reading the statements and filling in the past tense verbs. When you finish, check your spelling by looking at your partner's side of the page.

Follow this example:

Student A reads first: The United States grew quickly in the nineteenth century.
Student B writes *grew*.
Student B then reads: The territory expanded west of the Mississippi.
Student A writes *expanded*.

Student A: *Look here and cover the right side of the page.*

1. The United States grew quickly in the nineteenth century.
2. The territory _____ west of the Mississippi.
3. The United States paid France 11 million dollars.
4. The Louisiana Purchase _____ the size of the United States.
5. The United States received the Red River Basin in 1818.
6. Texas _____ a republic in 1836.
7. The Republic had many problems.
8. Texas _____ to be annexed.
9. They divided the Oregon Country.
10. The United States _____ half the land.
11. Mexico owned California.
12. The United States _____ some land for a railroad.
13. The United States purchased Alaska from Russia.
14. Alaska _____ 586,000 square miles.
15. Kings and queens governed Hawaii.
16. The businessmen _____ annexation.

Student B: *Look here and cover the left side of the page*

1. The United States _____ quickly in the nineteenth century.
2. The territory expanded west of the Mississippi.
3. The United States _____ France 11 million dollars.
4. The Louisiana Purchase doubled the size of the United States.
5. The United States _____ the Red River Basin in 1818.
6. Texas became a republic in 1836.
7. The Republic _____ many problems.
8. Texas agreed to be annexed.
9. They _____ the Oregon Country.
10. The United States received half the land.
11. Mexico _____ California.
12. The United States wanted some land for a railroad.
13. The United States _____ Alaska from Russia.
14. Alaska added 586,000 square miles.
15. Kings and queens _____ Hawaii.
16. The businessmen requested annexation.

Speak, Listen, and Write

In this exercise you will practice the pronunciation of years and large numbers while you learn about the population of the United States. Review the pronunciation of the years and large numbers. Repeat after your teacher and practice with your classmates.

1760　　　1800　　　1900　　　1770　　　1840　　　1910　　　1790　　　1850　　　1920

Large numbers

1,490,000	one million four hundred ninety thousand

1,000,000	6,000,000	11,000,000
1,200,000	8,200,000	22,500,000
1,250,000	9,390,000	31,670,000

As the territory of the United States grew, so did the population. In this exercise you and a partner are going to talk about how the population grew between 1760 and 1850. You have half the information and your partner has the other half. Fill in the years and populations as you work back and forth with your partner. When you finish, check your answers by looking at your partner's chart.

Follow this example:

Student A says:	The first year I have is 1760. What was the population in 1760?
Student B writes *1760* and says:	It was 1,600,000.
Student A writes *1,600,000*.	

Student B then says:	The next year I have is 1770. What was the population in 1770?
Student A writes *1770* and says:	It was 2,150,000.
Student B writes *2,150,000*.	

Student A: *Look here and cover the chart on the right.*

YEAR	POPULATION
1760	
	2,150,000
1780	
	4,000,000
1800	
	7,240,000
1820	
	12,900,000
1840	
	23,190,000

Student B: *Look here and cover the chart on the left.*

YEAR	POPULATION
	1,600,000
1770	
	2,780,000
1790	
	5,300,000
1810	
	9,600,000
1830	
	17,100,000
1850	

FOCUS ON CONTENT: THE CALIFORNIA GOLD RUSH AND THE "FORTY-NINERS"

In 1848, gold was discovered in California. By 1849, thousands of men *rushed* to California to look for gold. These men who went to California in search of gold were called "the Forty-Niners." In this section you will listen to a short lecture about the Gold Rush of 1849.

Vocabulary 📼

The following words are important in the lecture. Listen to the cassette and complete the sentences with words from the box.

settled	mule	wagon train	journeys
canoe	camps	discovered	equipment

1. The men lived outdoors in _____ , where they slept in tents and cooked on open fires.
2. A _____ is half donkey, half horse.
3. They needed special machines and other _____ to mine the gold.
4. The men _____ there and stayed permanently.
5. A _____ is a small, narrow boat.
6. A _____ _____ is a group of wagons pulled by horses.
7. Someone _____ gold in California in 1848. They later found gold in Canada.
8. The men traveled far to reach California. They had long _____ .

Listen and Write 📼

Listen to the lecture and fill in the notes on this page. Listen as many times as necessary in order to fill in all of the information.

_____ men went to California to find gold.

They took 3 routes: _____

_____

_____

$ _____ worth of gold was found between 1848 and 1852.

Populations: 1848   1852

San Francisco   _____   _____

California   _____   _____

Listen and Choose

Listen to the questions on the cassette and circle the letter of the best answer.

1. a. in 1848
    b. in 1849
    c. in 1852

2. a. because 49,000 men went
    b. because they went in 1849
    c. because they went 4900 miles

3. a. the first men who arrived
    b. 75,000 men
    c. the men who came after 1852

4. a. Many people died.
    b. Life in the mining camps was difficult.
    c. All of the easy-to-mine gold was gone.

5. a. They all returned to their families in the East.
    b. They all died.
    c. Many of them settled in California with their families.

Matching

In this exercise you will review the information in the lecture while you practice some irregular past tense verbs. Match the words and phrases on the left with the phrases on the right to make statements about the Gold Rush. Change the verbs in parentheses to past tense. Then write the letter of the answer on the line. Review the verbs in the box before you begin.

bring—brought	come—came	find—found
get—got	go—went	spend—spent

1. The Forty-Niners (go) _____
2. At first the men (find) _____
3. Many men (get) _____
4. They (spend) _____
5. After the Gold Rush, many men (bring) _____
6. Many men's families (come) _____

a. over the routes they opened.
b. to California by three routes.
c. gold easily.
d. their families to California.
e. rich, but many didn't.
f. a lot of their money for food and supplies.

Speak, Listen, and Decide

In this exercise, you and a partner will take turns reading statements about the Gold Rush and deciding if they are TRUE *or* FALSE. *Look back at your notes on page 59 if you can't remember an answer. When you finish, check your answers with your teacher.*

Follow this example:

Student A says: Gold was discovered in California in 1849.
Student B responds: That's False.
  and circles FALSE.

Student B reads: In 1849, many people wanted to go to California to get rich.
Student A responds: That's True.
  and circles TRUE.

Student A: *Look here and cover the right side of the page.*

1. Gold was discovered in California in 1849.
2. TRUE   FALSE

3. There were about 75,000 Forty-Niners.
4. TRUE   FALSE

5. The Forty-Niners crossed Panama by canoe and mule.
6. TRUE   FALSE
7. All of the Forty-Niners got rich.
8. TRUE   FALSE
9. Life in the mining camps was easy.
10. TRUE   FALSE
11. Many of the Forty-Niners stayed in California after the Gold Rush.
12. TRUE   FALSE

Student B: *Look here and cover the left side of the page.*

1. TRUE   FALSE
2. In 1849, many people wanted to go to California to get rich.
3. TRUE   FALSE
4. The Forty-Niners took 5 different routes to California.
5. TRUE   FALSE

6. The routes were easy journeys.
7. TRUE   FALSE
8. Food and supplies were expensive.
9. TRUE   FALSE
10. The Gold Rush continued for ten years.
11. TRUE   FALSE

12. The population of San Francisco grew from 800 to 25,000 in four years.

Talk About This!

The population of California grew quickly because of the Gold Rush of 1849. Has the population of an area in your country ever grown rapidly? Why? Tell your classmates.

PUT IT TOGETHER

Past Tense Sentence Combinations

Work with your classmates to combine the following into sentences about the information in this chapter. How many sentences can you make? Change all of the verbs to past tense.

Example:

Spain sold Florida to the United States for $5,000,000.

	spend	annexation in 1898.
Spain	become	Alaska from Russia.
France	want	routes to the West.
The United States	open	Florida to the United States for $5,000,000.
Texas	give	gold easily.
Hawaii	purchase	$11,000,000 for the Louisiana Purchase.
Mexico	pay	to go to California to look for gold.
Many men	find	California to the United States in 1848.
The "Forty-Niners"	go	the land from the Mississippi to the Rockies to the United States.
Some 49ers	request	all of their money on food and supplies.
	sell	to California by three routes.
		an independent republic in 1836.

Tic Tac Toe

Play Tic Tac Toe with your classmates. Your teacher will draw a big tic-tac-toe grid on the blackboard and fill in each square with a verb from this chapter.

Divide the class into two teams—X and O. X goes first. One student chooses a verb from the grid and makes a past tense statement about the territorial expansion of the United States or about the Gold Rush. If the statement is correct, the teacher erases the verb and writes an X. Then the other team has a chance. The purpose of the game is to get three Xs or three Os in a row.

Cloze 📼

Read the following information about the Gold Rush. Try to fill in the blanks with the correct word. After you have filled in as much as you can, listen to the lecture on your cassette again as many times as necessary to fill in all the blanks.

The California Gold Rush and the Forty-Niners

Gold was discovered in _____ in 1848. When news of the discovery reached the east coast in 1849, many people, mostly _____, wanted to go to California to find _____ and get rich. These men were called the "Forty-Niners." About _____ "Forty-Niners" went to California. They went by three different _____: across the land by wagon train, around Cape Horn (South America) by _____, and through Panama in Central America by ship, _____, mule, and another ship. All three routes were _____ journeys, and many people _____ or turned back before they reached California. But the routes that the "Forty-Niners" opened made travel easier and _____ for those who came later.

The first men who arrived in California _____ gold easily, almost on the top of the ground, and many men got rich. The rest of the 75,000 who came expected to get rich _____ and easily, but many people _____ find any gold, and the men who found only a _____ spent all of it living in California. They lived in _____ where food and supplies were very _____. Life in the camps was very difficult and _____, and many men died.

Between 1848 and 1852, about $250,000,000 worth of gold was found in California, but after that the gold rush was _____ and expensive equipment was needed to _____ any more gold. But many of the men who went looking for gold _____ in California and brought their families.

Between 1848 and 1852, the population of San Francisco _____ from 800 to 25,000 people. The population of California increased from 15,000 to 250,000 in that same time.

CHAPTER SEVEN

POPULATION GROWTH: THE GREAT IMMIGRATION

In 1850 the population of the United States was about 23,000,000. In 1930 it was 123,000,000. What was the average increase per year for that 80-year period?

Much of the great increase in population was due to a great immigration from abroad, mostly from Europe. Today, many people in the United States have ancestors who came during that time. In this chapter you will learn about the period of great immigration from 1850 to 1924. You will also learn about some of the ethnic groups living in the United States today.

SHOW WHAT YOU KNOW

Work with your classmates to make a list of the countries from which you think immigrants have come to the United States. Is your country on the list?

FOCUS ON CONTENT: THE GREAT IMMIGRATION

In this section you will listen to some information about the numbers of immigrants who arrived during certain years. You will learn which countries sent the most immigrants to the United States during the years of greatest immigration, from 1850 to 1924.

Listen and Write 📼

This chart shows some of the years in the period of great immigration, the number of immigrants who arrived in those years, and an example of the number who arrived from specific countries.

Listen to the information on the cassette as many times as you need to in order to fill in the years, numbers, and countries in the chart below.

YEAR	TOTAL NUMBER OF IMMIGRANTS THAT YEAR	COUNTRY	NUMBER OF IMMIGRANTS
1851			221,000
	428,000		215,000
1870		Great Britain*	
1873			20,000
	789,000	Scandinavia**	
	1,285,000	the former Soviet Union***	
1914			284,000
1921	805,000		

*   Includes England, Scotland, and Wales
** Includes Norway, Sweden, Finland, Denmark, and Iceland
***Includes countries of the former Soviet Union, such as Russia, the Ukraine, Estonia, Lithuania, and Latvia.

Listen and Choose 📼

Listen to the questions on your cassette and circle the letter of the best answer.

1. a. more than 50%
    b. fewer than 50%
    c. fewer than 25%

2. a. about 10%
    b. about 20%
    c. about 50%

3. a. England
    b. Scotland
    c. Ireland

4. a. more than 50%
    b. fewer than 10%
    c. more than 10%

5. a. Norway
    b. Finland
    c. Denmark

FACTS NOTE:

In 1924 the door was closed to immigrants from many countries when the National Origins Act went into effect. That law limited the number of immigrants per year from any country to 10% of the representation of that nationality in the 1890 census.

Read and Decide

1. Read each statement and decide if it is true or false. Write *T* or *F* on the line. If a statement is false, change it to make it true.

    1. _____ 221,000 people came from Ireland in 1851.
    2. _____ There were 428,000 immigrants in 1854.
    3. _____ Immigrants from Great Britain included people from England and France.
    4. _____ There were 460,000 immigrants in 1870.
    5. _____ 200,000 people came from China in 1873.
    6. _____ Immigrants from Scandinavia included people from Norway, Sweden, Denmark, and Iceland.
    7. _____ 1907 was the peak year of immigration, with 1,285,000 immigrants.
    8. _____ Immigrants from the former Soviet Union included people from Latvia.
    9. _____ 260,000 people immigrated from Italy in 1914.
    10. _____ In 1914 there were 95,000 immigrants from Poland.

2. A bar graph can help you to visualize how many immigrants came to the United States from some countries. Complete the bar graph below using information from the chart on the previous page.

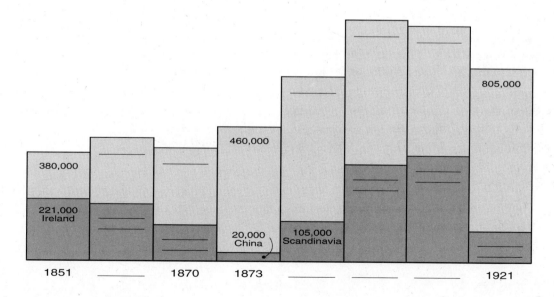

FOCUS ON SKILLS: PRONOUNCING COUNTRY NAMES, USING NATIONALITY WORDS AND PERCENTAGES

In this section you will practice the pronunciation of country names while talking about immigration in the United States and other countries. Then you will use nationality words and percentages to talk about large ethnic groups in the United States.

Pronunciation

Repeat the names of the countries after your teacher and practice with your classmates.

Countries that sent immigrants to the United States in the past:

Canada	France	Iceland	Lithuania	Scotland
China	Germany	Italy	Norway	Sweden
Denmark	Great Britain	Japan	Poland	the Netherlands
Estonia	Greece	Latvia	Portugal	Ukraine

Countries that have sent immigrants to the United States recently:

the Dominican Republic	Korea	Cuba	Mexico
the Philippines	Vietnam	India	

GRAMMAR NOTE:
Use *the* with names of countries that include the word *Republic* or a plural word.

Write the names of your classmates' countries on the blackboard. Practice the English pronunciation of those countries.

How do you pronounce the name of your country in your language? How do you say "the United States" in your language? Teach your classmates.

Speak, Listen, and Write

In this exercise you and a partner are going to talk about fifteen countries or regions that sent the most immigrants to the United States in the years between 1850 and 1924. You have half of the information and your partner has the other half. Ask and answer questions so that you and your partner can complete the charts below. When you are finished, check your answers by comparing your chart with your partner's chart.

Follow this example:

Student A says: Tell me about 1851.
Student B responds: In 1851, many people came from Ireland and France.
Student A writes *Ireland and France* on the line.

Student B then says: Tell me about 1881.
Student A responds: In 1881, many immigrants came from Norway, China, the Netherlands, and Germany.
Student B writes *Norway, China, the Netherlands, and Germany* on the line.

Student A: *Look here and cover the other chart.*

YEAR	COUNTRY/COUNTRIES
1851	
1881	Norway, China, the Netherlands, and Germany
1883	
1888	Great Britain
1907	
1919	Countries of the former Soviet Union and the Baltics
1921	
1924	Canada

Student B: *Look here and cover the other chart.*

YEAR		COUNTRY/COUNTRIES
1851		Ireland and France
1881		
1883		Sweden
1888		
1907		Italy, Japan, and Greece
1919		
1921		Poland and Portugal
1924		

Practice

You can make nationality words from country names. Nationality words are adjectives.

> He's from China. He's *Chinese*.

Study the patterns for nationality words and then fill in the nationality words for the countries below. When you finish, check your answers with your teacher. Then, write the name of your country and your nationality on the blackboard.

Pattern 1: *-ese* China–Chinese	Pattern 2: *-ish* Britain–British	Pattern 3: *-an* Germany–German	No Pattern France–French Greece–Greek
China _____ Japan _____ Vietnam _____ Portugal _____	Britain _____ Ireland _____ Poland _____	Germany _____ Italy _____ Korea _____ Canada _____ Mexico _____ Russia _____ Scandinavia* _____ *Scandinavia is a region.	France _____ Greece _____

Concentration

Play Concentration to memorize the nationality words. Make six pairs of cards with countries and nationality words on them. Mix up the cards and put them face down on a table. Get in groups. Take turns turning up two cards. If you have a match, keep the cards. If you don't have a match, turn the cards back over and the next person has a turn. Continue playing with more sets of six pairs.

Speak, Listen, and Change

In this exercise you and a partner are going to practice saying names of countries and nationality words. You will read a statement with a country name. Your partner will change it to a statement with a nationality word. Then you listen and change. Look at the Practice on page 67 if you can't remember the nationality words.

Follow this example:

Student A says:	He's from China.
Student B responds:	He's Chinese.
Student B then says:	She's from Canada.
Student A responds:	She's Canadian.

Student A: *Look here and cover the right side of the page.*

1. He's from China.
2.
3. She's from France.
4.
5. He's from Greece.
6.
7. She's from Britain.
8.
9. He's from Vietnam.
10.
11. She's from Poland.
12.

Student B: *Look here and cover the left side of the page.*

1.
2. She's from Canada.
3.
4. He's from Ireland.
5.
6. She's from Japan.
7.
8. He's from Italy.
9.
10. She's from Scandinavia.
11.
12. He's from Portugal.

Speak, Listen, and Write

In the United States, groups of immigrants often go to one state to settle. Their descendants continue to live there, and these large groups have an effect on the ethnic makeup of the state. In this exercise you will practice saying nationality words and percentages while you talk about the ethnic makeup of some states.

Practice the pronunciation of these percentages. Repeat the numbers after your teacher and practice the pronunciation with your classmates.

15%	20%	23%	34%	42%	57%	63%	98%	51%	65%	76%	29%

In this exercise you and a partner are going to talk about the people in sixteen states and learn about the nationalities of their ancestors. You have half the information and your partner has the other half. Work back and forth to fill in the missing percentages and nationalities on the maps. Think about which large percentages were not caused by immigration. When you finish, check your answers by looking at your partner's map.

Follow this example:

Student A says: Tell me about Georgia.
Student B responds: In Georgia, 32% of the people have British ancestors.
Student A writes *32%* and *British* on the state of Georgia.

Student B then says: Tell me about New York.
Student A says: In New York, 12% of the people have Italian ancestors.
Student B writes *12%* and *Italian* on the state of New York.

Student A: *Look here and cover the other map.*

Student B: *Look here and cover the other map.*

Talk About This!

Has there been immigration into your country? If so, where did the people immigrate from? Use this chart to poll your classmates about immigration in their countries. Write the names and countries of some of your classmates in the left column, and ask each one about immigration to his/her country. Make notes in the chart following the example for the United States. When your chart is complete, share what you learned with your classmates, and practice the pronunciation of any new country names that you discussed.

Name/Country	Immigrants?		If yes, from what countries? Recently or in the past?
U.S.A.	(yes)	no	In the past from Europe; recently from Southeast Asia and Latin America
	yes	no	
	yes	no	
	yes	no	

FOCUS ON CONTENT: ELLIS ISLAND, IMMIGRATION STATION

When many immigrants arrived in the United States from Europe by ship, most of them passed through an immigration station on Ellis Island in New York. In this section you will listen to a lecture to learn about that immigration station.

Listen and Write 🔲

Listen to the lecture about Ellis Island as many times as necessary in order to fill in the notes below.

Location:

Ellis Island is _____ _____ south of Manhattan Island, in New York City.
Near the Statue of _____.

Immigration Station:

From _____ to _____

Number of immigrants: _____ which was ____% of all immigrants during that period.

They arrived by _____.
They received _____ _____ and _____.
They bought _____ _____.

Museum:

1965: became part of the _____ ___ _____ National Monument.
It was renovated from _____ to _____.
1990: opened as an _____ _____.

Vocabulary

Are there any words in the lecture that you don't know? Write them here and ask a classmate or your teacher to explain.

Word   **Explanation, synonym, or example**

_____   _____

_____   _____

_____   _____

_____   _____

Speak, Listen, and Decide

In this exercise you and a partner will take turns reading statements about Ellis Island and deciding if they are true or false. Look back at your notes on page 70 if you can't remember the information. When you finish the exercise, check your answers with your teacher.

Follow this example:

Student A reads: Ellis Island is in New York.
Student B responds: That's TRUE.
   and circles TRUE.

Student B reads: Ellis Island is near the Statue of Liberty.
Student A responds: That's TRUE.
   and circles TRUE.

Student A: *Look here and cover the right side of the page.*	**Student B:** *Look here and cover the left side of the page.*
1. Ellis Island is in New York.	1. TRUE FALSE
2. TRUE FALSE	2. Ellis Island is near the Statue of Liberty.
3. Ellis Island was an immigration station from 1893 to 1903.	3. TRUE FALSE
4. TRUE FALSE	4. 20,000 immigrants passed through Ellis Island.
5. 90% of all immigrants passed through Ellis island.	5. TRUE FALSE
6. TRUE FALSE	6. The immigrants arrived by airplane.
7. Immigrants received medical exams on Ellis Island.	7. TRUE FALSE
8. TRUE FALSE	8. Immigrants bought train tickets at Ellis Island.
9. Ellis Island is an immigration station today.	9. TRUE FALSE
10. TRUE FALSE	10. Ellis Island is closed today.
11. In 1965, Ellis Island became part of the Statue of Liberty National Monument.	11. TRUE FALSE
12. TRUE FALSE	12. Ellis Island was renovated between 1983 and 1990.
13. Ellis Island is an immigration museum now.	13. TRUE FALSE
14. TRUE FALSE	14. The immigration museum at Ellis Island was opened in 1983.

PUT IT TOGETHER

Circulation

In this activity you will have the chance to speak with four different members of your class about immigration.

First, write the names of four classmates from four different parts of the world on the lines to the left of the questions. When everyone is finished, stand up, go to the person whose name appears next to the question, and ask the question. Write a short answer.

_____   Did any of your ancestors immigrate to your country?

                             If yes, where were they from?

                             _____

_____   Have people from your country immigrated into the
                             United States in the past?

                             If yes, what part have they settled in?

                             _____

_____   Are people immigrating into your country now?

                             If yes, where are they from?

                             _____

_____   Are people from your country immigrating into the
                             United States now?

                             If yes, which part of the country are they going to?

                             _____

Now share what you learned with the rest of the class.

Word Search Puzzle

Circle the 16 nationality words. They are horizontal and vertical.

```
( J  A  P  A  N  E  S  E )  P  K  O  R  E  A  N
  A  V  O  H  S  I  P  R  J  O  R  I  S  H  N
  P  I  R  O  B  R  I  T  I  S  H  K  R  E  P
  U  E  T  V  B  T  V  E  S  E  S  E  U  S  O
  I  T  U  T  A  N  S  C  I  S  G  S  S  E  L
  T  N  G  A  C  H  I  N  E  S  E  E  S  N  I
  A  A  U  A  A  R  M  A  I  R  R  L  I  O  S
  L  M  E  H  N  Y  D  N  A  L  M  I  A  R  H
  I  E  S  P  A  G  R  E  E  K  A  A  N  A  E
  A  S  E  M  D  O  G  Z  A  N  N  N  P  N  S
  N  E  M  E  I  R  I  S  H  R  I  S  H  O  E
  A  I  F  W  A  N  A  H  F  R  E  N  C  H  L
  I  S  H  O  N  O  N  O  N  I  N  I  S  H  M
  O  I  S  H  V  X  M  E  X  I  C  A  N  P  R
  S  C  A  N  D  I  N  A  V  I  A  N  A  N  N
```

Cloze 🔲

Read the following information about Ellis Island. Try to fill in the blanks with the correct word. After you have filled in as much as you can, listen to the lecture on the cassette again as many times as necessary to fill in all the blanks.

Ellis Island is _____ mile south of Manhattan Island in New York City, near the Statue of Liberty. It was an immigration station from _____ to _____ . In that time, _____ immigrants passed through Ellis Island. That was _____% of all immigrants who entered the United States in that period.

The immigrants arrived from _____ by ship. On Ellis Island they received _____ examinations and interviews about where they planned to _____ and _____ . Then they bought train tickets there and continued on to their new homes.

Ellis Island was closed for many years. In _____ , it became part of the Statue of Liberty National Monument. It was renovated between _____ and _____ , and it was opened as an immigration museum in 1990.

CHAPTER EIGHT

THE U.S.A. TODAY: THE TWENTIETH CENTURY

The United States became an important world leader in the twentieth century, and some of the events of the twentieth century have made the world what it is today. In this chapter you will talk about the most famous events and people of the twentieth century.

SHOW WHAT YOU KNOW

Work with your classmates to list some of the important events of the twentieth century. Did some of these events involve your country? How?

FOCUS ON CONTENT: THE DECADES OF THE TWENTIETH CENTURY

In this section you will learn about some major events that occurred in the United States in each decade of the twentieth century.

Matching

The boxes on this page contain lists of major events that occurred in the United States in the decades of the twentieth century. Work with your classmates and your teacher to match the events with the decades. Write the dates on the lines. The most important words and names are in **bold** letters. Look at them if you don't understand all of the vocabulary.

The Titanic sank, **Henry Ford** used the first assembly line to produce cars, and the United States fought in **World War I**.

Eisenhower was president, the United States fought in **the Korean War**. **Disneyland** opened, and schools were integrated.

The United States fought in the **Persian Gulf War,** and **Bill Clinton** was elected the first Democratic president since 1976.

President **Kennedy** was assassinated, the United States fought in the Vietnam War, the first men walked on the **moon**, the Woodstock Music and Art fair was held.

THE DECADES

1900–1909 ("the nineteen hundreds")
1910–1919 ("the nineteen teens")
1920–1929 ("the nineteen twenties")
1930–1939 ("the nineteen thirties")
1940–1949 ("the nineteen forties")
1950–1959 ("the nineteen fifties")
1960–1969 ("the nineteen sixties")
1970–1979 ("the nineteen seventies")
1980–1989 ("the nineteen eighties")
1990–present ("the nineteen nineties")

Anti-war protests were popular, **abortion** became legal, **Nixon** resigned as president over the **Watergate** scandal, and the United States celebrated its **bicentennial**.

Henry Ford produced the first **Model T Ford car, the Wright brothers** flew their airplane for the first time, and Admiral Peary went to the North Pole.

Women got the right to vote, Charles **Lindbergh** flew across the Atlantic, alcohol was prohibited in "Prohibition," Mickey Mouse made his first movie, and the **Stock Market crashed**.

Scientists built the first **atomic bomb** in the "Manhattan Project," the United States fought in **World War II,** and **the United Nations** met for the first time.

The Empire State Building was opened as the tallest building in the world, the "Prohibition" against alcohol ended, and **Franklin Roosevelt** was president during **the Great Depression**.

Reagan was president, **the Space Shuttle** program started, and the Olympics were in Los Angeles.

Vocabulary

In this exercise you will study some of the new vocabulary from the decades described on page 74.

Find a word in this decade	that means	and write it here:
1960s	killed a public person	_____
1920s	fell greatly and quickly	_____
1910s	place where workers stand in a factory	_____
1970s	an event that can ruin a career	_____
1930s	must not	_____
1970s	quit	_____
1950s	black and white people put together in one school	_____
1930s	a time when the economy was very bad	_____

Listen and Decide 🔲

Listen to the statements on the cassette and circle TRUE *or* FALSE.

1.	TRUE	FALSE		6.	TRUE	FALSE
2.	TRUE	FALSE		7.	TRUE	FALSE
3.	TRUE	FALSE		8.	TRUE	FALSE
4.	TRUE	FALSE		9.	TRUE	FALSE
5.	TRUE	FALSE		10.	TRUE	FALSE

Listen and Choose 🔲

Listen to the statements about twentieth century events on your cassette. Circle the correct decade for each statement.

1.	1930s	1940s	1950s	6.	1940s	1950s	1960s
2.	1920s	1930s	1940s	7.	1940s	1950s	1960s
3.	1930s	1940s	1950s	8.	1960s	1970s	1980s
4.	1920s	1930s	1940s	9.	1960s	1970s	1980s
5.	1930s	1940s	1950s	10.	1920s	1930s	1940s

Read and Decide

Work in groups to order the events in the twentieth century.

_____ Abortion became legal.

_____ Men walked on the moon.

_____ Lindbergh flew across the Atlantic.

___1___ Admiral Peary went to the North Pole.

_____ The United States fought in the Persian Gulf War.

_____ The Titanic sank.

_____ The United States fought in World War II.

_____ The Olympics were in Los Angeles.

_____ "Prohibition" ended.

_____ Disneyland opened.

SKILLS NOTE:

Use *in the* with decades:	In the 1920s
	In the 1960s
Use *in* with years:	In 1962
	In 1984

Speak, Listen, and Choose

You can use the past tense of *be* to talk about many past events.

When was World War II?	It was in the 1940s.
When was Woodstock?	It was in the 1960s.

In this exercise, you and a partner are going to take turns asking and answering questions about the twentieth century. Look at the information on page 74 if you can't remember. Circle the letter and say a long answer. When you finish, check your answers with your teacher.

Follow this example:

Student A asks first: When was World War II?
Student B responds: It was in the 1940s.
  and circles *a.*

Student B then asks: When was the Great Depression?
Student A responds: It was in the 1930s.
  and circles *a.*

Student A: *Look here and cover the right side of the page.*

1. World War II

2.   a.   1930s   b.   1950s

3. the crash of the Stock Market

4.   a.   1970s   b.   1990s

5. the Korean War

6.   a.   1920s   b.   1940s

7. Lindbergh's flight across the Atlantic

8.   a.   1960s   b.   1980s

9. abortion made legal

10.   a.   1930s   b.   1950s

11. Kennedy assassinated

12.   a.   1900s   b.   1980s

13. The Bicentennial

14.   a.   1920s   b.   1950s

Student B: *Look here and cover the left side of the page*

1.   a.   1940s   b.   1960s

2. the Great Depression

3.   a.   1920s   b.   1940s

4. the Persian Gulf War

5.   a.   1950s   b.   1970s

6. the Manhattan Project/first atomic bomb

7.   a.   1920s   b.   1960s

8. the first Space Shuttle flight

9.   a.   1940s   b.   1970s

10. Eisenhower president

11.   a.   1960s   b.   1980s

12. the Model T Ford first produced

13.   a.   1970s   b.   1990s

14. Mickey Mouse's first movie

Matching

Practice the irregular past tense verbs in the box while you review some of the events of the twentieth century. Match the words on the left with the phrases on the right to make statements about the events of the twentieth century. Change the verbs in parentheses to past tense. Review the verbs in the box before you begin.

become—became	fight—fought	get—got	make—made
build—built	fly—flew	go—went	sink—sank

1. Women (get) _____
2. The Titanic (sink) _____
3. The United States (fight) _____
4. Lindbergh (fly) _____
5. Mickey Mouse (make) _____
6. Admiral Peary (go) _____
7. Scientists (build) _____
8. Abortion (become) _____

a. to the North Pole in 1909.
b. in World War II.
c. in 1912.
d. his first movie in 1928.
e. across the Atlantic in 1927.
f. legal in 1973.
g. the first atomic bomb in the Manhattan Project.
h. the right to vote in 1920.

Concentration

Play Concentration to remember the events and the decades. Make six pairs of cards. Write a decade on one card and an event from that decade on the other card. Put the cards face down on a table or on the floor. Play in groups. Take turns turning up two cards. Try to match the event and the decade. If you don't make a match, turn the cards back over. If you make a match, keep the cards and have another turn.

Talk About This!

Many of the events in the recent history of the United States have been global, worldwide events. In this activity you will talk about some of the events and how they may have involved your country. First, read and answer the questions in the chart. Then get together with a partner and share your information. When your chart is complete, share what you learned with your classmates.

QUESTION	YOU	YOUR PARTNER
Did your country fight in World War I?		
Did anyone in your country build or experiment with early automobiles or airplanes?		
Were the people in your country very poor in the 1930s?		
Did your country fight in World War II?		
Did your country join the United Nations?		
Does your country have or participate in a space program?		
Has your country hosted the Olympics?		
Did your country fight in the Persian Gulf War?		

FOCUS ON CONTENT: FAMOUS NAMES OF THE TWENTIETH CENTURY

In this section you will learn about some of the famous people who have lived in the United States during the twentieth century.

Matching

You might recognize some of these famous twentieth century Americans. Work with your classmates to match the names with their accomplishments. Write the letter of the answer on the line. Check your answers with your teacher.

1.	Babe Ruth	_____	a.	first female vice-presidential candidate
2.	Al Capone	_____	b.	American Indian athlete in the 1912 Olympics
3.	Helen Keller	_____	c.	baseball player who hit 714 home runs
4.	Jim Thorpe	_____	d.	architect who designed prairie-style houses
5.	Geraldine Ferraro	_____	e.	Black Muslim leader
6.	Malcolm X	_____	f.	FBI Director, 1924–1972
7.	Shirley Temple	_____	g.	union organizer for farm workers
8.	J. Edgar Hoover	_____	h.	blind and deaf educator and writer
9.	Frank Lloyd Wright	_____	i.	child care expert and writer
10.	Dr. Benjamin Spock	_____	j.	organized crime leader
11.	Cesar Chavez	_____	k.	child actress of the 1930s

Speak, Listen, and Change

You can change a verb (action) into a noun (the person who does the action) by adding -er.

Use verbs to talk about what people do.			Use nouns to talk about the people.		
He	*plays*	baseball.	He	is a	*baseball player.*
She	*educates*	people.	She	is an	*educator.*
SUBJ	+ VERB	+ OBJECT	SUBJ	is + a/an	(+ADJ) + NOUN
					(VERB + er/or)

In this exercise you and a partner will take turns reading questions and making answers. If you hear a verb in the question, answer with a noun. If you hear a noun, answer with a verb. Some words in each answer are provided for you. When you finish, check your answers with your teacher.

Follow this example:

Student A reads:	Who plays baseball?
Student B responds:	A baseball player.
Student B then reads:	Who leads a union?
Student A responds:	A union leader.

GRAMMAR NOTE:
Change a verb to a noun by adding -er, -or, or sometimes -ess (for a woman).

Student A: *Look here and cover the right side of the page.*

1. Who plays baseball?
2. A union _____.
3. Who educates people?
4. A movie _____.
5. Who directs the FBI?
6. A _____.
7. Who organizes unions?
8. A farm _____.
9. What does a crime leader do?
10. She _____ people.
11. What does a movie actress do?
12. He _____ the FBI.
13. What does a writer do?
14. He _____ unions.
15. What does a farm worker do?
16. He _____ baseball.

Student B: *Look here and cover the left side of the page.*

1. A baseball _____.
2. Who leads a union?
3. An _____.
4. Who acts in movies?
5. The FBI _____.
6. Who writes books?
7. A union _____.
8. Who works on a farm?
9. He _____ criminals.
10. What does an educator do?
11. She _____ in movies.
12. What does the FBI Director do?
13. He _____ books.
14. What does a union organizer do?
15. He _____ on a farm.
16. What does a baseball player do?

Matching

In this exercise you will talk about famous names of the twentieth century while you practice some irregular and regular past tense verbs. Match the names on the left with the phrases on the right. Change the verbs in parentheses to past tense. Review the verbs in the box before you begin.

More Irregular Past Tense Verbs		Some Regular Past Tense Verbs
hit—hit	lead—led	act—acted
teach—taught	run—ran	direct—directed
fight—fought	write—wrote	design—designed

1. J. Edgar Hoover (*direct*) _____   a. for vice president in 1984.
2. Geraldine Ferraro (*run*) _____   b. homes and buildings.
3. Helen Keller (*teach*) _____   c. deaf children to communicate.
4. Dr. Benjamin Spock (*write*) _____   d. for rights for black people.
5. Malcolm X (*fight*) _____   e. in many movies.
6. Al Capone (*lead*) _____   f. the FBI for almost 50 years.
7. Shirley Temple (*act*) _____   g. 714 home runs.
8. Frank Lloyd Wright (*design*) _____   h. books about raising children.
9. Babe Ruth (*hit*) _____   i. organized crime for many years.

Who Am I?

In this game you will practice making *yes-no* questions while you review some of the famous names from this chapter and around the world. Your teacher will attach the name of a famous person to your back. You must find out who the famous person is by asking only *yes-no* questions. After everyone in the class has a name on his/her back, stand up, walk around, and ask and answer questions until you discover who "you are." Begin with some of these questions:

Am I living?
Am I a man?
Am I in politics?

Am I dead?
Was I a woman?
Was I a baseball player?

FOCUS ON CONTENT: MARTIN LUTHER KING, JR., CIVIL RIGHTS LEADER

The civil rights movement in the United States started during the 1950s with the integration of public schools and transportation. Martin Luther King, Jr., was an important figure in the movement. What do you know about him? In this section you will listen to a lecture about the life of Martin Luther King, Jr.

Vocabulary 📼

The following words are important in the lecture. Listen to the cassette and complete the sentences with words from the box.

assassinated	integration	minister	civil rights
theological seminary	delivered	boycott	jail

1. Martin Luther King, Jr., gave many speeches. He _____ his most important speech in front of the Lincoln Memorial in Washington, D.C.

2. There was a bus _____ in Montgomery, Alabama. As a protest, people stopped riding the buses.

3. He studied religion at a _____ _____.

4. The police arrested him and put him in _____.

5. The civil rights leaders worked for _____. They wanted black and white people to be able to live, study, and work together.

6. Martin Luther King, Jr., was _____ during the 1960s. More important people were murdered in the 1960s than in any other decade.

7. King was a _____, or pastor, of a church in Alabama.

8. In the fight for _____ _____, Martin Luther King, Jr., wanted blacks to have political, social, and economic equality with whites.

Listen and Write 📼

Listen to the lecture on the cassette as many times as necessary to in order to fill in the blanks.

Martin Luther King, Jr.

1929–	Born in _____ _____	1957–	helped start _____ _____
1948–	graduated from _____	1963–	the March on Washington and his _____ speech
1954–	_____ _____	1964–	_____ _____
1955–	received Ph.D. from _____	1968–	_____ _____
	and participated in the Montgomery bus boycott	1983–	Martin Luther King, Jr., Day became a federal holiday.

Read and Decide

Read each statement and decide if it is true or false. Write T or F on the line. If a statement is false, change it to make it true.

1. _____ Martin Luther King, Jr., was born in Montgomery, Alabama.
2. _____ He graduated from college when he was 19 years old.
3. _____ He received his Ph.D. from Boston University in 1955.
4. _____ He was a Baptist minister in Memphis, Tennessee.
5. _____ He was influenced by the teachings of Mahatma Gandhi on non-violent protest.
6. _____ He helped start the Southern Christian Leadership Conference.
7. _____ He delivered his famous speech, "I Have a Dream," in 1968.
8. _____ About 250,000 people attended the March on Washington in 1963.
9. _____ King received the Nobel Prize for physics in 1964.
10. _____ He was assassinated on April 4, 1968.

Speak, Listen, and Choose

In this exercise you and a partner will take turns asking and answering questions to review the information in the lecture about Martin Luther King, Jr. Circle the letter of the best answer and tell your partner the answer you chose. Look back at the information in the previous exercises if you can't remember an answer. When you finish, check your answers with your teacher.

Follow this example:

Student A asks first: When was Martin Luther King, Jr., born?
Student B responds: In 1929.
 and circles *a*.

Student A: *Look here and cover the right side of the page.*

1. When was Martin Luther King born?

2. a. in Boston
   (b.) in Atlanta

3. Where did he go after college?

4. a. Mahatma Gandhi
   b. Al Capone

5. Why did blacks boycott the buses in Montgomery?

6. a. for the bus boycott
   b. for his non-violent protests

7. When did he win the Nobel Peace Prize?

8. a. in 1964
   b. in 1968

Student B: *Look here and cover the left side of the page.*

1. (a.) in 1929
   b. in 1948

2. Where was he born?

3. a. to Montgomery
   b. to a theological seminary

4. Who influenced King?

5. a. to protest ticket prices
   b. to demand integration

6. Why was King sent to jail?

7. a. in 1964
   b. in 1968

8. When was King assassinated?

PUT IT TOGETHER

Past Tense Sentence Combinations

Work with your classmates to combine the following into sentences to review the information in this chapter. How many sentences can you make? Change all of the verbs to past tense.

		baseball.
Henry Ford		across the Atlantic.
The Titanic	fly	deaf children to communicate.
The Empire State Building	make	in 1955.
The Wright brothers	fight	in 1912.
Frank Lloyd Wright	teach	in World War I.
Shirley Temple	open	in many movies.
Babe Ruth	sink	in World War II.
Mickey Mouse	invent	the assembly line.
Manhattan Project scientists	resign	his first movie in 1927.
Richard Nixon	build	an airplane at Kitty Hawk.
Helen Keller	design	homes and buildings.
Charles Lindbergh	act	an atomic bomb.
The United States	play	in 1931.
Disneyland		in 1974.
		in the Korean War.

Jumble

Write the irregular past tense of the verbs in the box in the puzzle. Letters are written in to give you hints.

bring
come
pay
sell
make
fight
teach
sink
build
lead
run
write

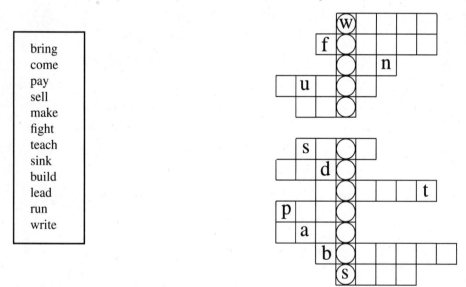

What words do the circled letters spell out? Write the words in this question:

The people in this chapter have been important in the United States.
Which ones do you consider to be _____ _____ also?

Tic Tac Toe

Play Tic Tac Toe with your classmates. Your teacher will draw a big tic-tac-toe grid on the blackboard and fill in each square with a verb from this chapter.

Divide the class into two teams—X and O. X goes first. One student chooses a verb and makes a statement about a person or event from the twentieth century. If the statement is correct, the teacher erases the verb and writes an X, and the other team has a chance. If the statement is incorrect, the teacher doesn't write an X, and the other team has a chance. If the other team makes a correct statement, the teacher erases the word and writes an O. Continue taking turns. The purpose of the game is to get three Xs or three Os in a row.

Cloze 🔲

Read the text of the lecture about Martin Luther King, Jr. Fill in as many blanks as you can. Then listen to the lecture again to fill in the rest.

Martin Luther King, Jr.

Martin Luther King, Jr., devoted his life to the fight for civil _____, including political, social, and economic equality for all people in the United States. King was born in _____, Georgia, on January 15, 1929. He graduated from Morehouse College in _____ at the age of 19. After that, he studied at a theological seminary where he received a bachelor of divinity degree. Then he studied at _____ University, where he received his Ph.D. in _____. During his _____, he was influenced by the teachings of Mahatma Gandhi and started to believe in the power of non-violent _____.

In 1954, King moved to Montgomery, _____, with his wife, Coretta Scott King. In that same year, in Montgomery, he became minister of a Baptist _____. In 1955, he was a leader in the Montgomery bus _____. That protest led to the _____ of public buses in Alabama. In 1957, he helped start the Southern Christian Leadership Conference, a _____ of organizations that worked for _____ rights. He was often sent to _____ for his participation in protests, even though they were _____. In the summer of 1963, King organized a _____ on Washington in which about 250,000 people demonstrated peacefully for civil rights. It was during the March on _____, on August 28, 1963, that King delivered his famous and powerful "I Have a _____" speech. He received the _____ Peace Prize in 1964.

On April 4, 1968, King was _____ in Memphis, Tennessee. In 1983, the third Monday in January became Martin Luther King, Jr., Day, in honor of his _____.

Here are some activities related to history for you to do on your own, with a small group, or with your whole class.

1. What was happening in your country around the year 1776? What was the form of government? How did the people live? Were the borders of your country the same as they are now? Prepare a 5-minute report answering these and other questions for your classmates. Use a poster, handout, or overhead to help your classmates understand your report.

2. Did your country ever receive independence from another country? Describe it for your classmates. Prepare a 5-minute report describing the events surrounding the independence. Bring to class visual aids such as a poster with a time line, pictures, or maps to make your speech more interesting.

3. Plan a trip to a local history museum to study one of the times described in this unit. When you return to class, share what you learned with your classmates.

4. If you are on the East Coast, plan a visit to Boston, Philadelphia, or Yorktown, and visit places that were important in the Revolutionary War. Before you go, contact tourist offices or the Chamber of Commerce for information, and share what you learned with your classmates when you return.

5. If you are on the West Coast, plan a trip to San Francisco or Sacramento to learn more about the 1849 Gold Rush. Before you go, contact tourist offices or the Chamber of Commerce for information, and share what you learned with your classmates when you return.

6. Interview some Americans about their ethnic backgrounds. What nationalities are represented in their families? Did any of them have ancestors who came during the period of great immigration (1850–1920)? Did they come through Ellis Island? Report what you find to your classmates, or invite the people to class and interview them in small groups.

7. If you are near New York, plan a trip to Ellis Island. Before you go, look in your local library for a book about Ellis Island. Share what you learned with your classmates when you return.

8. Plan a trip to a retirement home. Interview the people there about how life was during the Great Depression. Plan your questions in class, and share what you learned with your classmates when you return.

9. Choose someone from the exercise on "Famous Names of the Twentieth Century." Read about that person in the library and give a 5-minute report to your classmates. The children's or young adults' section of the library often has easy-to-understand books. Prepare a poster or overhead to help your classmates understand your speech, or bring visual aids such as pictures to make your speech more interesting.

10. "Who Am I?" Choose a famous person from this unit. Read about that person in the library. When you return to class, pretend to be that person while your classmates interview you for three to five minutes.

11. Check out and watch videos from your local library. Try to find Martin Luther King, Jr.'s, "I Have a Dream" speech, or President Kennedy's Inaugural Address, in which he said, "Ask not what your country can do for you; ask what you can do for your country." Or find a movie about one of the people in the unit, such as "The Miracle Worker," the story of Hellen Keller's early life.

We the People: The Government of the U.S.A.

CHAPTER NINE

SEPARATION OF POWER

The government of the United States is separated into three parts, as described in the United States Constitution. In this chapter you will learn about those different parts, called branches, and the powers they have. You will also learn about some very important changes to the United States Constitution.

SHOW WHAT YOU KNOW

Look at the illustration on page 89 which shows the different branches of the American government. Work with your classmates to fill in any information you already know about the different parts, where they are located, and the people who work in them. The lecture in the next section will help you fill in what you don't already know.

FOCUS ON CONTENT: THREE BRANCHES OF GOVERNMENT

In this section you will hear a short lecture about the three branches of the American government. You will learn about the people who work in them, where they work, how long they work in these positions, and their powers and responsibilities.

Vocabulary 📼

The following words are important in the lecture. Listen to the cassette and complete the sentences with words from the box.

judge	responsibility	bill	terms
representative	official	vetoed	enforce
abroad	legislative	judicial	branch

1. A _____ from each class participates in the student government and tells the school what his or her classmates want.

2. A _____ becomes a law when the president has signed it.

3. The _____ listened to the lawyers' arguments and decided not to send the man to jail.

4. Franklin D. Roosevelt was the only American president to serve three _____ in office.

5. The U.S. Navy is a _____ of the Armed Forces.

6. The president _____ the bill because it would cost too much money.

7. The _____ branch of government makes the laws.

8. The journalist talked to a government _____ about the new law.

9. It is the job of the local police to _____ the laws.

10. Both teachers and students have a _____ to prepare for class.

11. The _____ branch of the government involves the courts.

12. Many people go _____ to study foreign languages.

Listen and Write 🔲

Listen to the lecture on your cassette as many times as you need to in order to fill in the information about the U.S. government in the illustration.

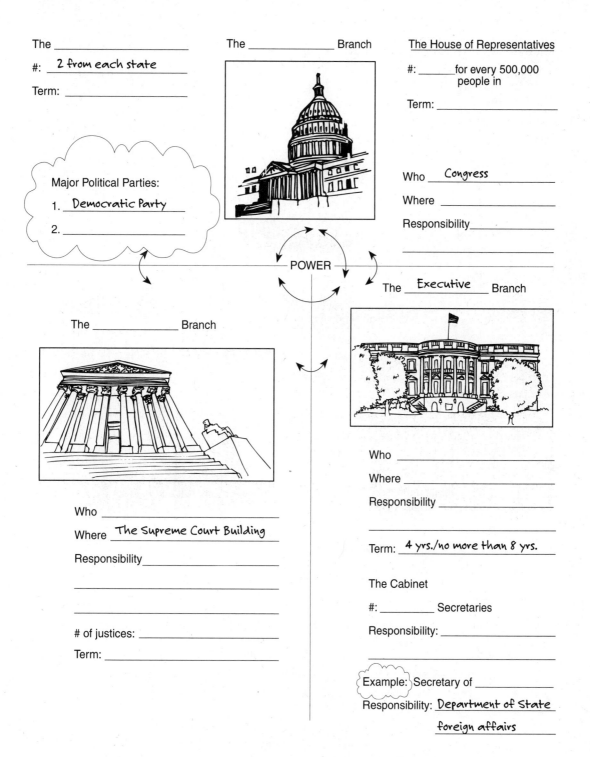

The _____

#: ___2 from each state___

Term: _____

Major Political Parties:

1. ___Democratic Party___

2. _____

The _____ Branch

The House of Representatives

#: _____for every 500,000 people in

Term: _____

Who ___Congress___

Where _____

Responsibility_____

_____

POWER

The ___Executive___ Branch

The _____ Branch

Who _____

Where ___The Supreme Court Building___

Responsibility_____

_____

_____

# of justices: _____

Term: _____

Who _____

Where _____

Responsibility _____

_____

Term: ___4 yrs./no more than 8 yrs.___

The Cabinet

#: _____ Secretaries

Responsibility: _____

_____

Example: Secretary of _____

Responsibility: ___Department of State foreign affairs___

Listen and Choose

Listen to the questions on the cassette and circle the letter of the best answer. Look back at the chart on page 89 if you can't remember the information.

1. a. the judicial branch
   b. the executive branch
   c. the legislative branch

2. a. 2 terms
   b. 1 terms
   c. 4 terms

3. a. the chief justice
   b. the senators
   c. the president

4. a. the chief justice
   b. the president
   c. the representatives

5. a. to make laws
   b. to explain laws
   c. to enforce laws

6. a. 50
   b. 100
   c. 435

7. a. 2 years
   b. 6 years
   c. life

8. a. the secretary of state
   b. the president
   c. the Congress

9. a. every 2 years
   b. every 4 years
   c. every 6 years

10. a. the White House
    b. the Capitol
    c. the Supreme Court

Read and Decide

In this exercise you will review information from the lecture describing how Congress works. Read and decide what order the statements go in. Number the statements from 1 to 8.

_____ People tell their elected officials what laws they want and how they want their tax money spent.

_____ Representatives and senators meet in committees to combine bills that the House and Senate have passed separately.

_____ If the bill is vetoed, Congress may vote and try to pass the law without the president's signature.

_____ The House and Senate vote again on the combined bills and, upon passage, send the bills to the president for his approval.

_____ People elect senators and representatives from their home states.

_____ The president either approves a bill and signs it into law or rejects it and vetoes it.

_____ Each house decides separately what issues are most important, writing and voting on bills, which are proposed laws.

_____ The senators and representatives tell their houses what the people from their districts and states want.

Talk About This!

How are laws made in your country? Is the process similar to law making in the U.S.A.?

1. As best you can, list the steps in making a law in your country.

2. Share this information with your classmates by making a short presentation. Draw a simple picture if it will help you explain.

FOCUS ON SKILLS: PRONOUNCING PLURAL NOUNS, USING TAG QUESTIONS

In this section you will practice the pronunciation of plural noun endings with words related to American government. You will also practice asking and answering tag questions about the information in the lecture.

Pronunciation

There are three different ways to pronounce plural noun endings. Study the rules below. Then listen to the cassette and practice the pronunciation.

Rule 1: The plural noun ending -s is pronounced [s] after most voiceless consonant sounds.	
[p] groups	The highest of all *courts* in the U.S.A. is the Supreme Court.
[t] departments	Many different *groups* make up a political party.
[k] breaks	American governmental *departments* are similar to ministries.
[f] chiefs	

Rule 2: The plural noun ending -s is pronounced [z] after most voiced consonant sounds and vowel sounds.		
[b] cabs	[r] years	Many *bills* in Congress do not become law.
[d] heads	[l] bills	Both political *parties* are represented in Congress.
[g] dogs	[m] terms	The representative from New York served for 2 *years*.
[v] representatives	[n] plans	
[vowel sound] parties, laws, days		

Rule 3: The plural noun ending -(e)s is pronounced [iz] after sounds like [s], [z], [s], [c], and [j].	
[s] justices	Only the country's best *judges* sit on the Supreme Court.
[z] causes	People don't like to pay *taxes*.
[c] branches	There are two *houses*, or chambers, in the Congress.
[j] judges	
[s] wishes	

Listen and Choose

Now you will hear some sentences about the U.S. government. Listen to the cassette and put a check under [s], [z], or [iz] depending on which type of noun you hear.

	[s]	[z]	[iz]
1.			
2.			
3.			
4.			
5.			
6.			
7.			
8.			
9.			
10.			

Speak, Listen, and Decide

In this exercise you and a partner will practice the pronunciation of plural noun endings in sentences about the branches of government. Take turns reading statements and deciding if the noun ends with [s], [z], or [iz]. Circle the correct pronunciation, and tell your partner what you decided. When you finish, check your answers by looking at your partner's side of the page.

Follow this example:

Student A says: There are nine *justices* [iz] on the Supreme Court. *justices*
Student B decides [s] [z] [iz].

Student B says: Representatives are elected from state *districts* [s]. *districts*
Student A decides [s] [z] [iz].

Student A: *Look here and cover the right side of the page.*

1. There are nine *justices* [iz] on the Supreme Court. *justices*
2. ([s])   [z]   [iz]
3. The government of the United *States* [s] is based on a constitution. *states*
4. [s]   [z]   [iz]
5. The Cabinet represents all the *departments* [s] of the government. *departments*
6. [s]   [z]   [iz]
7. There are two *senators* [z] from every state. *senators*
8. [s]   [z]   [iz]
9. There are two major political *parties* [z] in the United States. *parties*
10. [s]   [z]   [iz]
11. The Senate and House present the most important *bills* [z] to the president. *bills*
12. [s]   [z]   [iz]

Student B: *Look here and cover the left side of the page.*

1. [s]   [z]   ([iz])
2. Representatives are elected from state *districts* [s]. *districts*
3. [s]   [z]   [iz]
4. Three *branches* [iz] of the government share power. *branches*
5. [s]   [z]   [iz]
6. The Supreme Court is responsible for explaining the *laws* [z]. *laws*
7. [s]   [z]   [iz]
8. The number of *representatives* [z] depends on a state's population. *representatives*
9. [s]   [z]   [iz]
10. The chief justice is the head of all *judges* [iz]. *judges*
11. [s]   [z]   [iz]
12. All *states* [s] elect the same number of senators. *states*

Speak, Listen, and Decide

A *tag question* is a question that you add to the end of a statement. You can use the affirmative statement/negative tag pattern when they think the information is correct but you want to make sure.
Usually, if your information is correct, you will get a *yes* answer. However, if the information is incorrect, you'll get a *no* answer.

[+] Statement	[-] Tag	[+] Answer If You're Right!
Congress <u>is</u> in the Capitol,	<u>isn't</u> it?	Yes, it <u>is</u>.
Congress <u>makes</u> laws,	<u>doesn't</u> it?	Yes, it <u>does</u>.

[+] Statement	[-] Tag	[-] Answer If You're Wrong!
Congress <u>is</u> the judicial branch,	<u>isn't</u> it?	No, it <u>isn't</u>.
The president <u>serves</u> 2 years,	<u>doesn't</u> he?	No, he <u>doesn't</u>.

NOTE: For practice with negative sentences/affirmative tags, see page 183.

In this exercise you and a partner will practice making and answering tag questions while you review information about the U.S. government. Circle YES *or* NO *and say a short answer. If you answer* NO, *provide the correct information. Look at the illustration on page 89 if you can't remember. When you finish, check your answers with your teacher.*

Follow this example:

Student A asks: The president is the leader of the country, isn't he?
Student B answers: Yes, he is.
  and circles YES.

Student B then asks: The president serves for 3 years, doesn't he?
Student A answers: No, he doesn't. He serves for 4 years.
  and circles NO.

Student A: *Look here and cover the right side of the page.*

1. The president <u>is</u> the leader of the country, <u>*isn't he*</u>?

2. YES   No

3. The cabinet <u>is</u> made up of thirty secretaries, _____ it?

4. YES   No

5. The Senate <u>is</u> made up of 100 senators, _____ it?

6. YES   No

7. A justice of the Supreme Court <u>serves</u> for 6 years, _____ he?

8. YES   No

9. The secretary of state <u>gives</u> the president advice on foreign policy, _____ he?

10. YES   No

11. The Congress <u>decides</u> if laws are constitutional, _____ it?

12. YES   No

13. Senators <u>serve</u> 6-year terms, _____ they?

14. YES   No

Student B: *Look here and cover the left side of the page.*

1. YES   No

2. The president <u>serves</u> for 3 years, <u>*doesn't he*</u>?

3. YES   No

4. The president <u>is</u> the head of the Executive Branch, _____ he?

5. YES   No

6. Supreme Court justices <u>are</u> appointed by Congress, _____ they?

7. YES   No

8. The chief justice <u>signs</u> and vetoes bills, _____ he?

9. YES   No

10. People <u>elect</u> the president's cabinet, _____ they?

11. YES   No

12. The Constitution <u>describes</u> a separation of power, _____ it?

13. YES   No

14. The Constitution <u>divides</u> the government into three branches, _____ it?

Talk About This!

Now that you have learned about how the government in the United States is organized and operates, compare it to the government of your country. In the spaces under "In Your Country," write *similar to* or *different from* depending on how the U.S. government compares to your country's. Your partner will do the same. Then talk to your partner about the similarities and differences of your government and that of the U.S.A. Write down your partner's comparisons so that you can share some of the information with your classmates.

IN THE UNITED STATES	IN YOUR COUNTRY	IN YOUR PARTNER'S COUNTRY
The president is the head of the country.		
The law-making branch has two parts.		
People elect senators and representatives.		
The leader (president) chooses his advisors (cabinet).		
The leader chooses the judges for the highest court.		
Judges on the highest court are in office for life.		
The leader can veto a law.		
Congress can pass a law without the leader's signature.		
The people elect the leader.		

FOCUS ON CONTENT: CHANGES TO THE CONSTITUTION

In this section you will read and talk about important changes, or amendments, to the United States Constitution. The first ten amendments are called the Bill of Rights. They were added in 1791, just 2 years after the Constitution was written and accepted by the people. The Bill of Rights and later amendments define the basic rights of all Americans, rights which their government must respect. It is the job of the Supreme Court to determine if a government decision or law agrees with these amendments.

Read, Discuss, and Decide

You can use *must* (necessity) and *must not* (prohibition) to talk about the people's rights and the government's responsibilities as described in the Bill of Rights.

Use *must* when it is **necessary** that someone do something. There is no choice.

The government	must	guarantee	its citizens basic rights.
	must	BASE FORM	

Use *must not* when someone is **prohibited** from doing something.
There are rules or laws which say they are not allowed to do it.

The government	must not	pass	laws that take away basic rights.
	must not	BASE FORM	

In this exercise, you and a partner will:

1. First look in the box below at some of the amendments to the United States Constitution and discuss what they mean.
2. Then read the statements below about what the American government *must* and *must not* do, and match them with the correct amendment. When you are finished, check your answers with your teacher. Write the letter of each statement in the correct space beside the amendments.

The 1st Amendment: freedom of religion; freedom of speech; freedom of the press; freedom of assembly (the right to meet and organize in groups); the right to petition (to express opinions to the government)
The 4th Amendment: the right to privacy
The 6th Amendment: the right to a speedy and public trial
The 15th, 19th, and 26th Amendments: the right of all *male* citizens, of any race, to vote (1870); of all *female* citizens (1920); and of all citizens *18 or older* (1971)

Must/Must Not Statements:

a. The government must let people say what they think.
b. The government must not stop people from voting.
c. The government must not tell people what their religion should be.
d. The government must let people get together to talk about politics, or anything else they want.
e. The government must not tell a newspaper what it can print.
f. The government must not keep someone in jail for a long time without a trial.
g. The government must not enter a person's house without permission from a judge.
h. The government must let all adult citizens take part in elections.
i. The government must allow the public to come into a courtroom.
j. The government must permit newspapers to criticize it.
k. The government must not look for something in a car, book bag, or pockets without the person's permission.
l. The government must not punish people for expressing their opinions.
m. The government must accept letters, faxes, phone calls, and telegrams that express the people's opinions.
n. The government must allow people to practice all religions freely.
o. The government must not listen to your phone calls without your permission or permission from a judge.

Talk About This!

You have learned about some of the rights of American citizens as described in the Constitution. How do these rights compare with those of your country? What are some things your government *must* or *must not* do? Write them in the boxes below and explain them to your partner. Listen to what your partner has to say about his/her country. Be prepared to present some similarities and differences to the rest of the class.

THE GOVERNMENT	IN YOUR COUNTRY	IN YOUR PARTNER'S COUNTRY
must		
must not		

PUT IT TOGETHER

Find Someone Who . . .

Learn more about your classmates and the government of their countries. Go around the classroom and use questions beginning with "Are you . . . ?" and "Do you . . . ?" to find someone who can answer YES to the questions you ask from the information below. Once a person answers YES, write down his/her name and move on to a new student. When you're finished, discuss what you learned with the class and ask your classmates more questions.

Examples: *Do you* work for your government?   *Are you* allowed to vote in your country?

Find someone who . . .   **Write that person's name here:**

is old enough to vote in his/her country.   _____

knows a politician.   _____

wants to be a politician.   _____

is old enough to run for president in his/her country.   _____

belongs to a political party.   _____

lives in a country with a king, queen, or emperor.   _____

participates in a student government at school.   _____

lives in a country with a parliamentary government.   _____

works for the government of his/her country.

lives in a country with a state religion.

Tic-Tac-Toe: A Variation

Your teacher will divide the class into 2 teams, Xs and Os, and draw a big tic-tac-toe grid on the board.

In teams you will make up questions about the U.S. government, write them on pieces of paper and hand them to your teacher. You may look back to the chart on page 89 for ideas.

Your teacher will take turns asking each team questions from the other team's pile. A student from team X goes first. If an answer is correct, the teacher puts an X anywhere the team wants on the grid. Then, a student from team O tries to answer a question from team X.

The first team to get three Xs or three Os in a row is the winner of that round. Play as many rounds as you have time or questions for.

Cloze 🔈

Read the following information about the branches of the U.S. government. Try to fill in each blank with the correct word. After you have filled in as much as you can, listen to the lecture as many times as necessary to fill in all the blanks.

The Constitution of the United States, written over _____ years ago, gives Americans a set of rules to run their government. This document _____ the government into three branches, or parts, so no one group or person can have too much power.

The first _____ of government is called the executive branch. It is led by the president from the _____ in Washington, D.C. His responsibility is to see that all the _____ are enforced. He represents the country in all matters, both at home and _____. The president is elected for a term of 4 years and can serve for no more than _____ terms. He also chooses a "cabinet" of thirteen advisors, called _____. They give the president advice on what is happening in different parts of the government. One member of the _____ is the Secretary of State. He or she heads the Department of State and advises the president on _____ affairs.

The second branch of government is the _____ branch. It is made up of Congress, a group of elected _____ whose job is to make laws and decide how to spend the country's _____ . Congress is the largest part of the government and _____ in the Capitol Building, not too far away from the White House. It is _____ into two parts, the Senate and the House of Representatives. The Senate has _____ members—that's 2 senators from every state— who are elected for a _____ of 6 years. The House of Representatives includes one representative for about every 500,000 _____ living in each state. Now, there are 435 representatives. They serve for _____ years. It is interesting that small states with a lot of _____, like Delaware, send many more representatives to Congress than big states with _____ populations, like Wyoming.

The Congress works in this way: the people of the _____ tell their senators and representatives what laws they want made and how they want their _____ money spent. Then these elected officials go to Washington and give this _____ to their groups, either the Senate or the House of Representatives. Next the two groups meet together to _____ what is most important. They vote and send the most important plans for new laws, called _____, to the President. If the president signs the bill, it becomes a law. Sometimes the president _____ the bill, or refuses to sign it. In this case, the _____ can still pass a law if enough members vote for it.

Most _____ of Congress come from the two major political parties, the Democratic and the _____ parties. There are other parties in the U.S.A. such as the Socialist _____, but they are very small in comparison to the two big parties.

The _____ branch of government is the judicial branch, or the courts. There are several levels of _____ in the U.S.A. The Supreme Court is the highest and most _____ court in the country. It meets in the Supreme Court Building near the _____. The court is made up of nine judges, called justices, who are _____ by the president to serve for life. The leader of the judges is called the _____ justice. The job of the Supreme Court is to explain the meaning of _____. It decides if laws made by Congress and decisions of other _____ agree with the Constitution. Decisions of the Supreme Court can affect the _____ of millions of Americans.

CHAPTER TEN

PATRIOTIC SYMBOLS, SAYINGS, AND SONGS

All countries have ways to express what is important to them and ways for citizens to show their patriotism—that is, their love, respect, and support of their country. In this chapter, you will look at some of the patriotic symbols, sayings, and songs of the United States and learn more about what the American government and people value most. You will listen to the national anthem, "The Star-Spangled Banner."

SHOW WHAT YOU KNOW

The illustrations below show some symbols, sayings, and songs that have patriotic meaning for many Americans. The names of each appear in the box. Look at the next section and work with your classmates to write a name under each illustration. Check your answers with your teacher.

WHAT IS IT CALLED?		
a rattlesnake	the Liberty Bell	"In God We Trust"
a bald eagle	the Statue of Liberty	Uncle Sam
a donkey	the Stars and Stripes	"The Star Spangled Banner"
an elephant	the Great Seal	

FOCUS ON CONTENT: STORIES BEHIND THE SYMBOLS, SAYINGS, AND SONGS

In this section you will learn about the history of the symbols, sayings, and songs associated with American patriotism.

Think and Connect

Now work with your classmates to draw lines from the words and phrases in the boxes out to the illustrations. Check your answers with your teacher.

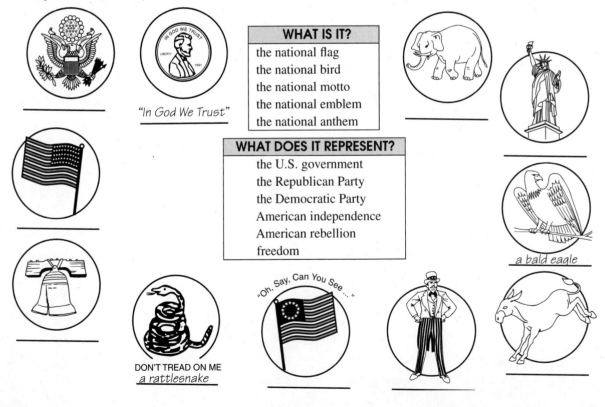

"In God We Trust"

WHAT IS IT?
the national flag
the national bird
the national motto
the national emblem
the national anthem

WHAT DOES IT REPRESENT?
the U.S. government
the Republican Party
the Democratic Party
American independence
American rebellion
freedom

a bald eagle

"Oh, Say, Can You See ..."

DON'T TREAD ON ME
a rattlesnake

Vocabulary

The following words are important to know in order to talk about American patriotic symbols, sayings, and songs. Check your knowledge by completing the sentences with the correct vocabulary word from the box. Compare your answers with a classmate, and check with your teacher.

liberty	seal	power	motto
emblem	symbolizes	tread	anthem

1. The athlete's _____ was "No pain, no gain." He said it every time he exercised.
2. The dean put the university _____ on every official letter she signed.
3. _____ is another word for *step*.
4. My new car has more_____ than my old one. It can go faster.
5. The dove, a beautiful white bird,_____ peace.
6. People are fighting for _____ from governments that won't let them be free.
7. The national _____ of the United States is a difficult song to sing.
8. You can buy lots of souvenirs with the football team's _____ on them.

Matching

Match the descriptions below with the names of the symbols that appear in the box under Show What You Know *on page 98. Write the correct name on the line after each description.*

The Continental Congress decided this animal best symbolized the power and honor of the U.S.A. Benjamin Franklin was upset because a turkey was not chosen. _____

This emblem is used on official government documents, medals, buttons of soldiers' uniforms, and the dollar bill. _____

This is a symbol of the more conservative of the two major political parties in the U.S.A., the Republican Party.

_____

This is a song written about the flag by Francis Scott Key during a difficult battle in the War of 1812. It later became the national anthem of the U.S.A. _____

This is a nickname for the American flag. _____

This stands in the New York City harbor. It has been a welcome sign to immigrants for a long time. It was a gift to the U.S.A. from France. _____

This is a symbol of the more liberal of the two major political parties in the U.S.A., the Democratic Party.

_____

This figure's name came from a man, Sam Wilson, who supplied the American Army with meat during the War of 1812. He used to stamp all the supplies with "U.S.," which meant "United States," but the soldiers gave it Wilson's nickname. _____

This national motto was chosen by Congress in 1956 and put on all coins and money bills. It expresses the belief that God protects America, a belief that goes back to the beginning of American history.

_____

Located at Independence Hall in Philadelphia, this rang out on July 4, 1776, to declare the independence of the 13 colonies. _____

This symbol appeared on American flags during the Revolutionary War. It was used by the 13 colonies to show their rebellion against the British, warning them not to "tread" or step on the colonists.

_____

Listen and Decide ▱

Listen to the statements on your cassette and circle TRUE *or* FALSE. *Look back at the exercises on pages 98–99 if you can't remember the information.*

1.	TRUE	FALSE	6.	TRUE	FALSE
2.	TRUE	FALSE	7.	TRUE	FALSE
3.	TRUE	FALSE	8.	TRUE	FALSE
4.	TRUE	FALSE	9.	TRUE	FALSE
5.	TRUE	FALSE	10.	TRUE	FALSE

Listen and Choose ▱

Listen to the questions on the cassette and circle the letter of the best answer. Look back at the exercises on pages 98–99 if you can't remember the information.

1. a. Benjamin Franklin
   b. Francis Scott Key
   c. Sam Wilson

2. a. a rattlesnake
   b. an elephant
   c. a donkey

3. a. Philadelphia
   b. New York City
   c. Boston

4. a. It represents power.
   b. It symbolizes freedom.
   c. It stands for rebellion.

5. a. in the 1700s
   b. in the 1800s
   c. in the 1900s

6. a. during the War of 1812
   b. during the Revolution
   c. during World War II

7. a. in 1776
   b. in 1812
   c. in 1956

8. a. Uncle Sam
   b. the Great Seal
   c. the Liberty Bell

9. a. the Republican Party
   b. rebellion
   c. the American government

10. a. United States
    b. Uncle Sam
    c. the American Army

Talk About This!

What patriotic symbol, saying, or song comes to mind when you think of your country? For example, does your country have a national bird? If so, why do you think this bird was chosen? What does it symbolize? What appears on your country's money? What does it symbolize?

Walk around the room and ask a few of your classmates about patriotic symbols, sayings, or songs from their countries, and fill in the chart below. When your chart is complete, discuss what you found out with the whole class.

WHO	COUNTRY	PATRIOTIC SYMBOL, SAYING, OR SONG	MEANING OR SYMBOLISM
You			
Classmate 1			
Classmate 2			
Classmate 3			

FOCUS ON SKILLS: USING ARTICLES, PRONOUNCING PRESENT VERBS

In this section you will practice using the articles *a/an* and *the* with certain groups of nouns. You will also practice the pronunciation of the *-s* verb ending.

Use *A* or *An* with Singular Count Nouns	Use *The*
A general example, not a specific thing in mind *Example:* A symbol may have a strong patriotic meaning.	Only one of its kind, both the speaker and listener have the same thing in mind *Example:* The national bird of the U.S.A. symbolizes power and honor.
Use *A/An* or *The*	**Don't Use Any Article**
An animal, when it represents the whole group or species *Example:* A/The donkey is a symbol of the Republican Party.	people's names *Example:* Uncle Sam lived in New York. abstract ideas *Example:* Freedom is a basic right.

Practice

Read the sentences below and write a *or* an, the, *or* X *(for no article) in the blanks. Compare your answers with a classmate's by reading them out loud. Then check them with your teacher.*

1. _____ Liberty Bell rang out _____ independence in 1776.
2. _____ Uncle Sam represents _____ U.S. government.
3. _____ bald eagle is a bird that symbolizes _____ power and _____ honor.
4. _____ motto is a saying or idea we want to live by.
5. _____ national flag of the U.S.A. is red, white, and blue.
6. _____ elephant is the symbol of _____ Republican Party.
7. "In God We Trust" has been _____ national motto of the U.S.A since 1956.
8. A symbol of _____ rebellion during _____ American Revolution was _____ rattlesnake.
9. _____ national emblem of the U.S.A. is _____ Great Seal.
10. _____ anthem is a country's most important song.
11. "_____ Star Spangled Banner" is _____ national anthem of the U.S.A.
12. _____ Sam Wilson supplied _____ American army during _____ War of 1812.

PRONUNCIATION NOTE:
Remember:
Pronounce *the* with a final [i] sound before vowel sounds.
Pronounce *the* with a final [ë] sound before consonant sounds.

Try these examples with your teacher:

[i]	the uncle	the elephant	the eagle	the American
[ë]	the bell	the bird	the donkey	the government

Speak, Listen, and Choose

In this exercise you and a partner will practice using articles by asking and answering questions about American symbols, sayings, and songs. Listen to the question your partner asks. Circle the best answer, filling in an article if necessary, and answer with a full sentence. When you're finished, check your answers with your teacher.

Follow this example:

Student A asks first: What is the symbol for the Republican Party?
Student B responds: It's *an/the* elephant.
and circles *b*, writing in *an/the*.

Student B then asks: What does the rattlesnake symbolize?
Student A responds: It symbolizes rebellion.
and circles *a*.

Student A: *Look here and cover the right side of the page.*

1. What is the symbol for the Republican Party?

2. a. _____ rebellion   b. _____ honor

3. What does the Statue of Liberty stand for?

4. a. during _____ War   b. during _____
   of 1812   American Revolution

5. What is the nickname for the American Flag?

6. a. _____ motto   b. _____ anthem

7. What did Francis Scott Key write?

8. a. _____ eagle   b. _____ turkey

9. What symbol do you see on the dollar bill?

10. a. _____ patriotic   b. _____ national
    symbol   motto

11. What do you find on American coins?

12. a. _____ United   b. _____ American
    States   Army

13. Which American political party is more liberal?

14. a. _____ rebellion   b. _____ honor

Student B: *Look here and cover the left side of the page.*

1. a. _____ donkey   b. _____ elephant

2. What does the rattlesnake symbolize?

3. a. _____ freedom   b. _____ U.S. government

4. When did a rattlesnake symbolize rebellion?

5. a. _____ Stars and Stripes b. _____ Great Seal

6. What do you call a country's national song?

7. a. "_____ Star Spangled b. _____ national motto
   Banner"

8. What was Ben Franklin's choice for the national bird?

9. a. _____ Liberty Bell   b. _____ Great Seal

10. What is the American flag?

11. a. _____ flag   b. _____ national motto

12. What does "Uncle Sam" stand for?

13. a. _____ Republican   b. _____ Democratic Party
    Party

14. What does the bald eagle symbolize?

Pronunciation 📼

There are three ways to pronounce the -s in 3rd person singular verbs. Follow the same pronunciation rules you learned to use with the plural noun endings on page 91. Review the rules below. Then listen to the cassette and practice the pronunciation.

Rule 1: The 3rd person singular verb ending -s is pronounced [s] after most voiceless consonant sounds.	
[p] stamps [t] represents [k] asks	He *stamps* his letters with his personal seal. The President *asks* for the Great Seal to stamp documents. A dove *represents* peace.

Rule 2: The 3rd person singular verb ending -s is pronounced [z] after most voiced consonant sounds and vowel sounds.	
[b] stabs [l] calls [d] stands [m] comes [g] rings [n] means [v] lives [r] hears [vowel sounds] [signifies, supplies]	The university bell *rings* every hour. The supermarket nearby *supplies* the office with coffee. A symbol always *means* something more.

Rule 3: The 3rd person singular verb ending -*(e)s* is pronounced [iz] after sounds like [s], [z], [š], [č], and [ǰ].	
[s] expresses [z] symbolizes [č] watches [ǰ] judges [š] wishes	The U.S. government *uses* the Great Seal on soldiers' uniforms. My personal motto *expresses* optimism. An eagle *symbolizes* strength.

Listen and Choose 📼

Now you will hear some sentences about patriotic symbols. Listen and put a check under [s], [z], or [iz], depending on which type of verb you hear.

	[s]	[z]	[iz]
1.			
2.			
3.			
4.			
5.			
6.			
7.			
8.			
9.			
10.			

Present Tense Sentence Combinations

In this exercise you and a partner will practice the pronunciation of the 3rd person singular verb endings while you review symbols, sayings, and songs. Take turns making up sentences using the words below by drawing lines. Work back and forth until you've made at least one sentence for each. Then go back and try to make new combinations. How many sentences can you make?

The Liberty Bell		independence.
"In God We Trust"	means	immigrants to the U.S.A.
A donkey	flies over	rebellion.
"The Star Spangled Banner"	stands for	pride in the flag.
A rattlesnake	appears on	honor and power.
The Statue of Liberty	represents	the U.S. government.
An elephant	expresses	freedom.
Uncle Sam	rings out	the Republican Party.
The Great Seal	symbolizes	the Democratic Party
The national flag	signifies	American embassies.
A bald eagle	welcomes	the dollar bill.
		an American belief that God protects the country.

Talk About This!

1. Think about a patriotic symbol, saying, or song from your own country. It can be one you talked about earlier in the chapter. Describe it to your partner using some of the verbs above.

2. In addition to the words "In God We Trust," another motto is found on American money. It is the Latin saying *E Pluribus Unum*, which means "One from many." It signifies the union of the American states.

   A. Does your country have a national motto or mottoes? Is there a story behind it?
   Make some notes here, and then present the information to your classmates.

   The Motto _____
   What does it mean? _____
   Where does it come from? _____
   Where/When is it used? _____

   B. Some people have their own personal motto to live by. Do you? If so, tell your classmates about it. What is it? When do you think about it?

FOCUS ON CONTENT: FRANCIS SCOTT KEY AND "THE STAR SPANGLED BANNER"

In this section you are going to learn how the national anthem of the United States was written. It is a very dramatic story. The author, Francis Scott Key, is remembered in American history for just one poem he wrote during one event in his life.

Vocabulary

The words in the box are important to the story you will hear. Do you know what they mean? Review them with your teacher before listening to the lecture.

prisoner	port	fort	battle	inspire

Listen In 📼

Listen to the lecture about Francis Scott Key, but don't write anything while listening. When you're finished, write any main points of the story that you remember, and discuss them with a partner.

_____

_____

_____

_____

Listen and Write 📼

Listen for specific information. Listen to the lecture on the cassette as many times as you need to in order to fill in the blanks below.

1. two nationalities _____ _____
2. three locations _____ _____ _____
3. four buildings _____ _____
   _____ _____

Read and Decide 📼

Read the following sentences and write T *for True or* F *for False. Listen to the lecture again if you can't remember all of the information. If a sentence is false, change it to make it true.*

_____ 1. The American president during the War of 1812 was Thomas Jefferson.

_____ 2. Francis Scott Key was a doctor by profession.

_____ 3. He lived and worked in Georgetown, which was near the District of Columbia.

_____ 4. During the War of 1812, Baltimore was an important port.

_____ 5. Key went to Baltimore to help free a British prisoner.

_____ 6. The doctor was freed, and he went with Key directly to Fort McHenry.

_____ 7. From his boat, Key watched the British bomb the fort.

_____ 8. The battle was difficult, but the British won.

_____ 9. When he returned to Georgetown, Key began to write a poem about the battle he saw.

_____ 10. Key's poem was put to music and named "The Stars and Stripes."

Speak, Listen, and Choose

In this exercise, you and a partner will ask and answer questions about Francis Scott Key and the American national anthem. Circle the letter of the best answer and tell your partner the answer you chose using a complete sentence. When you finish, check your answers with your teacher.

Follow this example:

Student A asks first: Who wrote the national anthem of the U.S.A.?
Student B responds: Francis Scott Key did.
and circles *a*.

Student B then asks: Who was President of the U.S.A. when the anthem was written?
Student A responds: James Madison was.
and circles *b*.

Student A: *Look here and cover the right side of the page.*

1. Who wrote the national anthem of the U.S.A.?

2. a. George Washington
   (b.) James Madison

3. What was the second American war with Great Britain?

4. a. Fort McHenry
   b. The Capitol Building

5. Where did Francis Scott Key live and work as a lawyer?

6. a. in 1812
   b. in 1814

7. Where were the British ships waiting?

8. a. the British ships
   b. the American boat

9. When did Key finally see the flag still flying?

10. a. on the boat
    b. in Georgetown

11. When was "The Star Spangled Banner" first sung in Washington?

12. a. in a museum
    b. in the White House

Student B: *Look here and cover the left side of the page.*

1. (a.) Francis Scott Key
   b. Benjamin Franklin

2. Who was president of the United States when the anthem was written?

3. a. the War of 1812
   b. the Revolutionary War

4. What building did the British burn down towards the end of the war?

5. a. in Georgetown
   b. in Baltimore

6. When did Key go to Baltimore to help the prisoner?

7. a. in the Potomac River
   b. in the port of Baltimore

8. Who bombed Fort McHenry?

9. a. at night
   b. in the morning

10. Where did Key begin to write the anthem?

11. a. in September, 1814
    b. in December, 1814

12. Where is the flag from Fort McHenry now?

$\mathcal{S}ong$

"The Star Spangled Banner" by Francis Scott Key

Listen and Write 🔲

Now that you know the story behind the writing of the national anthem, listen to the song on the cassette and fill in the missing words below.

1. Oh, say, can you _____,
   By the dawn's early _____,
   What so proudly _____ hailed
   At the twilight's _____ gleaming?

2. Whose broad_____ and bright _____,
   Through the perilous _____,
   O'er the ramparts we _____
   Were _____ gallantly streaming?

3. And the rocket's ____ glare,
   The bombs bursting in _____,
   Gave proof _____ the night
   That our _____ was still there.

4. Oh, say, does that _____ Spangled
   Banner yet wave
   O'er the land of the _____
   And the _____ of the brave?

Talk About the Song

1. Study the vocabulary.

Find a word in	that means	and write it here:
Verse 1	time when sun goes up	_____
	time when sun goes down	_____
	saluted, greeted	_____
	shining	_____
Verse 2	wide	_____
	dangerous	_____
	part of wall around fort	_____
	bravely	_____
Verse 3	a very bright	_____
	exploding	_____
Verse 4	a flag	_____

2. What do you know about your country's national anthem?
   Is there a story behind it? Write a little about your anthem here, and then tell a classmate about it.
   Name of anthem (translated): _____
   What is it about? _____
   Who wrote it? _____
   When do you sing it?_____

3. It is interesting to look at how people behave when their national anthem is being played.
   Usually, Americans put their right hands over their hearts and sing along when "The Star Spangled Banner" is being played.
   What do you do when your national anthem is played? Ask a few classmates about their countries.

Who	Country	What do you do when your national anthem is being played?
You		
Classmate 1		
Classmate 2		
Classmate 3		

PUT IT TOGETHER

Crossword

Fill in the blanks with words from the chapter.

ACROSS

1. This party's symbol is an elephant.
4. A bald eagle is the national ____.
7. It represents the Republican Party.
8. The Great ___ is on the dollar bill.
9. An eagle is a symbol of ____.
10. The national ___ is on all official government documents.
12. He wrote the national anthem.
14. Another word for freedom.
16. During the Revolutionary War, a rattlesnake meant ____.

DOWN

1. A symbol of rebellion.
2. A symbol of the U.S. government.
3. A bell____.
5. This party's symbol is a donkey.
6. The Stars and _____.
11. This rang out in 1776.
13. The Statue of Liberty is in the harbor of this city (abbreviation).
15. The Great Seal is on a one dollar _____.

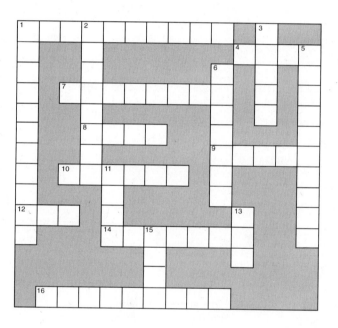

Password

You will play a game with your class using vocabulary words you've learned in this chapter.

A. Your teacher will divide the class into two teams, Team A and Team B. Within each team, everyone will find a partner.

B. Your teacher will put two sets of two chairs each at the front of the room. They will be for the pairs from each team. Your teacher will stand in the middle and serve as the game leader.

C. On small pieces of paper, your teacher will have written down vocabulary words from the chapter. There will be two copies of every word so that one member of each pair gets a copy.

D. The game will begin with a pair from each team at the front of the room. Each pair sits facing one another. The teacher will give one member of each pair a piece of paper with the same vocabulary word. Their partners will not be able to see the word.

E. A member of Team A's pair will begin by giving his/her partner a one-word clue. The partner will have 10 seconds to guess the word. If he/she doesn't, Team B's pair will take a turn. One member of the pair will give the partner another one-word clue. The partner will have 10 seconds to guess the word. If he/she doesn't, the game will go back to Team A, and so on, taking turns.

The winner of the round is the pair that guesses the word first, based on the clues given. This pair's team will get one point.

F. A new round will begin each time a word is guessed. A new pair from each team will go to the front of the room and receive a new vocabulary word to play with.

G. The team with the most points wins.

Cloze

Read the following information about Francis Scott Key and "The Star Spangled Banner." Try to fill in the blanks with the correct word. After you have filled in as much as you can, listen to the lecture as many times as necessary to fill in all the blanks.

FRANCIS SCOTT KEY AND "THE STAR SPANGLED BANNER"

During the _____ American war with Great Britain, the War of _____ , the British army burned down the Capitol building and set fire to the _____ House. They also took a well-known American doctor as _____ . The American president at that time, James Madison, was worried about the doctor. He found a _____ named Francis Scott Key to go to the _____ and ask for the doctor's freedom.

In September, 1814, Francis Scott _____ was living and working in Georgetown, an area close to Washington, D.C. In order to help the President, Key went to _____ , Maryland to look for the British ships. Baltimore was an important _____ and center of trade during the war and the British wanted to take control of it. But the American Fort McHenry was there to _____ it. Over the fort flew an extremely large American _____ , which could be seen from far away. It was a _____ of the American goal to defeat the British.

The British ships were waiting in the port of Baltimore for the perfect time to _____ the fort. Francis Scott Key went out to the ships on a small _____ and convinced the British to give the American doctor his _____ . Both Key and the doctor returned to the American boat, but they could not go back to land because the British had attacked Fort McHenry. The British ships _____ the fort all night. Key spent the night on his boat watching the _____ . The battle was so tough that he did not know who was winning. He wondered if he would see the American flag in the morning. When the _____ finally ended and the sun came up, Key saw that "the flag was still there." The Americans had won the battle.

In his happiness, Francis Scott Key immediately began to write a _____ about the battle. In the poem, he described what he saw from the boat. When he returned to Baltimore, the patriotic poem was printed in a local _____ . By December of that year, 1814, _____ was written for the poem and it was sung for the first time in Washington under the name of "The Star Spangled Banner."

Today, the famous flag from Fort McHenry that inspired Francis Scott Key to write the national _____ can be seen in the Smithsonian Museum in _____ , D.C.

CHAPTER ELEVEN

A CLOSER LOOK AT THE STARS AND STRIPES

A flag is perhaps the most patriotic of all national symbols. In this chapter you will learn how and why the American flag has changed over the years. You will also look at American state flags and practice describing them. Finally, you will learn how Americans show respect for their flag.

SHOW WHAT YOU KNOW

1. The design of a flag usually represents ideas, values, or events that are important to a country.

   Work with a partner and discuss what you think the design of the American flag symbolizes.

The Colors	The Shapes
Red _____	Stars _____
White _____	Stripes _____
Blue _____	

2. Legend has it that George Washington described the symbolism of the American flag in his own way.

   "We take the stars from heaven, the red from our Mother Country, separated by white stripes to show that we have separated from Her and to represent liberty."

   Do you know who "The Mother Country" is? _____

FOCUS ON CONTENT: FLAGS OF AMERICAN HISTORY

In this section you will hear a short lecture about how and why the design of the American flag has changed throughout the history of the United States.

Vocabulary 🔲

The following words are important in the lecture. Listen to the cassette and complete the following sentences with words from the box.

adopts	cross	design	row
background	stripes	nickname	version

1. The first _____ of this song was too hard to sing, so the composer changed it.
2. His real name is James, but his friends call him by his _____, Jimmy.
3. The flag of France has three _____ of blue, white, and red.
4. The Japanese flag has a red circle in the middle of a white _____.
5. Most flags have a simple _____ so that they are easy to recognize.
6. It is very rare that Congress _____ changes to the Constitution.
7. At the United Nations, the flags of all countries fly next to each other in a _____.
8. A _____ is a design that looks like the letter "X."

Listen and Write

Listen to the lecture as many times as necessary in order to fill in the illustration below about changes to the American flag.

FLAGS OF AMERICAN HISTORY

1.

Name: _____

Date: _____

Colors: _____

2.

Name:_____

Date:_____

Nickname: _____

3.

Name: _____

Date: _____

Importance: *First flag of American Revolution*

4.

Name:_____

Date:_____

Importance: _____

_____

5.

Name: *First National Flag*

Date: _____

Holiday: _____

6.

Name: _____

Date: _____

New States: _____

_____

7.

Name: *Stars and Stripes of today*.

Date: _____

Stars: _____ Stripes: _____

Listen and Choose 📼

Listen to the questions on the cassette and circle the letter of the best answer. Look back at the illustration on page 111 if you can't remember the information.

1. a. circle of stars
    b. rattlesnake
    c. a cross

2. a. from the first Stars and Stripes
    b. from the Rattlesnake Flag
    c. from the Union Jack

3. a. Vermont and Hawaii
    b. Hawaii and Alaska
    c. Vermont and Kentucky

4. a. 13
    b. 15
    c. 50

5. a. in 1977
    b. in 1777
    c. in 1607

6. a. in a cross
    b. in a row
    c. in a circle

7. a. the Stars and Stripes
    b. the Rattlesnake Flag
    c. the Union Jack

8. a. the Flag of 15 Stripes
    b. the Grand Union Flag
    c. the Union Jack

Read and Decide

Below is information from the lecture about flags of American history. Read and decide what order they go in. Number the sentences from 1 to 7.

_____ The earliest version of the Stars and Stripes first flew in the Battle of Bennington, Vermont.

_____ The 13 colonies showed one of their first signs of rebellion in the symbols of the Rattlesnake Flag.

_____ The Flag of 15 Stripes became the official flag after the new states of Vermont and Kentucky were added.

__1__ The Union Jack was the flag of the British colonies and one of the first flags to fly in America.

_____ Congress adopted the first national flag on June 14, 1977.

_____ With the addition of Hawaii, the U.S. flag has 50 stars and stripes.

_____ The Grand Union Flag was the first flag of the American Revolution.

Speak, Listen, and Decide

You can use *there + be* to describe flags.

There	are	thirteen stripes on the U.S. flag today.
There	*be* (present)	
There	were	stripes on the Union Jack.
There	*be* (past)	

In this exercise you and a partner will take turns reading statements about flags of American history and deciding if they are TRUE *or* FALSE. *Look back at the illustration on page 111 if you can't remember an answer. When you finish, check your answers with your teacher.*

Follow this example:

Student A says: There was a rattlesnake on the Navy Jack.
Student B responds: That's true.
  and circles TRUE.

Student B says: There were two crosses on the Grand Union Flag.
Student A responds: That's true.
  and circles TRUE.

Student A: *Look here and cover the right side of the page.*

1. a rattlesnake—the Navy Jack
2. TRUE   FALSE
3. 15 stripes—the flag today
4. TRUE   FALSE
5. rows of stars—the Flag of 15 Stripes
6. TRUE   FALSE
7. a red cross—the Union Jack
8. TRUE   FALSE
9. a circle of stars—the Bennington Flag
10. TRUE   FALSE
11. 13 stripes—the flag today
12. TRUE   FALSE

Student B: *Look here and cover the left side of the page.*

1. TRUE   FALSE
2. 2 crosses—the Grand Union Flag
3. TRUE   FALSE
4. a circle of stars—the First National Flag
5. TRUE   FALSE
6. 13 red and white stripes—the Navy Jack
7. TRUE   FALSE
8. a blue square—the Navy Jack
9. TRUE   FALSE
10. 50 stars—the flag today
11. TRUE   FALSE
12. a small Union Jack—the Grand Union Flag

Talk About This!

1. Has your country's flag changed over time? If so, make some notes here about the change and then tell your classmates.

   How has it changed? _____

   What was the reason for the change? _____

2. There are a lot of popular stories, or legends, about the American flag. No one is really sure if they are true or not, but here are a few of them.

   A. The most famous seamstress in American history is a woman named Betsy Ross. Legend has it that this seamstress from Philadelphia designed and sewed the first national flag with stars and stripes. If someone calls you "Betsy Ross" today, it means you have a talent for sewing.

   B. The American flag has lots of nicknames: the "Stars and Stripes," the "Red, White, and Blue," the "Star Spangled Banner." Another popular nickname is "Old Glory." The story has it that a Massachusetts ship captain named William Diver was given a beautiful handmade flag by his mother before setting sail for a trip around the world in the early 1800s. He was so excited by the gift that he shouted to his shipmates "My flag! I think I'll call her 'Old Glory.'" This nickname has stayed with us until today.

Do you know any stories about your flag or any nicknames for your flag? Make some notes here and then present the information to your classmates.

A story about the origin or symbols of your national flag:

_____

_____

A special nickname for your flag:

_____

_____

FOCUS ON SKILLS: DESCRIBING DESIGNS, SHAPES, AND LOCATIONS

In this section you will learn how to describe shapes and designs and their locations on a flag. You will practice these skills by describing the state flags of the United States.

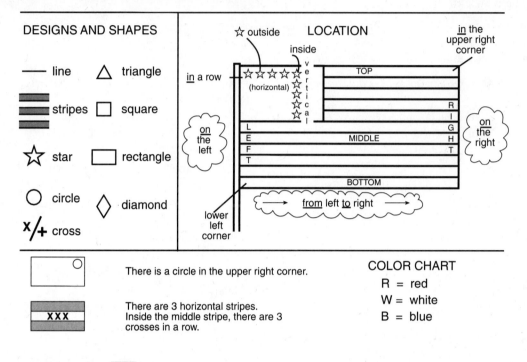

Listen and Decide 📼

In this exercise you will listen to descriptions of eight flags on the cassette. For each item, decide which flag is being described and circle it. After you listen and decide, go back and practice describing the flags to a partner.

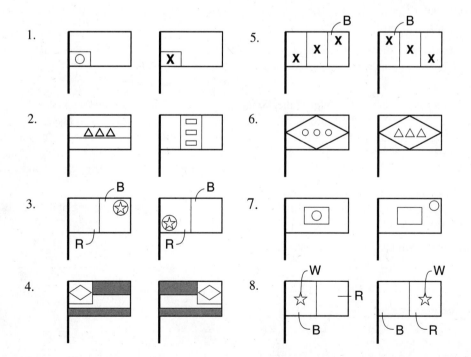

Speak, Listen, and Draw

There is only one national flag of the U.S.A. However, every state also has its own flag. So does the District of Columbia. In this exercise you will work with a partner to describe and draw the state flags below. Use the designs, shapes, and locations that you've already practiced. You may add colors, if you'd like. When you are finished, compare your drawings. They should look similar.

Follow this example:

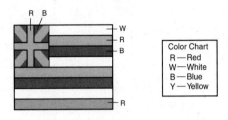

Color Chart
R—Red
W—White
B—Blue
Y—Yellow

Student A describes: The flag of Hawaii has eight stripes of white, red, and blue. In the upper left corner, there is a square. Inside the square, there are two red crosses. One goes from top to bottom, and the other goes from corner to corner. The crosses are on a blue background.

Student B draws the flag and writes down the state name.

Student A: *Look here and cover the right side of the page.*

Student B: *Look here and cover the left side of the page.*

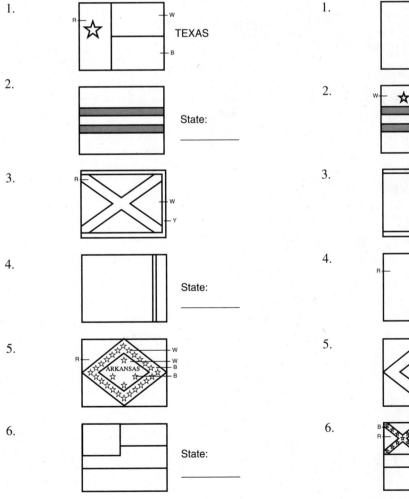

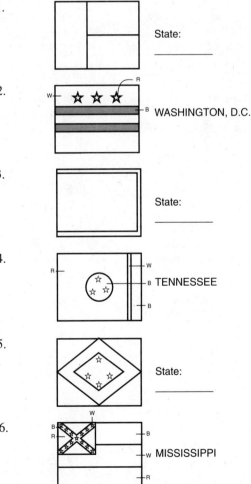

FOCUS ON CONTENT: RESPECTING THE FLAG

In this section you will learn about how the American people treat their flag with respect.

One way Americans show respect for the flag is by saying "The Pledge of Allegiance." "The Pledge of Allegiance" is a short speech that all Americans memorize when they are children. It is a promise of loyalty to the American flag and everything it symbolizes. There are many situations in which Americans are supposed to say "The Pledge of Allegiance" as a sign of respect. It is said by children in schools every morning, by boy scouts and girl scouts at the beginning of their troop meetings, and by immigrants to the U.S.A. at their official citizenship ceremonies.   Read the "Pledge" and ask your teacher about any words you don't understand.

THE PLEDGE OF ALLEGIANCE

"I pledge allegiance to the flag of the United States of America and to the republic for which it stands, one nation under God, indivisible, with liberty and justice for all."

Speak, Listen, and Change

When you say "The Pledge of Allegiance," you are supposed to stand up, face the flag, and put your hand over your heart. You are supposed to take your hat off, too. The United States Flag Code describes more rules about how people are expected to act toward the flag.

When you talk about what someone expects or requires you to do, you can use *supposed to* or the imperative. The imperative is stronger than *supposed to*.

Be + Supposed To + BASE FORM	THE IMPERATIVE
You are supposed to treat the flag with respect.	Treat the flag with respect.
You are not supposed to walk on the flag.	Don't walk on the flag.

In this exercise, you and a partner are going to practice talking about more expected behavior toward the American flag using *supposed to* and the imperative. Your partner will read a statement in the imperative. You should respond by restating it with *you are/aren't supposed to*. Some of the words are written in to help you.

Here's some tricky vocabulary:

mast—flagpole   display—show   dispose of—throw away

Follow this example:

Student A reads: Don't hang the flag on a wall with the stars on the right side.
Student B responds: You are not supposed to hang the flag on a wall with the stars on the right
                          side.

Student B then reads: Display the flag on all national holidays.
Student A responds: You are supposed to display the flag on all national holidays.

Student A: *Look here and cover the right side of the page.*

1. Don't hang the flag on a wall with the stars on the right side.
2. _____ display the flag on all national holidays.
3. Don't let the flag touch the ground.
4. _____ higher than the United States flag.
5. Fly the flag from sunrise to sunset.
6. _____ school during school days.
7. Don't fly the flag in bad weather.
8. _____ fly the flag at half mast when someone important has died.
9. Fly the flag at half mast until noon on Memorial Day.
10. _____ in a respectful way.
11. Stand and face the flag during the national anthem.
12. _____ when you are in serious trouble.

Student B: *Look here and cover the left side of the page.*

1. _____ hang the flag on a wall with the stars on the right side.
2. Display the flag on all national holidays.
3. _____ touch the ground.
4. Don't fly any state flags higher than the United States flag.
5. _____ from sunrise to sunset.
6. Display the flag near every school during school days.
7. _____ in bad weather.
8. Fly the flag at half mast when someone important has died.
9. _____ until noon on Memorial Day.
10. Dispose of worn flags in a respectful way.
11. _____ during the national anthem.
12. Fly the flag upside down when you are in serious trouble. (On a ship, for example.)

Talk About This!

Are there any special rules in your country for respecting your flag? How is the way Americans are supposed to treat their flag different from the way you are supposed to treat yours? Fill in any special rules about your country. Then get together with a partner and ask your partner about how the flag is supposed to be treated in his/her country.

SPECIAL RULES ABOUT THE FLAG IN YOUR COUNTRY

SPECIAL RULES ABOUT THE FLAG IN YOUR PARTNER'S COUNTRY

PUT IT TOGETHER

Circulation

Find out some information about the national flags of your classmates. In the spaces below, write the names of five students from five different countries. Then ask each of those students to describe their flag while you try to draw it.

STUDENT	COUNTRY	FLAG

Cloze 📼

Read the following information about flags of American history. Try to fill in the blanks with the correct words. After you have filled in as much as you can, listen to the lecture on your cassette again as many times as necessary to fill in all the blanks.

Flags have always played an important _____ in American history. The way the flag has changed _____ the growth of a nation.

One of the _____ flags to fly in America was called the "_____ Jack." It was the flag of all the British _____, and it flew from 1607 to 1776. It had a _____ background with two crosses: one red, going from _____ to bottom and left to right, and one _____, going from corner to corner. All the American _____ that followed took their colors from the Union _____ . (By the way, a "jack" is another _____ for a flag.)

In 1775, the thirteen American colonies _____ to fly a flag of their own—the Navy Jack. It was also _____ as the "Rattlesnake Flag" because of the _____ in the middle, a symbol of rebellion. It was the _____ flag to have a background of _____ red and white stripes going from top to bottom and _____ the thirteen colonies.

One of the first flags to be _____ in the American Revolution was the Grand Union Flag starting in _____. It was a combination of British and revolutionary _____ because it had a small union jack in the upper left _____ on a background of red and white stripes.

This was _____ in 1777 by the Bennington Flag, named after the _____ in Vermont where an important battle took place. This is an _____ version of the American national flag because it _____ the first to have white stars on a blue _____ , with a background of stripes. To this day, a _____ for the flag of the U.S.A. is the "Stars and Stripes."

The first _____ flag of the 13 United States was adopted by Congress on _____ 14, 1777. It had a circle of 13 stars on a blue square in the _____ left corner, with a background of 13 red and white stripes. June 14 became a national _____ and is celebrated every year as Flag Day, the _____ of the American flag.

As time passed, new states were _____ to the U.S.A. and this changed the design of the _____ . The second national flag, known as the "Flag of 15 _____ " was adopted in 1795 to represent the _____ states of Vermont and Kentucky. It had 15 stars, in _____ instead of in a circle, and 2 more stripes were _____ . It was flown during the _____ of 1812 and was the flag that the American _____ anthem — "The Star Spangled Banner" — was named after.

The Stars and _____ of today have been in use since 1960 after the last _____, Alaska and Hawaii, became part of the U.S.A. A new star was _____, to the blue square for each state, which means _____ are now 50 stars. However, the number of stripes returned to _____ to represent the country at its birth.

ON YOUR OWN   WE THE PEOPLE: THE GOVERNMENT OF THE U.S.A.

Here are some activities related to government for you to do on your own, with a small group or with your whole class.

1. Work with a group of classmates to design a flag for your class. Use colored paper, cloth, magic markers, and other materials to make it look nice. Be prepared to describe the flag to your classmates, explaining the symbols, designs, shapes, and colors you chose.

2. Prepare a 5-minute speech about your country's government. Tell your classmates about such things as the form of government and how it is similar to or different from the U.S.A., the leader's name, the major political parties, the constitution (if there is one), and popular elections. You may need to go to the library. Use a poster, overhead, or handout to help your classmates understand your speech.

3. Invite an American student who is a member of a student government to be interviewed in class. Prepare questions about the student government to find out how it is similar to or different from the U.S. government. Interview the student either in a small group or as a class.

4. Interview a student who is a member of a political party in the U.S.A. Ask what the party stands for, why he/she is a member, and what he/she does for the party. Give a 3-minute report to your class in a group discussion.

5. Present to your class one of your country's national symbols, such as an emblem, seal, or symbol on money. Prepare a picture or other visual aid and explain the meaning and history behind the symbol.

6. Find out about the local government in the community where you are studying. Divide the class into groups to research the executive, judicial, and legislative branches. Find out where they are located and plan a visit. Report to the class with information, such as the name, where they're located, what they do. You may want to bring in a map of the place to show where the government offices can be found.

7. Prepare a 5-minute role play with a partner. One of you will take on the role of a famous political leader in your country, and the other will be an international TV reporter. He/she will ask you questions about your daily life, issues that are important to you and your country, what party you belong to, and what it stands for. Practice several times and present the role play to your class.

8. If possible, plan a trip to Washington, D.C. to visit the branches of the federal government mentioned in this chapter. Take a tour of the Capitol, the White House, and the Supreme Court. Attend an open session of Congress and see senators and representatives discuss and vote on bills.

9. Go to the library and watch the classic American film about a young politician, *Mr. Smith Goes to Washington*. Watch it with a small group and report back to your class with a summary. Discuss how the movie related to what you had learned about American government.

Unit 4

Names to Know in the U.S.A.

CHAPTER TWELVE

THE WRITTEN WORD: AMERICAN AUTHORS AND POETS

American authors have produced a wide variety of novels, short stories, and poems over the past two hundred years. In this chapter you will learn more about American authors and poets, from writers who lived around the time of the Revolution to twentieth century writers.

SHOW WHAT YOU KNOW

Have you ever read a book or part of a book by an American author? What is the title of the book? Was the book in English or translated into your language? Tell your classmates about your experiences reading American literature.

Which of these authors do you recognize? Have you ever read a book by one of them?

Louisa May Alcott	Ernest Hemingway	John Steinbeck
Maya Angelou	Washington Irving	Harriet Beecher Stowe
F. Scott Fitzgerald	Herman Melville	Mark Twain
Nathaniel Hawthorne		

FOCUS ON CONTENT: AMERICAN AUTHORS

In this section you will learn more about the books and short stories written by the authors you discussed in the previous section.

Matching

Work with your classmates to write the authors' names from the box above on the book covers. You will hear the correct answers in the Listen and Write exercise on page 125.

Listen and Write 🔊

In this exercise you will learn more about the authors from page 124. Listen to the statements on the cassette and fill in the dates. After you finish this exercise, return to the exercise on page 124 and finish filling in the information on the book covers.

1. *The Great Gatsby* was written in by F. Scott Fitzgerald in _____.
2. Washington Irving wrote "The Legend of Sleepy Hollow" in _____.
3. Maya Angelou was born in _____.
4. *For Whom the Bell Tolls* was written by Ernest Hemingway in _____.
5. *Little Women* was written by Louisa May Alcott in _____.
6. John Steinbeck died in _____.
7. Mark Twain wrote *The Adventures of Huckleberry Finn* in _____.
8. Harriet Beecher Stowe was born in _____.
9. Herman Melville wrote *Moby Dick* in _____.
10. *I Know Why the Caged Bird Sings* was written by Maya Angelou in _____.
11. Ernest Hemingway died in _____.
12. Nathaniel Hawthorne wrote *The Scarlet Letter* in _____.
13. Washington Irving was born in _____.
14. *The Grapes of Wrath* was written by John Steinbeck in _____.
15. F. Scott Fitzgerald died in _____.
16. Harriet Beecher Stowe wrote *Uncle Tom's Cabin* in _____.

Listen and Decide 🔊

Listen to the statements on the cassette and circle TRUE *or* FALSE. *Look at the book covers on page 124 if you can't remember the information.*

1.	TRUE	FALSE		6.	TRUE	FALSE
2.	TRUE	FALSE		7.	TRUE	FALSE
3.	TRUE	FALSE		8.	TRUE	FALSE
4.	TRUE	FALSE		9.	TRUE	FALSE
5.	TRUE	FALSE		10.	TRUE	FALSE

Talk About This!

Many of these books have been translated into your language. Do you recognize the titles? Often, titles do not translate exactly. If you know, tell your classmates how the titles of these books have been translated into your language. Is the meaning exactly the same or a little different?

Speak, Listen, and Write

You can ask about people's lives using questions with *when* and *what did*.

When	did	John Steinbeck	live?	He	lived	*from 1902 to 1968.*
What	*did*	John Steinbeck	write?	He	wrote	*The Grapes of Wrath.*
Wh-	*did*	SUBJECT	BASE FORM	SUBJ	PAST VERB	COMPLEMENT

In this exercise you and a partner will talk about when some authors lived and what they wrote using past tense questions and answers. Take turns asking and answering questions to fill in the missing information on the chart. When you finish, check your answers by looking at your partner's chart.

Follow this example:

Student A asks: When did Nathaniel Hawthorne live?
Student B responds: He lived from 1804 to 1864.
Student A writes in *1804* and *1864*.

Student B then asks: What did he write?
Student A responds: He wrote *The Scarlet Letter.*
Student B writes in *The Scarlet Letter.*

Student A: *Look here and cover the other chart.*

AUTHOR	LIVED FROM	TO	WROTE
Nathaniel Hawthorne	*1804*	*1864*	*The Scarlet Letter*
Ernest Hemingway	1899	1961	
Washington Irving	1783	1859	
Herman Melville			*Moby Dick*
Harriet Beecher Stowe			*Uncle Tom's Cabin*
Mark Twain	1835	1910	

Student B: *Look here and cover the other chart.*

AUTHOR	LIVED FROM	TO	WROTE
Nathaniel Hawthorne	1804	1864	*The Scarlet Letter*
Ernest Hemingway			*For Whom the Bell Tolls*
Washington Irving			"The Legend of Sleepy Hollow"
Herman Melville	1819	1891	
Harriet Beecher Stowe	1811	1896	
Mark Twain			*The Adventures of Huckleberry Finn*

Matching

In this exercise you will read short descriptions of each book and story mentioned so far. The "jacket," or paper covering of a book, often includes a short description of the book which can help you decide if you want to read the book. Work with your classmates to write a title from page 124 on the line above each description. Use the cues in the description and what you have already learned about the books and authors to help you guess each title.

_____

This autobiography, written in 1970, tells about the life of a young black girl growing up in a racist, segregated environment in Arkansas during the Great Depression of the 1930s.

_____

This novel is set in a seventeenth century New England colonial settlement. It tells about Hester Prynne, a woman who has been sent away from the village for adultery and later makes up for her sin by serving others.

_____

This novel tells the story of a millionaire living in the wealthy society of New York City and Long Island, New York, during the Jazz Age of the 1920s.

_____

This novel tells the story of the Joad family. They leave their "dustbowl" home in Oklahoma during the difficult economic times of the Great Depression of the 1930s and travel to the rich farmland of California to look for work.

_____

In this novel, a man named Ishmael tells the story of Captain Ahab's hunt for the great white whale that has defeated him before. The book includes details of the whaling industry and the natural history of the whale.

_____

This novel follows the adventures of Robert Jordan, an American volunteer fighting on the side of the Loyalist forces in the Spanish Civil War during the 1930s. The author wrote about his experiences in Spain during the war.

_____

This novel, written ten years before the Civil War (1861–1865), depicts the evils of slavery and tells about how families were broken up as members were sold "down the river" in Kentucky.

_____

This short story is one of the first examples of American literature, appearing in a collection called _The Sketch Book_ in 1820. In the story, Ichabod Crane is a greedy, superstitious schoolmaster who has a strange encounter with the ghost of the headless horseman.

_____

In this novel, four sisters—Meg, Jo, Beth, and Amy— grow up in Massachusetts during the Civil War. The story shows both the happiness and the sadness of family life in the nineteenth century.

_____

This novel tells about a boy traveling down the Mississippi River on a raft with his friend, a runaway slave named Jim. They have various adventures on the river, including surviving a crash with a steamboat.

Vocabulary

Are there any words in the descriptions above that you don't know? Write them here and look in your dictionary or ask a classmate or your teacher to explain:

Word   **Explanation, synonym, or example:**

_____   _____

_____   _____

_____   _____

Present Tense Sentence Combinations

Work with your classmates to combine the following into sentences about the books and stories in the Matching exercise. How many sentences can you make? All of the verbs are present tense.

		during the Great Depression.
Moby Dick		an adulterous relationship.
		in New York City.
The Grapes of Wrath	takes place	adventures on the Mississippi.
		four sisters.
The Great Gatsby	describes	in Massachusetts.
		in the nineteenth century.
The Scarlet Letter	tells about	in the twentieth century.
		during the Spanish Civil War.
I Know Why the Caged Bird Sings	includes	the evils of slavery.
		in Arkansas.
For Whom the Bell Tolls	follows	in the seventeenth century.
		racism.
"The Legend of Sleepy Hollow"	shows	in New England.
		a millionaire.
Uncle Tom's Cabin	depicts	the Joad family.
		on a whaling boat.
Little Women		information about whales.
		the adventures of Robert Jordan.
The Adventures of Huckleberry Finn		in Kentucky.
		the ghost of a headless horseman.
		family life in the nineteenth century.

Talk About This!

Decide which of the books described here you would most like to read. Why?
Write your decision here. Then interview three classmates about their decisions.

WHO	TITLE	REASON
You		
Classmate 1		
Classmate 2		
Classmate 3		

Your teacher can help you find copies of books you would like to read.

FOCUS ON CONTENT: AMERICAN POETS

In this section you will listen to the beginning of a famous poem by Henry Wadsworth Longfellow and learn about some other famous poets.

"Paul Revere's Ride" was written by Henry Wadsworth Longfellow. Paul Revere was a silversmith who rode his horse across the Massachusetts countryside on the night before the Battle of Lexington and Concord in 1775, the first battle of the Revolutionary War. He warned the colonists that the British troops were coming. Because of Paul Revere's warning, the colonists were ready to fight the next day.

Listen and Write 🔲

Listen to the beginning of the poem on the cassette and fill in the missing words below.

"Paul Revere's Ride"

1. Listen, my _____, and you shall hear
2. Of the midnight _____ of Paul Revere,
3. On the eighteenth of _____, in Seventy-five;
4. Hardly a man is now alive
5. Who _____ that famous day and year.
6. He said to his _____, "If the British march
7. By _____ or _____ from the town tonight,
8. Hang a _____ aloft in the belfry arch
9. Of the North _____ tower as a signal light, —
10. _____, if by land, and _____, if by sea;
11. And I on the opposite shore will be,
12. Ready to _____ and spread the alarm
13. Through every Middlesex village and _____,
14. For the _____ folk to be up and to arm."

Vocabulary

Study some of the new vocabulary that appears in the poem.

Find a word in line	that means	and write it here:
1	will	_____
2	12:00	_____
4	barely, scarcely	_____
8	lamp, light	_____
8	high above the ground	_____
8	tower	_____
8	curved opening	_____
11	edge of the river	_____
12	warning	_____
13	small town	_____
14	people	_____
		_____

Speak, Listen, and Connect

You can talk about poets and poems using passive voice. In passive voice, the poem is the subject of the sentence.

PASSIVE: "Paul Revere's Ride"	was	written	by	Longfellow.
POEM	*be*	PAST PARTICIPLE	*by*	POET

In this exercise you and a partner will practice making statements in passive voice while you learn about more American poets and the titles of the poems they wrote. Make statements in passive voice by following the lines connecting the poems with the poets. Work back and forth with your partner until both charts are complete. When you finish, check your answers by looking at your partner's chart.

Follow this example:

Student A says: *Leaves of Grass* was written by Walt Whitman.
Student B connects *Leaves of Grass* with Walt Whitman.

Student B then says: "The Road Not Taken" was written by Robert Frost.
Student A connects "The Road Not Taken" with Robert Frost.

Student A: *Look here and cover the other chart.*

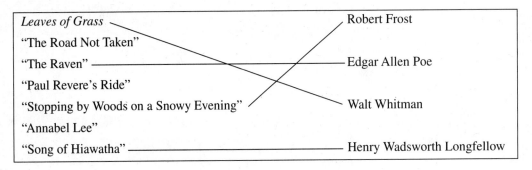

Student B: *Look here and cover the other chart.*

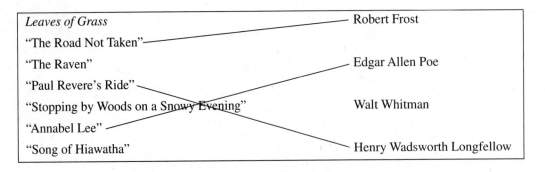

FACTS NOTE:

Leaves of Grass is a collection of poems.

Speak, Listen, and Change

You can vary your sentence patterns with both active and passive voice when you talk about poets and poems. Use active voice to talk about the poet. Use passive voice to talk about the poem.

ACTIVE VOICE:	Longfellow	wrote		"Paul Revere's Ride."	
	POET	ACTIVE VERB		POEM	
PASSIVE VOICE:	"Paul Revere's Ride"	was	written	by	Longfellow.
	POEM	*be*	PAST PARTICIPLE	*by*	POET

In this exercise you and a partner will practice changing active voice to passive voice while you talk about the poems and poets. Your partner will read a sentence in active voice. You should respond by changing it to passive voice. Some words are written in to help you form the passive sentences.

Follow this example:

Student A reads: Robert Frost wrote "The Road Not Taken."
Student B responds: "The Road Not Taken" was written by Robert Frost.

Student B then reads: Walt Whitman wrote *Leaves of Grass*.
Student A responds: *Leaves of Grass* was written by Walt Whitman.

Student A: *Look here and cover the right side of the page.*

1. Robert Frost wrote "The Road Not Taken."

2. *Leaves of Grass* _____ by _____ Whitman.

3. Henry Wadsworth Longfellow wrote "The Song of Hiawatha."

4. "The Raven" _____ by Edgar Allen _____.

5. Robert Frost wrote "Stopping by Woods on a Snowy Evening."

6. "The Song of Hiawatha" _____ by _____ Wadsworth _____.

7. Edgar Allen Poe wrote "The Raven."

8. "The Road Not Taken" _____ by _____ _____.

9. Walt Whitman wrote *Leaves of Grass*.

10. "Stopping by Woods on a Snowy Evening" _____ by _____ _____.

Student B: *Look here and cover the right side of the page.*

1. "The Road Not Taken" _____ by Robert _____.

2. Walt Whitman wrote *Leaves of Grass*.

3. "The Song of Hiawatha" _____ by Henry Wadsworth _____.

4. Edgar Allen Poe wrote "The Raven."

5. "Stopping by Woods on a Snowy Evening" _____ by _____ Frost.

6. Henry Wadsworth Longfellow wrote "The Song of Hiawatha."

7. "The Raven" _____ by _____ _____ _____.

8. Robert Frost wrote "The Road Not Taken."

9. *Leaves of Grass* _____ by _____ _____.

10. Robert Frost wrote "Stopping by Woods on a Snowy Evening."

PUT IT TOGETHER

Find Someone Who

In this activity you will use questions beginning with "Have you read . . . ?" to talk to your classmates about what they have read by American authors and poets. When you find someone who says yes, *fill in the information on the right side of the page. After you finish, share what you learned with your classmates.*

    Examples: *Have you read* anything by Louisa May Alcott?

                 Have you read any poems in English?

Find someone who has read something by . . .   **Write this information:**

1.   Ernest Hemingway.

                                            Student's name: _____

                                            Title: _____

                                            English or translated?_____

2.   John Steinbeck.

                                            Student's name: _____

                                            Title: _____

                                            English or translated?_____

3.   Mark Twain.

                                            Student's name: _____

                                            Title: _____

                                            English or translated?_____

4.   Maya Angelou.

                                            Student's name: _____

                                            Title: _____

                                            English or translated?_____

5.   Herman Melville.

                                            Student's name: _____

                                            Title: _____

                                            English or translated?_____

6.   another American author:

                                            Student's name: _____

    _____

             (name of author)   Title: _____

                                            English or translated?_____

Crossword

Fill in with the names of the writers.

ACROSS

1. *The Scarlet Letter*
3. *Moby Dick*
5. *For Whom the Bell Tolls*
7. *Leaves of Grass*
9. *The Grapes of Wrath*
11. "The Legend of Sleepy Hollow"
12. *Little Women*
13. "Paul Revere's Ride"

DOWN

2. *I Know Why the Caged Bird Sings*
4. *The Great Gatsby*
6. "The Raven"
8. *The Adventures of Huckleberry Finn*
10. *Uncle Tom's Cabin*
14. "Stopping by Woods on a Snowy Evening"

CHAPTER THIRTEEN

AMERICAN INNOVATION: INVENTORS AND INVENTIONS

Each century of American history has been marked by inventions that have influenced the way people live. In this chapter you will talk about some of those inventors and their inventions.

SHOW WHAT YOU KNOW

1. Inventions often change the way people live. Talk with your classmates to list some inventions, and try to decide how the inventions changed people's lives. The inventions can be as old as the wheel or as new as the personal computer.

Invention	How it changed people's lives
_____	_____
_____	_____
_____	_____
_____	_____

2. Here are some things that were invented in the United States in the eighteenth and nineteenth centuries. Many of them helped to shape the country as we know it today. Work with your classmates to match the names of the inventions in the box with the pictures below. Check your answers with your teacher.

eyeglasses (bifocals)	Franklin stove	lightning rod	submarine
cotton gin	telephone	phonograph	steamboat
light bulb	moving picture camera		

   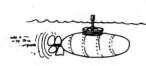      

_____   _Franklin stove_   _____   _____

      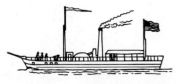

_____   _____   _____

_____   _____   _____

FOCUS ON CONTENT: INVENTORS AND INVENTIONS

In this section you will hear a lecture about five famous American inventors. Look at the names of the inventors before you listen. Do you recognize any of them? Do you know any of their inventions?

Listen and Write 🔲

Listen to the lecture as many times as necessary to in order to fill in the dates and inventions.

INVENTOR	LIVED		INVENTION(S)
	FROM	TO	
Benjamin Franklin	1706		
Robert Fulton			
Eli Whitney			
Alexander Graham Bell		1922	
Thomas Alva Edison		1931	

Listen and Choose 🔲

Listen to the questions on the cassette and circle the letter of the best answer.

1. a. in the seventeenth century
    b. in the eighteenth century
    c. in the nineteenth century

2. a. the lightning rod
    b. the electric light
    c. the telephone

3. a. They helped people see.
    b. They made houses warm.
    c. They helped people live safely and comfortably.

4. a. a fireplace
    b. the steamboat
    c. bifocal glasses

5. a. Robert Fulton
    b. Eli Whitney
    c. Benjamin Franklin

6. a. They helped the economy.
    b. They made people comfortable.
    c. They helped people have fun.

7. a. Fulton and Franklin
    b. Bell and Whitney
    c. Bell and Edison

8. a. Alexander Graham Bell
    b. Thomas Edison
    c. Eli Whitney

Listen and Write 🔲

Listen to the statements on the cassette and fill in the dates.

1. Bell invented the telephone in _____.
2. Edison invented the phonograph in _____.
3. The cotton gin was patented in _____.
4. Fulton invented the steamboat in _____.
5. The light bulb was invented in _____.

Read and Decide

Read each statement and decide if it is true or false. Write T *or* F *on the line. If a statement is false, change it to make it true.*

1. _____ Benjamin Franklin was an inventor, author, and diplomat.

2. _____ Franklin worked around the time of the American Revolution.

3. _____ Franklin invented a type of boat.

4. _____ Franklin's inventions influenced the economy of the eighteenth century.

5. _____ Robert Fulton and Eli Whitney were born in 1765.

6. _____ Robert Fulton and Eli Whitney were both educated at home by their mothers.

7. _____ Eli Whitney's cotton gin helped the economy in the nineteenth century.

8. _____ Fulton's submarine made transportation on the Mississippi cheaper.

9. _____ Alexander Graham Bell invented the telephone.

10. _____ Thomas Edison invented the television.

Vocabulary

Study the vocabulary from the lecture. Then match the word or phrase on the left with the phrase on the right. Write the letter of the best answer on the line.

1. Lightning is _____
2. To experiment is _____
3. A fireplace _____
4. To patent is _____
5. Bifocal eyeglasses _____
6. A steamboat _____
7. A submarine _____
8. A cotton gin _____
9. The Franklin stove is _____
10. A phonograph is _____
11. A telephone _____

a. heats a room by burning wood.
b. a record player.
c. to register an invention with a government agency.
d. transmits signals over wires.
e. cleans cotton.
f. electricity appearing in the sky.
g. an iron fireplace.
h. to try out new ideas, usually in a laboratory.
i. combine two types of glass in one lens.
j. uses a steam engine to drive a wheel.
k. can go under water.

Speak, Listen, and Choose

You can ask questions about inventors and inventions using *what did.*

Review the formation of past tense questions:

What	did	Edison	invent?		Edison	invented	the light bulb.
What	*did*	SUBJ	BASE FORM		SUBJ	PAST VERB	OBJECT

In this exercise you and a partner will review the information and vocabulary from the lecture while you ask and answer questions in the past tense. Take turns forming questions with the cues and answering them by choosing and circling the correct illustration. Look at page 135 if you can't remember the vocabulary or the information. When you finish, check your answers with your teacher.

Follow this example:

Student A asks first: What did Benjamin Franklin invent?
Student B responds: He invented bifocals.
  and circles the illustration of the bifocals.

Student B then asks: What did Robert Fulton invent?
Student A responds: He invented the steamboat.
  and circles the illustration of the steamboat.

Student A: *Look here and cover the right side of this page.*

Student B: *Look here and cover the left side of this page.*

1. Benjamin Franklin

1.

2. 

2. Robert Fulton

3. Eli Whitney

3. 

4. 

4. Benjamin Franklin

5. Thomas Edison

5.

6.

6. Alexander Graham Bell

7. Robert Fulton

7.

8. 

8. Thomas Edison

FOCUS ON SKILLS: PRONOUNCING PAST VERBS, USING RELATIVE CLAUSES AND PASSIVE VOICE

In this section you will practice the pronunciation of regular past tense verbs and make sentences with relative clauses and passive voice while you talk about inventors and inventions.

Pronunciation

There are three ways to pronounce regular past tense verb endings. Study the rules below. Then listen to the cassette and practice the pronunciation.

Rule 1:	The past tense verb ending *-ed* is pronounced [t] after voiceless sounds except *t*. Do not add an extra syllable.	
[p] helped		The cotton gin *processed* cotton.
[k] liked		Edison *equipped* a laboratory in New Jersey.
[s] processed		Edison *worked* night and day.
[s̆] published		
Rule 2:	The past tense verb ending *-ed* is pronounced [d] after voiced sounds except *d*. Do not add an extra syllable.	
[v] lived		Franklin *believed* that lightning was electricity.
[r] hired		Bell *lived* in Scotland.
[g] begged		Fulton *died* in 1815.
[vowel sounds] died, married		
Rule 3:	The past tense verb ending *-ed* is pronounced [id] after *t* and *d*. Add an extra syllable.	
[t] edited		Edison *invented* the phonograph.
[d] added		Franklin *experimented* with electricity.
		Whitney *patented* the cotton gin in 1794.

Listen and Choose 🔲

Now you will hear some sentences about inventors and inventions. Listen to the cassette and put a check under [t], [d], or [id] depending on which type of verb you hear.

	[t]	[d]	[id]
1.			
2.			
3.			
4.			
5.			
6.			
7.			
8.			

Speak, Listen, and Decide

In this exercise you and your partner will practice the pronunciation of regular past tense verbs in sentences about inventors and inventions. Take turns reading statements and deciding if the verb ends with [t], [d], or [id]. Circle the correct pronunciation, and tell your partner what you decided. When you finish, check your answers by looking at your partner's side of the page.

Follow this example:

Student A reads: Benjamin Franklin published a newspaper. *published*
Student B decides [t].

Student B then reads: Eli Whitney invented the cotton gin. *invented*
Student A decides [id].

Student A: *Look here and cover the right side of the page.*

1. Ben Franklin *published* [t] a newspaper. *published*
2. [t]   [d]   ([id])
3. Bell *helped* [t] deaf people speak and hear. *helped*
4. [t]   [d]   [id]
5. Bell *patented* [id] the telephone in 1876. *patented*
6. [t]   [d]   [id]
7. Robert Fulton *died* [d] in 1815. *died*
8. [t]   [d]   [id]
9. Franklin *experimented* [id] with lightning. *experimented*
10. [t]   [d]   [id]
11. Bell *invented* [id] the telephone. *invented*
12. [t]   [d]   [id]
13. Fulton *believed* [d] that a steam engine could run a boat. *believed*
14. [t]   [d]   [id]
15. Fulton *worked* [t] in France and the United States. *worked*
16. [t]   [d]   [id]
17. Franklin *lived* [d] in the eighteenth century. *lived*
18. [t]   [d]   [id]

Student B: *Look here and cover the left side of the page.*

1. ([t])   [d]   [id]
2. Eli Whitney *invented* [id] the cotton gin. *invented*
3. [t]   [d]   [id]
4. Ben Franklin *believed* [d] that lightning was electricity. *believed*
5. [t]   [d]   [id]
6. Edison *worked* [t] long hours in his laboratory. *worked*
7. [t]   [d]   [id]
8. Bell *lived* [d] in England, Scotland, and Canada. *lived*
9. [t]   [d]   [id]
10. Edison *edited* [id] a small newspaper. *edited*
11. [t]   [d]   [id]
12. Inventions have *helped* [t] people live better. *helped*
13. [t]   [d]   [id]
14. Edison *patented* [id] hundreds of inventions. *patented*
15. [t]   [d]   [id]
16. Edison *died* [d] in 1931. *died*
17. [t]   [d]   [id]
18. Edison's inventions *changed* [d] the way people live. *changed*

Sentence Combinations with Relative Clauses

You can use relative clauses to talk about inventions.

Use a relative clause to describe a noun. The relative clause comes after the noun that it describes. You can use a relative clause to make a complex sentence from two simple sentences:

The Franklin stove is a fireplace.   It is made of iron instead of bricks.

Main clause: **Relative clause:**

The Franklin stove is a fireplace   that   is made of iron instead of bricks.
                     NOUN   *that*   VERB

Replace *it* with *that*.

In this exercise you will make sentences about inventions using relative clauses. Work with your classmates to combine the following parts into statements using relative clauses. How many statements can you make?

				sends voice signals long distance.
				influenced the economy of the nineteenth century.
The lightning rod				attracts lightning.
Bifocals		a type of boat		runs on a steam engine.
The submarine		a sharp point		have 2 types of glass.
The cotton gin	is	of metal	that	have 2 types of glass.
The telephone	are	a device		turns electricity into light.
The light bulb		eyeglasses		can go under water.
The Franklin stove		an invention		helped to shape the way we live today.
The steamboat		a fireplace		cleans cotton.
				plays back music on disks.
				helped people live more safely and comfortably in the eighteenth century.

What is it?

Think of an invention. It can be one of the inventions above, another invention from history, or a modern invention such as the personal computer or the microwave oven. Prepare as many statements about the invention as you can. Use relative clauses.

> This is a machine that cleans cotton.
> It is an invention that influenced the economy of the nineteenth century.
> It is an invention that was important to cotton farmers.
> (Answer: the cotton gin)

Say your statements to your classmates. The first classmate to guess the correct invention is the winner. The winner has the next turn.

Speak, Listen, and Change

You can vary your sentence patterns with both active and passive voice when you talk about inventors and inventions. Use active voice to talk about the inventor. Use passive voice to talk about the invention.

ACTIVE VOICE:	Bell	invented	the telephone.
	INVENTOR	ACTION VERB	INVENTION
PASSIVE VOICE:	The telephone	was invented	by Bell.
	INVENTION	be + PAST PARTICIPLE	+ by + INVENTOR

In this exercise you and a partner will talk about inventors and their inventions using active voice and passive voice. Your partner will read a sentence in active voice. You should respond by changing it to passive voice. Some words are written in to help you form the passive sentences.

Follow this example:

Student A reads: Franklin invented bifocals.
Student B responds: Bifocals were invented by Franklin.

Student B then reads: Fulton invented the steamboat.
Student A responds: The steamboat was invented by Fulton.

Student A: *Look here and cover the right side of the page.*

1. Franklin invented bifocals.

2. The steamboat ——————— by ———————

3. Whitney invented the cotton gin.

4. The phonograph ——————— by ———————.

5. Bell invented the telephone.

6. The lightning rod ——————— by ———————.

7. Edison invented the light bulb.

8. The moving picture camera ——————— by ———————.

9. Edison invented the phonograph.

10. The telephone ——————— by ———————.

11. Franklin invented the lightning rod.

12. The light bulb ——————— by ———————

Student B: *Look here and cover the left side of the page.*

1. Bifocals ——————— by ———————.

2. Fulton invented the steamboat.

3. The cotton gin ——————— by ———————.

4. Edison invented the phonograph.

5. The telephone ——————— by ———————.

6. Franklin invented the lightning rod.

7. The light bulb ——————— by ———————.

8. Edison invented the moving picture camera.

9. The phonograph ——————— by ———————

10. Bell invented the telephone.

11. The lightning rod ——————— by ———————.

12. Edison invented the light bulb.

Talk About This!

In this activity you will talk to your classmates about other inventions using passive voice. Tell about inventions from your country or inventions that are useful for you. Tell who invented it if you know. Use *by* + *name*.

If you don't know the inventor, you can use passive voice without *by* to tell when or where it was invented. Study the use of passive voice without *by*.

Instead of *by* + INVENTOR, you can tell *when* or *where* the invention was made by using a PREPOSITIONAL PHRASE.			
The wheel	was invented	in prehistoric times.	(when)
Chopsticks	were invented	in Asia.	(where)
INVENTION	*be* + PAST PARTICIPLE	PREPOSITIONAL PHRASE	

INVENTION		INVENTOR, WHEN, OR WHERE
	was invented	
	was invented	
	was invented	
	was invented	
	was invented	

Here are some ideas for inventions if you can't think of any on your own:

the Walkman	the airplane	the television
the personal computer	Nintendo	forks and knives
the bicycle	Coca Cola	the ballpoint pen
the microwave	the CD player	the radio

PUT IT TOGETHER

Tic Tac Toe

Play Tic Tac Toe to review the information in this chapter and practice the pronunciation of past tense verbs. Your teacher will draw a tic-tac-toe grid on the blackboard and fill in the spaces with the regular past tense verbs from this chapter. The two teams take turns making past tense statements about inventions, following the rules for Tic Tac Toe in Chapter Four on page 37.

Cloze

Read the following information about American inventors and inventions. Try to fill in the blanks with the correct word. After you have filled in as much as you can, listen to the lecture on the cassette again as many times as necessary to fill in all the blanks.

American Inventors and Inventions

Since the early days of the country, American _____ have made important contributions to the way people live in the United States and in the world.

One of the first and most _____ inventors in American history was Benjamin Franklin. Franklin was an inventor, _____, and diplomat who worked around the time of the American _____. He lived from 1706 to 1790. He _____ with a kite during a thunderstorm and demonstrated that _____ is electricity. This discovery led to his _____ of the lightning _____, a device that can attract lightning and keep it away from buildings. Two of his other inventions were a type of iron _____ called the Franklin _____, and bifocal _____ or bifocals, which combine two types of glass in one lens. Franklin's inventions were important because they helped the people of the eighteenth century live more safely and comfortably.

Two other inventors born in the eighteenth century were _____ Fulton and Eli _____. Robert Fulton was born in 1765 and died in 1815. He invented a type of _____, which is a boat that can go under water, and a _____, or a boat powered by a steam engine. Eli Whitney was also born in 1765, and he died in 1825. Whitney invented the _____ gin, a machine that processed cotton. Fulton and Whitney are considered _____ because their inventions changed the _____ of the country. Fulton's steamboat made _____ on the _____ cheaper, and Whitney's cotton gin helped farmers to sell their cotton for a good _____.

The two _____ famous American inventors are Alexander Graham _____ and Thomas Alva _____. There are many _____ between Bell and Edison. They were born in the same year, 1847. They were both educated at home by their _____. And both Bell and Edison patented inventions that would become part of everyday life in the _____ century. Bell invented the _____, and Edison invented the _____, moving picture camera, and the light _____. Bell and Edison lived into the twentieth century to see their inventions change the way people live.

CHAPTER FOURTEEN

AMERICAN MUSIC: SINGERS, SONGWRITERS, AND COMPOSERS

Music is an important part of American culture, and American musicians have originated or developed several styles of music. In this chapter you will learn about American musicians and the songs they wrote and sang. You will learn the names of musical instruments as you talk about music. You will also listen to one of the first songs written in the United States.

SHOW WHAT YOU KNOW

1. Do you like music? What is your favorite type of music? Work with your classmates to list as many types or styles of music as you can. Talk about which types you like and which you don't like. Write them here:

   _____   _____   _____

   _____   _____   _____

2. In the box below are names of ten famous singers, songwriters, and composers who have worked with six styles of American music through the nineteenth and twentieth centuries. Which names do you recognize? Do you know what styles of music some of them are famous for?

Irving Berlin	Chuck Berry	George M. Cohan	Bob Dylan
Duke Ellington	Stephen Foster	George Gershwin	Woody Guthrie
Hank Williams	John Philip Sousa		

FOCUS ON CONTENT: SINGERS, SONGWRITERS, AND COMPOSERS

In this section you will hear a lecture about the musicians you talked about in the section above. You will learn about the songs they composed and sang.

Vocabulary 🔲

The following words are important in the lecture. Listen to the cassette and complete the sentences with words from the box.

parade	patriotic	combine	minstrel shows
dialects	Broadway	marches	cultural heritage

1. _____ is the center of the theater district in New York City.
2. In a _____, performers walk in the street playing music.
3. In _____ _____, during the nineteenth century, performers painted their faces black and sang and danced.
4. _____ songs show love for one's country.
5. _____ are varieties of a language in which pronunciation and some words are changed.
6. All of a country's traditions form its _____ _____.
7. _____ are songs played by bands in parades.
8. Some styles of music _____ or mix together two styles.

Listen and Write

Look at the six types of music below. Under each type of music are examples of songs and some other information. Look over the chart and try to fill in the names of the musicians from the box on page 144. Then listen to the lecture on the cassette as many times as necessary in order to fill in the rest of the names.

Popular Traditional Music

from the nineteenth century:

_____

"Oh! Susanna"   "Camptown Races"   "Swanee River"

from the early twentieth century:

_____

"God Bless America"   "White Christmas"

Broadway show tunes:

_____

"I'm a Yankee Doodle Dandy"   "You're a Grand Old Flag"

Marches

_____

"Stars and Stripes Forever"   "The Washington Post March"

Jazz

_____

"Mood Indigo"

with classical:

_____

" An American in Paris"   "Rhapsody in Blue"

Country and Western

_____

"Hey, Good Lookin'"   "Cold, Cold Heart"

Folk Music

from the 1930s to the 1950s:

_____

"This Land Is Your Land"

from the 1960s:

_____

"Blowin' in the Wind"   "The Times They Are a Changin'"

Rock and Roll

_____

"Roll Over Beethoven"   "Rock and Roll Music"   "Maybelline"

Listen and Choose 🔲

Listen to the questions on the cassette and circle the letter of the best answer.

1. a. Duke Ellington
   b. George Gershwin
   c. Stephen Foster

2. a. John Philip Sousa
   b. Hank Williams
   c. George Gershwin

3. a. Irving Berlin
   b. Bob Dylan
   c. Woody Guthrie

4. a. Bob Dylan
   b. Hank Williams
   c. Chuck Berry

5. a. John Philip Sousa
   b. George M. Cohan
   c. Duke Ellington

6. a. Hank Williams
   b. Duke Ellington
   c. Chuck Berry

Listen and Write 🔲

Listen to the statements on the cassette and fill in the dates.

1. Stephen Foster was born in _____ and died in _____.
2. John Philip Sousa was born in _____ and died in _____.
3. George M. Cohan lived from _____ to _____.
4. Irving Berlin was born 10 years after Cohan, in _____, and died at the age of 100, in _____.
5. George Gershwin lived from _____ to _____.
6. Duke Ellington was born in _____ and died in _____.
7. Woody Guthrie lived from _____ to _____.
8. Hank Williams was born in _____ and died at the age of 30, in _____.
9. Chuck Berry was born in _____ and is still living.
10. Bob Dylan was born in _____ and is still living.

Listen and Decide 🔲

Listen to the statements on the cassette and circle TRUE or FALSE.

1. TRUE   FALSE   6. TRUE   FALSE
2. TRUE   FALSE   7. TRUE   FALSE
3. TRUE   FALSE   8. TRUE   FALSE
4. TRUE   FALSE   9. TRUE   FALSE
5. TRUE   FALSE   10. TRUE   FALSE

Speak, Listen, and Choose

You can ask about songwriters and composers with questions beginning with *who*.

QUESTION		ANSWER	
Who	wrote "Blowin' in the Wind"?	Bob Dylan.	
Who	VERB	Bob Dylan	did.
		Bob Dylan	wrote "Blowin' in the Wind."
		SUBJ	*(did)*
			(VERB + COMPLEMENT)
Past tense subject questions use statement word order *who* + PAST VERB. Do not use *did*. The answer is the SUBJECT of the sentence.			

In this exercise you and a partner will take turns asking and answering questions about the musicians from the lecture. Make subject questions from the cues, changing the verbs to past tense. Circle the letter of the best answer, and tell your partner which musician using a short or long answer. When you finish, check your answers with your teacher.

Follow this example:

Student A asks first: Who wrote country and western music?
Student B responds: Hank Williams did.
  and circles *a*.

Student B then asks: Who composed "Mood Indigo"?
Student A responds: Duke Ellington composed that.
  and circles *a*.

Student A: *Look here and cover the right side of the page.*

1. write—country and western music

2.   a. Duke Ellington
    b. Irving Berlin

3. mix—jazz and classical styles

4.   a. Hank Williams
    b. John Philip Sousa

5. write—"White Christmas"

6.   a. Hank Williams
    b. Chuck Berry

7. write—1960s protest songs

8.   a. Woody Guthrie
    b. Stephen Foster

9. write—music for Broadway shows

10.   a. Woody Guthrie
    b. Hank Williams

Student B: *Look here and cover the left side of the page.*

1.   a. Hank Williams
    b. George Gershwin

2. composed—"Mood Indigo"

3.   a. Elvis Presley
    b. George Gershwin

4. write—marches

5.   a. Irving Berlin
    b. Woody Guthrie

6. write—"Maybelline"

7.   a. Hank Williams
    b. Bob Dylan

8. write—popular songs in the nineteenth century

9.   a. George M. Cohan
    b. George Gershwin

10. write—folks songs in the 1930s

Talk About This!

You have studied six types of music from the United States. In this activity you will talk to your classmates about types of music that are popular in your countries.

1. Circle the styles of music on this list that are popular in your country and give an example of a composer, singer, or songwriter from your country. Then share what you circled and wrote with your classmates.

TYPE	EXAMPLE
Jazz	_____
Folk	_____
Rock & Roll	_____
Popular/show tunes	_____
Country	_____
Marches	_____

2. Now share a type of music from your country that is not on the list above. Follow the example below and fill in the box with a style of music, a short description and the name of at least one famous musician. After you have written the information, share what you wrote with your classmates. Bring a cassette of music from your country to class so your classmates can listen.

STYLE/COUNTRY	DESCRIPTION	MUSICIANS
Folk music/U.S.A.	Singing with acoustic guitars. The words often talk about social problems.	Woody Guthrie, Bob Dylan, Joan Baez, Pete Seeger

STYLE/COUNTRY	DESCRIPTION	MUSICIANS
Marches/U.S.A.	Marching bands including horns, flutes, drums. No singing. Often played in parades. Often patriotic.	John Philip Sousa

STYLE/COUNTRY	DESCRIPTION	MUSICIANS

FOCUS ON SKILLS: SAYING NAMES OF MUSICAL INSTRUMENTS

In this section you will talk about musical instruments and learn the names of some twentieth century American musicians.

Matching

1. Match the name of the musical instrument with the picture in the box.

clarinet	drums	cello	trumpet
electric guitar	acoustic guitar	banjo	violin
piano	saxophone	flute	

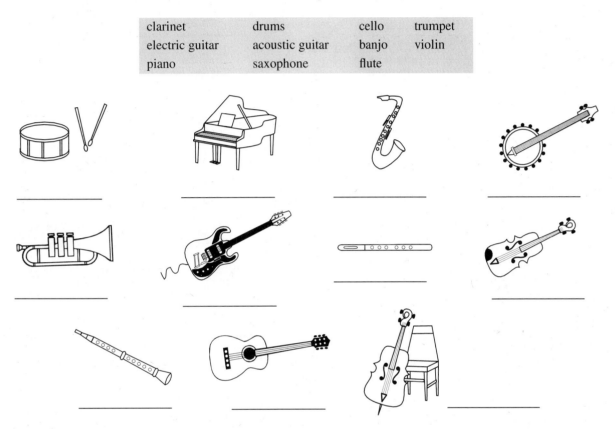

2. The box below contains names of twentieth century American musicians who have worked with four styles of music. How many do you recognize? Work with your classmates and your teacher to write the name of the style of music at the top of each list of names. Then practice the pronunciation of the names. Repeat the names after your teacher and practice with your classmates.

Styles: Folk or Country   Classical   Jazz   Rock or Popular

_____	_____	_____	_____
Louis Armstrong	Joan Baez	Billy Joel	Yo-Yo Ma
Kenny G.	Earl Scruggs	Jimi Hendrix	Itzhak Perlman
Benny Goodman	Pete Seeger	Paul Simon	Van Cliburn
Buddy Rich		Carole King	
Charlie Parker			
Herbie Mann			
Artie Shaw			
Dizzy Gillespie			
Stan Getz			
Miles Davis			

Speak, Listen, and Answer

You can talk about musicians and their instruments with questions with *what*.

What	did	Louis Armstrong	play?	He	played	the trumpet.
What	does	Joan Baez	play?	She	plays	the guitar.
What +	*did* +	SUBJ	BASE FORM	SUBJ +	VERB +	OBJECT
	does					

In this exercise you and a partner will review the names of musical instruments while you practice pronouncing the names of the musicians on page 149. Take turns making questions with what do, *if the musician is living, and* what did, *if the musician is dead. Then look at the illustration and make an answer. When you finish, check your answers with your teacher.*

Follow this example:

Student A asks: What did Louis Armstrong play?
Student B responds: He played the trumpet.

Student B then asks: What does Billy Joel play?
Student A responds: He plays the piano.

> **SKILLS NOTE:**
> Use *the* before names of musical instruments.
>
> I play *the* piano. Do you play *the* guitar?

Student A: *Look here and cover the right side of the page.*

1. Louis Armstrong   (past)

2.

3. Kenny G.   (present)

4.

5. Joan Baez   (present)

6.   (violin image)

7. Buddy Rich   (past)

8.   (electric guitar image)

(continued on next page)

Student B: *Look here and cover the left side of the page.*

1.   (trumpet image)

2. Billy Joel   (present)

3.   (saxophone image)

4. Benny Goodman   (past)

5.   (guitar image)

6. Itzhak Perlman   (present)

7.   (snare drum image)

8. Jimi Hendrix   (past)

(continued on next page)

Student A: *Look here and cover the right side of the page.*

9. Van Cliburn   (present)

10.

11. Earl Scruggs   (present)

12.

13. Artie Shaw   (present)

14.

15. Yo-Yo Ma   (present)

16.

17. Carole King   (present)

18.

19. Pete Seeger   (present)

20.

Student B: *Look here and cover the left side of the page.*

9.

10. Charlie Parker   (past)

11.

12. Herbie Mann   (present)

13.

14. Dizzy Gillespie   (past)

15.

16. Paul Simon   (present)

17.

18. Stan Getz   (past)

19.

20. Miles Davis   (past)

♪ ong

"Oh! Susanna" by Stephen Foster

As you heard in the lecture, Stephen Foster, who lived from 1826 to 1864, is considered to be the first American songwriter.

"Oh! Susanna" was Foster's first successful song. He wrote it in 1848. It became a favorite song of the "Forty-niners" of the California gold rush in 1849.

Foster was a great songwriter, but a poor businessman. He earned only $100 for "Oh! Susanna."

Stephen Foster's most popular songs are "Oh! Susanna," "Swanee River," "My Old Kentucky Home," "Camptown Races," "Beautiful Dreamer," and "Jeanie with the Light Brown Hair." Although he lived and worked most of his life in New York, his songs were often about the South.

Listen and Write 🔲

Listen and fill in the blanks below.

1.   I come from _____

       With my _____ on my knee;

       I'm goin' to _____,

       My true _____ for to see.

2.   It _____ all night the day I left,

       The _____ it was dry;

       The sun so _____ I froze to death.

       Susanna, don't you cry.

Chorus:

        Oh! Susanna,

        Oh! don't you _____ for me.

        I come from _____

        With my _____ on my knee.

3.   I had a _____ the other night,

       When _____ was still;

       I thought I saw _____ dear,

       A-coming down the hill.

4.   The buckwheat cake was in her _____,

       The tear was in her _____.

       Said I, I'm coming from the _____,

       Susanna, don't you _____.

Chorus:

        Oh! Susanna,

        Oh! don't you _____ for me.

        I come from _____

        With my _____ on my knee.

Talk About the Song

1.   Stephen Foster often wrote about the South. What two states appear in Verse 1?

     _____   _____

2.   Verse 2 is a nonsense verse. What are the two contradictions there?_____

     _____

3.   What musical instrument appears in the chorus? _____

4.   Find the word in Verse 3 that means calm and quiet: _____

5.   Find the word in Verse 4 that means a type of pancake: _____

PUT IT TOGETHER

Find Someone Who . . .

Use questions beginning with "Do you . . . ?" to find someone for each of the items on the left. BE CAREFUL. Sometimes you need a yes *answer and sometimes you need* no. *When you hear the answer you are looking for, write the person's name in the space. After you have asked all of the questions, share what you learned about your classmates with the class.*

Examples: *Do you* know how to play the guitar?
           Do you like country music?

Find someone who . . .	Write that person's name here:
knows how to play the guitar.	_____
likes country music.	_____
knows how to play the piano.	_____
doesn't like rock music.	_____
likes jazz.	_____
knows how to read music.	_____
likes folk music.	_____
doesn't know how to sing well.	_____
knows how to play more than one musical instrument. (What instruments?)	_____
doesn't like classical music.	_____
likes to go to concerts.	_____

Crossword

Fill in with the names of the musicians, songs, or instruments.

ACROSS

1. Irving _____
3. Louis _____
6. Chuck Berry song
7. Billy Joel plays the _____.
10. "Mood Indigo" composer
13. Popular jazz saxophone player _____.
14. Itzhak Perlman plays the _____.
17. Joan Baez plays the _____.
19. Irving Berlin song, "God _____ America"
21. John Philip Sousa wrote _____.
22. Foster song "_____! Susanna"
23. Yo-Yo Ma plays the _____.
24. Classical piano player Van _____

DOWN

1. 1960s folk singer/songwriter
2. Gershwin wrote "_____ in Blue."
4. Woody Guthrie song, "_____ Land Is Your Land"
5. Earl Scruggs plays the _____.
6. Duke Ellington wrote "_____ Indigo."
8. Benny Goodman played the _____.
9. Nineteenth-century songwriter Stephen _____
11. Carole _____ plays the piano.
12. Country music singer Hank _____
15. Buddy Rich played the _____.
16. Dizzy Gillespie played the _____.
18. Woody _____
19. Bob Dylan song, "_____' in the Wind"
20. Sousa march, "Stars and _____ Forever"

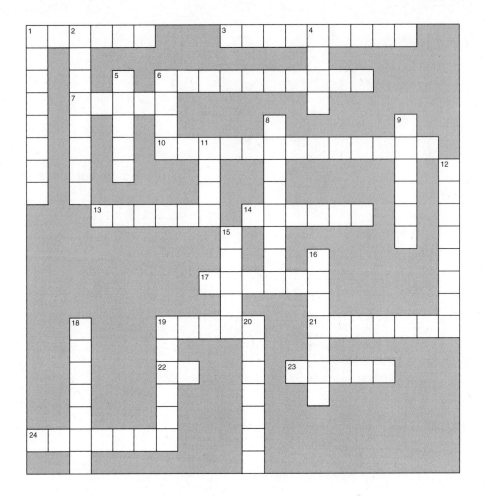

CHAPTER FIFTEEN

BUSINESS IN AMERICA: MONEY MAKERS, MONEY GIVERS, AND HOUSEHOLD NAMES

When many people think about the United States, they think of business. In this chapter you will learn about some businessmen from the nineteenth and twentieth centuries. You will hear about Sam Walton, who was the richest man in the United States when he died in 1992. You will learn about some other very wealthy people and how they have helped other people with their money. And you will learn about the people behind some famous products.

SHOW WHAT YOU KNOW

Sam Walton was the owner of Wal-Mart Stores. Wal-Mart is a large, discount department store. Discount department stores, such as Wal-Mart and K-Mart, sell a wide variety of products at low prices. They are just one of many kinds of stores and shops in the United States. Work with your classmates to list some different types of stores, with examples of each from the area you are living in.

Type of Store	Example
Discount department store	Wal-Mart, K-Mart, Caldor
Drugstore	

FOCUS ON CONTENT: SAM WALTON

In this section you will learn about Sam Walton, who owned Wal-Mart Stores and was the richest man in the country when he died. Have you ever shopped in a Wal-Mart? If you live in a large city, you may not have a Wal-Mart near you. Listen to the lecture to find out why.

Vocabulary 🔲

The following words are important in the lecture. Listen to the cassette and complete the sentences with words from the box.

chain	chairman	annual	old-fashioned
style	employees	profit	billion

1. More than one _____ people live in China. (1,000,000,000)

2. _____ means every year.

3. He is the director, or _____, of the company.

4. His business _____ is the way he does business.

5. The workers are the _____.

6. The money you keep after you pay your expenses is called your _____.

7. He's not modern. He is _____.

8. McDonald's is a _____. There are McDonald's restaurants throughout the United States.

Listen and Write 🔲

Listen to the lecture on the cassette as many times as necessary in order to fill in the information about Sam Walton.

Sam Walton   born: _____   died: _____

He was the _____ man in the United States. He was worth _____ billion dollars.

Opened his first store in _____.

YEAR	NUMBER OF STORES
1970	_____
1972	_____
_____	_____
_____	_____

Listen and Choose 🔲

Listen to the questions on the cassette and circle the letter of the best answer.

1. a. $18,200,000,000
   b. $18,200,000
   c. $80,200,000

2. a. 1952
   b. 1962
   c. 1972

3. a. It didn't grow.
   b. It grew very slowly.
   c. It grew very fast.

4. a. because he lived in a small town
   b. because there were already too many stores in big cities
   c. because there were more people in small towns

5. a. modern
   b. old-fashioned and direct
   c. cold and distant

6. a. He flew his own plane.
   b. He drove his own car.
   c. He sailed his own boat.

7. a. a few
   b. about half
   c. almost all

8. a. in a hotel
   b. in a small house
   c. in a large house

9. a. a pickup truck
   b. a sports car
   c. a luxury car

10. a. He retired when he was 65.
    b. He never retired.
    c. He retired when he was 70.

Listen and Write 🔲

In this exercise you will to hear some more information about Sam Walton and Wal-Mart Stores. Listen to the statements on the cassette and fill in the numbers.

1. Sam Walton was _____ years old when he died.
2. In 1972, Wal-Mart had _____ million dollars in annual sales.
3. In 1992, Wal-Mart had _____ billion dollars in annual sales.
4. Wal-Mart employs _____ workers.
5. Wal-Mart opens _____ new stores every year.
6. In 1987, there were _____ Wal-Mart stores.
7. In 1989, Wal-Mart had _____ billion dollars in annual sales.
8. There were Wal-Mart stores in _____ states in 1992.
9. Sam Walton also opened _____ Sam's warehouse stores for small businesses.
10. Sam's sells products at ___ to _____ % over cost.
11. Another Walton store called Hypermart, U.S.A. is the size of ___ regular Wal-Marts.

Matching

Review the information and new vocabulary from the lecture. Match the phrases on the left with the phrases on the right.

1. Sam Walton was the _____	a. *shares* profits with employees.
2. Walton had a _____	b. *discount department stores.*
3. Wal-Mart and K-Mart are _____	c. *chairman* of Wal-Mart Stores.
4. Sam Walton _____	d. *piloted* his own plane.
5. When he died, Walton's _____	e. *direct* style of management.
6. The Wal-Mart Corporation _____	f. *net worth* was $18.2 billion.

Talk About This!

1. Sam Walton was very unusual. He was the richest man in the United States when he died, but in many ways he did not act the way you would expect a rich business leader to act. Below are some examples of the way Sam Walton lived and worked. Work with your classmates to decide how you might expect a very wealthy businessperson to act. Use present tense verbs in your description.

What he did (past verbs)	What wealthy, successful business leaders usually do (present verbs)
He opened stores in small towns, where people don't have a lot of money.	
He piloted his own small airplane.	
He visited all of his stores every year and talked to his employees in person.	
He shared profits with his employees.	
He lived in a small house.	
He drove a pickup truck.	
He worked full time until he died at the age of 74.	

2. If you were a wealthy business leader, would you be more like Sam Walton, or the typical businessperson you described? Why?

FOCUS ON CONTENT: MONEY MAKERS AND MONEY GIVERS

Many very wealthy business leaders in the United States have given money to others. Such people are called *philanthropists*. In this section you will learn about wealthy philanthropists from the nineteenth and twentieth centuries.

Philanthropists use their money in many ways. What ways can you think of for a philanthropist to use his or her money?

Speak, Listen, and Write

In this exercise you and your partner will talk about seven philanthropists. You will exchange information on when they lived, how they made their money, and how they gave it away. Work back and forth, asking and answering questions so that you each complete your chart. When you finish, check your answers by looking at your partner's chart.

Follow this example:

1. **Student A says:**	Tell me about Andrew Carnegie.	5. **Student A then asks:**	How did he make his money?
2. **Student B looks at the information.**		6. **Student B responds:**	In iron, steel, and railroads.
3. **Student A asks:**	When did he live?	7. **Student A asks:**	What did he do with his money?
4. **Student B responds:**	From 1835 to 1919.	8. **Student B responds:**	He gave it to educational institutions and libraries.

Student A: *Look here and cover the other chart.*

Name	Lived From – To	Business	Gave Money To
Andrew Carnegie			
Henry Ford	1836–1947	automobiles	science, education, and the arts
Armand Hammer			
William Randolph Hearst	1863–1951	newspapers	art museums
J. P. Morgan			
John D. Rockefeller	1839–1937	oil	medical education and research
Cornelius Vanderbilt			

Student B: *Look here and cover the other chart.*

Name	Lived From – To	Business	Gave Money To
Andrew Carnegie	1835–1919	iron, steel, railroads	educational institutions and libraries
Henry Ford			
Armand Hammer	1898–1990	oil	art museums
William Randolph Hearst			
J. P. Morgan	1837–1913	banking and finance	churches, hospitals, and schools
John D. Rockefeller			
Cornelius Vanderbilt	1794–1877	shipping and railroads	a university

Speak, Listen, and Decide

In this exercise you and a partner will take turns reading statements about the information in your completed charts and deciding if they are TRUE *or* FALSE. *When you finish the exercise, check your answers with your teacher.*

Follow this example:

Student A reads:	Andrew Carnegie made his money in steel and railroads.
Student B responds:	That's true.
and circles TRUE.	
Student B then reads:	Henry Ford made his money in airplanes.
Student A responds:	That's false.
and circles FALSE.	

Student A: *Look here and cover the right side of the page.*

1. Andrew Carnegie made his money in steel and railroads.

2. TRUE   FALSE

3. J. P. Morgan gave his money to schools.

4. TRUE   FALSE

5. Cornelius Vanderbilt lived in the twentieth century.

6. TRUE   FALSE

7. William Randolph Hearst made his money in oil.

8. TRUE   FALSE

9. Armand Hammer was 92 years old when he died.

10. TRUE   FALSE

11. Henry Ford gave his money to art museums.

12. TRUE   FALSE

Student B: *Look here and cover the left side of the page.*

1. TRUE   FALSE

2. Henry Ford made his money in airplanes.

3. TRUE   FALSE

4. Armand Hammer gave his money to medical research.

5. TRUE   FALSE

6. John D. Rockefeller made his money in oil.

7. TRUE   FALSE

8. Andrew Carnegie gave his money to public libraries.

9. TRUE   FALSE

10. J. P. Morgan made his money in steel.

11. TRUE   FALSE

12. John D. Rockefeller gave his money to medical research.

Talk About This!

1. Does your country have any famous philanthropists? Tell your class about them or any other philanthropists you know.

2. Before Andrew Carnegie died, he gave away $350 million. He said, "The man who dies rich dies disgraced." What did he mean? Do you agree with that?
   If you were very rich, would you be a philanthropist, or would you prefer to keep your money in your family? Why?

3. Group Discussion
   If you worked for a philanthropic organization today, how would you give away your money? Look at the chart below. On the left are institutions that received money from the philanthropists in the previous exercise. Work with your classmates to fill in at least three more institutions (homeless shelters? family planning clinics? animal causes?). Then decide what percentage of your money will go to each institution. You can write any percentage from 0% to 100% — as long as your total is not more than 100%. Give a reason for each percentage. When your group is finished, share what you decided with your classmates.

INSTITUTION	PERCENTAGE	REASON
Elementary and secondary schools		
Libraries		
Art museums		
Religious institutions		
Hospitals		
Medical and science research institutions		
Universities		
TOTAL:	100%	

FOCUS ON CONTENT: HOUSEHOLD NAMES IN THE U.S.A.

Do you wear Calvin Klein jeans and chew Wrigley's gum? Have you ever eaten Baskin Robbins ice cream or Kellogg's cornflakes cereal? In this section will learn about the names behind some famous products.

Matching

Work with your classmates to match the people on the left with the products that they made. Draw a line between the name and the product. When you finish, check your answers with your teacher.

Dan Gerber	cars
Calvin Klein	ice cream
Louis Chevrolet	ketchup
Will K. Kellogg	sewing machines
Burton Baskin and Irving Robbins	baby food
Joseph Campbell	soup
Maurice and Richard McDonald	vacuum cleaners
Isaac Merritt Singer	hamburgers
William Wrigley, Jr.	jeans
William H. Hoover	chewing gum
Henry J. Heinz	cereal

Speak, Listen, and Decide

You can ask about events in the past with *yes – no* questions beginning with *did.*

Did	Henry Ford	make	cars?	Yes,	he	did.
Did	Henry Ford	make	airplanes?	No,	he	didn't.
Did	SUBJ	BASE FORM	OBJECT		PRONOUN	*did(n't)*

In this exercise you and a partner are going to take turns making yes/no *questions about the information from the matching exercise above. Circle* yes *or* no *and say a short answer. When you finish, check your answers with your teacher.*

Follow this example:

Student A asks:	Did William H. Hoover make vacuum cleaners?
Student B responds: and circles YES.	Yes, he did.
Student B then asks:	Did Will K. Kellogg make cereal?
Student A answers: and circles YES.	Yes, he did.

Student A: *Look here and cover the right side of the page.*

1. William H. Hoover/vacuum cleaners
2. YES   NO
3. Joseph Campbell/cereal
4. YES   NO
5. Dan Gerber/baby food
6. YES   NO
7. Louis Chevrolet/ice cream
8. YES   NO
9. Calvin Klein/jeans
10. YES   NO
11. Burton Baskin and Irving Robbins/ice cream
12. YES   NO

Student B: *Look here and cover the left side of the page.*

1. YES   NO
2. Will K. Kellogg/cereal
3. YES   NO
4. Maurice and Richard McDonald/ketchup
5. YES   NO
6. Isaac Merritt Singer/cars
7. YES   NO
8. William Wrigley, Jr./chewing gum
9. YES   NO
10. Henry J. Heinz/cereal
11. YES   NO
12. Will K. Kellogg/soup

Talk About This!

1. In your country, can you buy a McDonald's hamburger or drive a Chevrolet? In this activity you will talk about American products that are available in your country. Look at the list of products below. Put a check in the block next to the ones that you can buy in your country. Then, get together with a partner and share your information. Check off the products that your partner mentions and talk about whether you use the products, if they are expensive in your country, and so on.

PRODUCT	IN YOUR COUNTRY	IN YOUR PARTNER'S COUNTRY
Baskin Robbins ice cream		
Calvin Klein jeans		
Campbell soup		
Chevrolet cars and trucks		
Gerber baby products		
Heinz ketchup		
Hoover vacuums		
Kellogg's cornflakes, "Special K"		
McDonald's restaurants		
Wrigley spearmint gum		

2. Are there any other American products that are popular in your country? Tell the class about them.

PUT IT TOGETHER

"I'm thinking of a person who . . ."

In this activity you will review the names of the people in this chapter. Sit in a circle. One student will choose a name from the chapter and make a statement with a relative clause. The first classmate to call out the answer goes next. Continue until everyone has had a chance to speak.

Follow this example:

One student says: I'm thinking of a person who put baby food in jars.

A classmate shouts: Gerber!
   and that student goes next.

Role Play

You learned that Wal-Marts open more frequently in small towns than in large cities. Work in groups of four to six on a role play about the possibility of a Wal-Mart opening in a small town. Practice your role play and present it to the class. Here are your roles:

Student A: You are a representative from Wal-Mart Stores. You think that opening a Wal-Mart in this small town is a good idea. People will be able to buy things at a good price. People will find jobs, especially around Christmas time.

Student B: You are the owner of a small variety store on Main Street. You think that opening a Wal-Mart is a bad idea. You can't match Wal-Mart's low prices because your business is much smaller than a Wal-Mart. You will lose customers. Your customers will lose the personal service you give.

Student C: You are a person in the town. You think the Wal-Mart is a good idea. You can get many things at Wal-Mart that you can't find in the stores on Main Street, and the prices are better.

Student D: You are a union leader. You work for good pay, working conditions, and benefits (such as health insurance and vacation time) for workers. You think the new Wal-Mart is a bad idea. Most of the workers will be paid a low hourly wage with no benefits and no job security. Many of the workers will lose their jobs if business is slow.

Use these extra roles if your group has five or six members:

Student E: You are the owner of a small dress shop on Main Street. Your opinions are similar to those of Student B.

Student F: You are an unemployed person in the town. You think that the new Wal-Mart is a good idea, because you hope to get a job there.

Cloze 🔲

Read the following information about Sam Walton. Try to fill in the blanks with the correct word. After you have filled in as much as you can, listen to the lecture on the cassette again as many times as necessary to fill in all the blanks.

Sam Walton was born in 1918, and when he died in 1992, he was worth 18.2 _____

dollars. That made him the _____ man in the United States. How did he become so

rich? He was chairman of Wal-Mart _____ , the largest chain of discount department

stores in the country.

Sam Walton wasn't always rich. He started out with _____ store, which he opened

in 1962. His business grew _____ at first. In 1970, he had 24 stores. He had 64 stores in

1972. At that time, Sears was the largest discount store in the United States, and K-Mart was the

_____ largest. But Wal-Mart began to _____ very quickly. In

1983, there were 642 Wal-Mart stores. More than 100 stores _____ each year after that.

First, Wal-Mart replaced K-Mart as number two; then it replaced Sears as number one in 1992. By 1992, there

were 1,650 Wal-Marts in 43 _____ , with $40 billion in _____

sales.

Why was Sam Walton so _____ ? For one thing, he opened his Wal-Mart stores in

small cities and _____ , not in big cities where there were already many large stores. And

he had a direct, old-fashioned _____ of management. He traveled around the country in

a small _____ , which he piloted himself, and visited almost all of his stores every year.

He believed in getting to know his employees personally and sharing _____ with them.

In spite of his great wealth, he lived in a small house, drove a _____ truck, and continued

to work full-time until he died.

ON YOUR OWN NAMES TO KNOW IN THE U.S.A.

Here are some activities related to famous people for you to do on your own, with a small group, or with your whole class.

1. Choose an author from Chapter 12. Go to the library and find a book that he/she wrote. Look through the book, and read parts or all of it. Bring the book to class to share with your classmates.

2. Bring cassettes to class to listen to music by the musicians in Chapter 14. You can borrow cassettes from friends, teachers, or the library if you don't want to buy one.

3. Share music from your country with your classmates. Bring cassettes to class, and be prepared to explain a little about the type of music and the musicians.

4. Give a 5-minute oral report on the life of one of the people in this unit. Find out about the person's life in the library. You can use an encyclopedia or other reference materials. Ask the reference librarian for information. Also, the children's biography section has easy-to-understand books about many of the people in this unit. Prepare a handout, overhead, or poster on the life of the person to help your classmates understand your speech.

5. Give a 5-minute oral report on the life of a famous person from your country. Try to think of an author, inventor, musician, or business leader that your classmates would like to hear about. Follow the directions in item 4.

6. Work in pairs to research the life of one of the people in this unit. Find information in the library, using materials suggested in item 4 above. Plan and present a role play for the class in which one partner plays the famous American and the other partner is a talk-show interviewer. Your interview should last about 5 minutes.

7. Plan a trip to a local concert. Begin by looking in the newspaper. What kind of music do you want to hear? Jazz? Folk? Rock? Attend the concert with your classmates. Report to your class about the concert afterward.

8. Look in the local newspaper and learn about local radio stations. Is there a jazz station? A country music station? Bring a radio to class, and using the guide from the newspaper, try to identify the various stations. Or call a station and arrange a tour.

9. Visit a museum about American history. How many of the names in this unit can you find in the museum? Report to your class on what you found.

10. Invite the manager of a local Wal-Mart to come to your class and talk about the company. Find out how Wal-Mart is different from other companies. What has made it so successful? Visit a Wal-Mart and report to the class about it.

11. Wal-Mart Stores has a warehouse division called Sam's. Sam's is not open to the general public. Call a local Sam's (or Price Club) to find out about the store. Who can shop there? How are the prices? Report to your class.

12. Find out if there is an office of a large philanthropic organization in your city. Look for the Ford Foundation, the Rockefeller Foundation, or the Carnegie Institute. Invite someone from the organization to talk to your class about philanthropy in the United States, or find out if your class can visit the office of the organization to learn more.

Unit

Celebrating Holidays
in the U.S.A.

CHAPTER SIXTEEN
THE HOLIDAYS AT A GLANCE

Holidays are special days of celebration that form an important part of every country's culture. American holidays come throughout the year and in all varieties. In this chapter, you will learn about the different types of holidays that Americans celebrate and when throughout the calendar year Americans celebrate them.

SHOW WHAT YOU KNOW

What American holidays do you already know? Work with a partner and write the names of some holidays and something you know about them in the spaces below. Share the information with your class and together try to decide what types of holidays they are.

Name of Holiday	Something We Know
Christmas	It's a Christian holiday.
New Year's Day	It's in January.

FOCUS ON CONTENT: TYPES OF AMERICAN HOLIDAYS

In this section you will hear a short lecture about the different types of holidays celebrated in the United States.

Vocabulary 📼

The following words are important in the lecture. Listen to the cassette and complete the sentences with words from the box.

background	religious	patriotic	celebrated
honors	ethnic	observe	tradition

1. The students _____ the end of the school year with concerts, picnics, and parties.
2. When an employee retires, the company usually_____ him or her with a big farewell party and a nice present.
3. Chinatown in New York City is an example of an _____ neighborhood.
4. The family was very _____ and flew the American flag in front of their house on every holiday.
5. People all over the world _____ a New Year's holiday.
6. John F. Kennedy was an American president of Irish _____.
7. Christians, Jews, and Muslims are examples of _____ groups in the United States.
8. It is a birthday _____ in the U.S.A. to have a cake with the same number of candles as the person's age.

Listen and Write 📼

Listen to the lecture on the cassette as many times as necessary in order to complete the diagram about types of American holidays. Fill in with the names of holidays in the box.

Earth Day	Independence Day	New Year's Day
Easter	Memorial Day	Presidents' Day
Halloween	Mother's Day	Valentine's Day

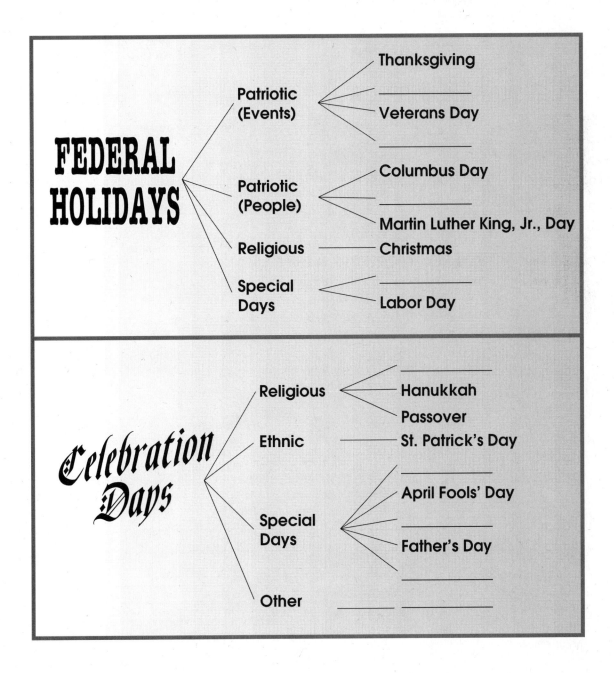

Listen and Choose 📼

Listen to the questions on the cassette and circle the letter of the best answer. Look back at the information on pages 170 and 171 if you don't remember an answer.

1. a. All private businesses are closed.
   b. Only schools and banks are closed.
   c. Federal offices, banks, and post offices are closed.

2. a. at least five
   b. at least nine
   c. at least eleven

3. a. Christmas
   b. Thanksgiving
   c. Hanukkah

4. a. Halloween and April Fools' Day
   b. Easter and Passover
   c. Earth Day and St. Patrick's Day

5. a. a great civil rights leader
   b. an important event in the country's history
   c. the Irish background of many Americans

6. a. on Valentine's Day
   b. on Thanksgiving
   c. on Halloween

7. a. on Mother's and Father's Days
   b. on Labor Day
   c. on Memorial Day

8. a. April Fools' Day
   b. Earth Day
   c. Veterans Day

Read and Decide

Read each statement and decide if it is true or false. Write *T* or *F* on the line. If a statement is false, change it to make it true.

1. _____ All states celebrate ten federal holidays.
2. _____ Thanksgiving is a day to remember the first people who came and settled in America.
3. _____ Independence Day is an example of a patriotic holiday.
4. _____ Columbus Day honors an American president.
5. _____ Martin Luther King, Jr., Day remembers an event in American history.
6. _____ Most religious holidays are also federal holidays.
7. _____ Labor Day honors working people.
8. _____ There is usually no school or work on Halloween and Valentine's Day.
9. _____ Father's Day is a special day when Americans remember their ethnic backgrounds and traditions.
10. _____ Earth Day is a special day that honors nature.

Talk About This!

What types of holidays are celebrated in your country?

In this activity you will share information about some holidays that you celebrate in your country. Fill in one or two examples of holidays for each category if you celebrate that type of holiday in your country. Put a check (✓) after the holidays that are days off from work or school. After you have filled in examples from your country, get together with a partner, and share your information. Fill in the information about your partner's country. When your chart is complete, share what you learned with your classmates.

TYPE OF HOLIDAY	THE U.S.A.	YOUR COUNTRY	YOUR PARTNER'S COUNTRY
Patriotic (Events)	Independence Day		
Patriotic (People)	Martin Luther King, Jr., Day		
Religious	Christmas		
Ethnic	St. Patrick's Day		
Special Days	Halloween		

FOCUS ON CONTENT: THE HOLIDAY CALENDAR

In this section, you will learn about when Americans celebrate their holidays. You will practice the pronunciation of months, days, and dates, and use them with prepositions of time to talk about holidays.

Pronunciation

Review the pronunciation of months, days, and ordinal numbers with your teacher and your classmates.

January	March	May	July	September	November
February	April	June	August	October	December

Sunday	Monday	Tuesday	Wednesday	Thursday	Friday	Saturday

1st–first	11th–eleventh	21st–twenty-first
2nd–second	12th–twelfth	22nd–twenty-second
3rd–third	13th–thirteenth	23rd–twenty-third (and so on)
4th–fourth	14th–fourteenth	
5th–fifth	15th–fifteenth	30th–thirtieth
6th–sixth	16th–sixteenth	31st–thirty-first
7th–seventh	17th–seventeenth	
8th–eighth	18th–eighteenth	
9th–ninth	19th–nineteenth	
10th–tenth	20th–twentieth	

> **GRAMMAR NOTE:**
>
> Always use *the* before ordinal numbers, except when the ordinal comes after the name of a month. Then it's optional. You can say "January first" or "January the first."

Listen and Write 🔲

Listen to the cassette for the description of the holiday calendar. In the chart below, write in the ordinal numbers you hear. Note that some holidays are celebrated on the same date every year, and others are always celebrated on the same day of the month.

	JANUARY	FEBRUARY	MARCH	APRIL
Same Date Every Year	New Year's Day: the _____	Valentine's Day: the _____	St. Patrick's Day: the _____	April Fools' Day: the _____
Same Day Every Year	Martin Luther King, Jr., Day: the _____ Monday	Presidents' Day: the _____ Monday		

	MAY	JUNE	JULY	AUGUST
Same Date Every Year			Independence Day: the _____	
Same Day Every Year	Mother's Day: the _____ Sunday Memorial Day: the _____ Monday	Father's Day: the _____ Sunday		

	SEPTEMBER	OCTOBER	NOVEMBER	DECEMBER
Same Date Every Year		Halloween: the _____	Veterans Day: the _____	Christmas: the _____
Same Day Every Year	Labor Day: the _____ Monday	Columbus Day: the _____ Monday	Thanksgiving: the _____ Thursday	

Speak, Listen, and Write

You can say and write the date in a variety of ways in English.

On applications, letters, and other forms in the United States, *write* the date in the following ways: January 25, 1990   or   1/25/90 The short form is more informal for letters and more common for forms.
Say the date like this: January twenty-fifth, nineteen ninety   or   January the twenty-fifth, nineteen ninety

In this exercise you will practice saying and writing dates. You and a partner are going to take turns reading dates and writing them using the short form. When you finish, check your answers by looking at your partner's side of the page.

Follow this example:

Student A says: July fourth, nineteen sixty-two
Student B writes 7/4/62.

Student B then says: January the first, nineteen seventy-five
Student A writes 1/1/75.

Student A: *Look here and cover the right side of the page.*	**Student B:** *Look here and cover the left side of the page.*
1. 7/4/62	1. _____
2. _____	2. 1/1/75
3. 5/31/87	3. _____
4. _____	4. 2/14/24
5. 10/31/91	5. _____
6. _____	6. 11/11/52
7. 9/2/59	7. _____
8. _____	8. 4/1/46
9. 8/15/93	9. _____
10. _____	10. 9/12/82
11. 3/17/67	11. _____
12. _____	12. 6/4/76

Talk About This!

1. Find a calendar for this year. Look at the holidays in the chart on page 173. Look for the holidays that are celebrated on the same day, but on a different date, each year. What date are they on this year?

2. Look at the holidays that are celebrated on the same date every year. What day of the week do they fall on this year?

3. What is your birthday? What other dates are important to you? Your wedding anniversary? The date on which you came to the United States? Share these dates with your classmates.

Speak, Listen, and Decide

You can use the prepositions of time *on* and *in* to talk about when holidays are celebrated.

Use *on* with a day or date.	Labor Day is celebrated on the first Monday in September. Christmas is celebrated on December 25.
Use *in* with a month.	Labor Day is celebrated in September.

In this exercise you and a partner are going to practice prepositions of time by asking and answering questions about the American holiday calendar. Listen to the question your partner asks. Circle the letter of the best answer, fill in the correct preposition, and answer with a full sentence. Refer to the chart on page 173 if you can't remember an answer. When you're finished, check your answers with your teacher.

Follow this example:

Student A asks: When is Independence Day?
Student B responds: It's on July fourth.
  and circles *b*, filling in *on*.

Student B then asks: When is Thanksgiving?
Student A responds: It's on the fourth Thursday in November.
  and circles *b*, filling in *on* and *in*.

Student A: *Look here and cover the right side of this page.*

1. Independence Day?

2. a. _____ the third Thursday_____ November
   b. _____ the fourth Thursday_____ November

3. Mother's Day?

4. a. _____ February 2nd
   b. _____ February 14th

5. Martin Luther King, Jr., Day?

6. a. _____ May
   b. _____ June

7. Christmas?

8. a. _____ March 17th
   b. _____ May 17th

9. Memorial Day?

10. a. _____ October
    b. _____ August

11. Columbus Day?

12. a. _____ the third Monday _____ February
    b. _____ the first Monday _____ February

Student B: *Look here and cover the left side of this page.*

1. a. _____ July 14th
   b. _____ July 4th

2. Thanksgiving?

3. a. _____ September
   b. _____ May

4. Valentine's Day?

5. a. the first Monday _____ January
   b. the third Monday _____ January

6. Father's Day?

7. a. _____ December 25th
   b. _____ December 31st

8. St. Patrick's Day

9. a. the fourth Monday _____ May
   b. the first Monday _____ September

10. Halloween?

11. a. _____ October
    b. _____ April

12. Presidents' Day?

Talk About This!

Where do the names of the months come from? Believe it or not, the names of the months in English do have meanings. They have Latin roots and come from the time of the ancient Romans. The original Roman calendar had only 10 months. Later, when the 12-month calendar was adopted, January and February were added at the beginning. For example, October comes from the Latin word *octo* for eight, and was originally the eighth month.

1. Work with a partner to see if you can match some of the months with their origins.

    1.   March _____   a.   from the Latin *novem* for nine or ninth month
    2.   July _____   b.   named after the Roman god for beginnings, gates, or doors, who was named Janus
    3.   December _____   c.   named after the Roman leader, Augustus Caesar
    4.   August _____   d.   named after the Roman leader, Gaius Julius Caesar
    5.   November _____   e.   named after the Roman god of war, Mars
    6.   January _____   f.   from the Latin *decem* for ten or tenth month

2. In your country, do you use the same 12-month calendar as Americans do? If your calendar is different, bring one in and explain the differences to your classmates.

3. Think about the meaning of the names of the months in your own language. Are they different from English? If so, tell a classmate/your class the names of the months in your language, then explain:
    where the names come from: _____
    what they mean: _____

PUT IT TOGETHER

Circulation

In this activity you will have the chance to speak to 10 different members of your class and find out more about the holidays in their countries.

First, write the name of a different classmate on each line to the left of the questions. Then, stand up, go to your classmates whose names you have written, and ask the questions next to their names. Write short answers and be ready to share them with your classmates when you finish.

_____ Do you celebrate an Independence Day? If you do, when is it?
                 _____

_____ Do you have a favorite holiday? What holiday and when?
                 _____

_____ Do you have a holiday that is celebrated *only* in your country? What holiday and when? _____

_____ Is there a holiday in your country just for children? If there is, when is it?
                 _____

_____ Do you celebrate the birthday of a famous person? Who and when?
                 _____

_____ Do you have any month in your calendar that has no holidays? Which one?
                 _____

_____ Do you celebrate birthdays in your country? When is yours?
                 _____

_____ Do you celebrate a Mother's Day? When? _____

_____ Do you have a holiday especially for fathers? When? _____

_____ Do you have a special day to celebrate nature or the weather? What and when?
                 _____

Concentration

Play a game of Concentration matching the holidays with the months during which they are celebrated. Prepare packets of twelve cards, six with names of holidays and six with the months during which they are celebrated.

Cloze 🔊

Read the lecture below about the types of American holidays. Try to fill in the blanks with the correct words. After you have filled in as much as you can, listen to the lecture on the cassette again as many times as necessary to fill in all the blanks.

Americans love holidays and celebrate a variety of days all through the _____ . They observe federal holidays, which give them a _____ off from school or work, and other celebration days without a day off.

The government of the United States has declared ten _____ holidays. On these holidays, all federal government offices, banks, and post offices are _____ . Since the American states have their own governments, each _____ has a right to decide which of the federal holidays it will _____ . Private businesses can decide which of these federal holidays their employees will observe with a _____ day. As it happens, most states and businesses _____ at least _____ of the federal holidays, so everyone can have at least nine days off from _____ or _____ every year.

There are several different _____ of federal holidays. Some are _____ holidays, which remember important _____ in the history of the United States. For instance, Thanksgiving is a day to remember the very beginnings of the _____ and the first people that came and _____ in America. Another holiday, Independence Day, celebrates the American colonies' Declaration of Independence from _____ and the birth of the United States. Veterans Day and _____ Day honor Americans who have fought and died in wars.

Other federal holidays are patriotic in a different way. They remember important _____ in the country's history. For example, Columbus Day _____ Christopher Columbus, the _____ explorer financed by Spain who opened America to European exploration. Two presidents, George _____ and Abraham Lincoln, are honored February on Presidents' Day. Finally, Martin Luther King, Jr., Day honors a _____ African American civil rights leader.

Some federal holidays are special days that are also _____ in other countries, but perhaps in different ways and at different times of the year. New _____ Day is one of these special days. Labor Day, a holiday which honors all _____ people, is another.

Most _____ holidays are not federal holidays because the American constitution separates the government from the church. However, there is one religious holiday that is also a federal holiday, and that is _____ .

There are also many _____ days of celebration in the United States that are not observed with _____ from school or work. These days are celebrated with their own special _____ , either by all Americans or by specific _____ or religious groups. Some different types of these celebration days are religious holidays and ethnic holidays.

Religious holidays are celebrated by Americans of different religious _____ . For example, Easter is a day celebrated by Christians, and Hanukkah and Passover are examples of _____ holidays.

Ethnic holidays are celebrated with special traditions brought to this country by the many _____ who came to the United States from all over the world. For example, St. Patrick's Day is a holiday which celebrates the _____ background of many Americans.

Americans also have a number of special celebrations just for fun, _____ , and family, such as _____ , a special day on which children dress up in _____ and eat lots of candy. April Fools' Day is celebrated by playing little _____ on friends. There are also holidays to _____ parents, such as Mother's Day and Father's Day, and a holiday just for _____ , Valentine's Day.

As time goes on, other days become part of the American holiday _____ . One example of this is Earth Day, a special day in April that honors _____ . This day is observed by more and more Americans each year who are interested in _____ the earth.

Although it is difficult to get the Congress to agree to add a new federal holiday to the American calendar, there is always room for new celebrations.

Holidays always bring with them celebrations or ceremonies of some kind. In this chapter you will learn how Americans celebrate their holidays. You will also look at the holiday tradition of sending cards and look at some of the legends and superstitions that go along with some holiday celebrations.

SHOW WHAT YOU KNOW

How do Americans celebrate their holidays? Look at the list of holidays in the center box below. Together with a partner, choose a few holidays you know something about and discuss what special things Americans do on these days.

Holiday	How celebrated?
Christmas	*People give gifts.*
_____	_____
_____	_____
_____	_____

FOCUS ON CONTENT: HOW AMERICANS CELEBRATE

In this section you will talk about some American holiday traditions.

Matching

The boxes on this page and the next contain short descriptions of how the holidays you talked about in Chapter Sixteen are celebrated. Work with your classmates and your teacher to match the celebrations with the names of the holidays in the center of the page. Write the letter or letters of the descriptions next to the names of the holidays. When you finish, review the information for the following exercises.

a. Green clothes are worn by Irish Americans, and parades are held in Irish American neighborhoods.

b. Eggs are dyed and hidden, and a bunny gives candy to children.

c. Gifts are exchanged around a tree.

d. Turkey is eaten as part of a large meal.

HOLIDAYS

April Fools' Day	____
Christmas	____
Columbus Day	____
Easter	____
Father's Day	____
Halloween	____
Hanukkah	____
Independence Day	____
Labor Day	____
Martin Luther King, Jr., Day	____
Memorial Day	____
Mother's Day	____
New Year's Day	____
Presidents' Day	____
St. Patrick's Day	____
Thanksgiving	____
Valentine's Day	____
Veterans Day	____

e. Cards are sent by sweethearts, and heart-shaped boxes of candy are given as gifts.

f. Jokes are played on friends and colleagues.

g. Mothers are treated to breakfast in bed and a day of rest.

h. Songs of freedom and equality are sung.

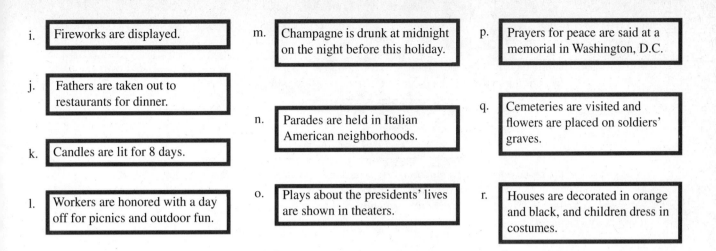

i. Fireworks are displayed.

j. Fathers are taken out to restaurants for dinner.

k. Candles are lit for 8 days.

l. Workers are honored with a day off for picnics and outdoor fun.

m. Champagne is drunk at midnight on the night before this holiday.

n. Parades are held in Italian American neighborhoods.

o. Plays about the presidents' lives are shown in theaters.

p. Prayers for peace are said at a memorial in Washington, D.C.

q. Cemeteries are visited and flowers are placed on soldiers' graves.

r. Houses are decorated in orange and black, and children dress in costumes.

Vocabulary

Are there any words in the descriptions that you do not know? Write them here and ask your classmates or teacher to explain.

Word   **Explanation, Synonym, or Example**

_____   _____

_____   _____

_____   _____

Listen and Decide 🔲

Listen to the statements on the cassette and circle TRUE or FALSE. Look at the Matching exercise on page 178 and above if you can't remember all the information.

1. TRUE   FALSE   6. TRUE   FALSE
2. TRUE   FALSE   7. TRUE   FALSE
3. TRUE   FALSE   8. TRUE   FALSE
4. TRUE   FALSE   9. TRUE   FALSE
5. TRUE   FALSE   10. TRUE   FALSE

Listen and Choose 🔲

Listen to the questions on the cassette and circle the letter of the best answer. Look at the Matching exercise on page 178 and above if you can't remember all the information.

1. a. on Halloween
   b. on Valentine's Day
   c. on St. Patrick's Day

2. a. on Thanksgiving
   b. on Independence Day
   c. on Memorial Day

3. a. on Valentine's Day
   b. on Mother's Day
   c. on Christmas

4. a. on Easter
   b. on Christmas
   c. on Hanukkah

5. a. on St. Patrick's Day
   b. on Columbus Day
   c. on Veterans Day

6. a. on Halloween
   b. on Christmas
   c. on Easter

7. a. on Veterans Day
   b. on Christmas
   c. on Labor Day

8. a. on Father's Day
   b. on Mother's Day
   c. on Veterans Day

Speak, Listen, and Connect

You can talk about holidays using present tense passive voice. In passive voice, the object associated with the holiday is the subject of the sentence. The name of the holiday is last, after a preposition.

PASSIVE:	Costumes	are	worn	on	Halloween.
	OBJECT	*be*	PAST PARTICIPLE	PREP.	HOLIDAY

In this exercise you and a partner are going to learn more American holiday traditions while you practice making statements in passive voice. Make statements by following the lines connecting the phrases on the left with the holidays on the right. Work back and forth until both charts are complete. When you finish, check your answers by looking at your partner's chart.

Follow this example:

Student A says: Handmade cards are given to Dad on Father's Day.
Student B connects the two parts of the sentence.

Student B then says: Cherry pie is eaten on Presidents' Day.
Student A connects the two parts of the sentence.

Student A: *Look here and cover the other chart.*

Handmade cards are given to Dad	on Mother's Day.
Cherry pie is eaten	on Thanksgiving.
Red and white carnations are worn by sons and daughters	on Halloween.
Romantic cards are chosen for sweethearts	on Father's Day.
New clothes are worn to church	after Labor Day.
Carols are sung	on New Year's Day.
A candle is lit each night	on St. Patrick's Day.
Cookouts and picnics are held	on Presidents' Day.
Green beer is sometimes drunk	during Hanukkah.
"April fool!" is shouted after jokes	on Valentine's Day.
Black-eyed peas are eaten in the South	on Independence Day.
Football games are shown on television	on April Fools' Day.
Pools are closed for the summer	on Christmas.
"Trick or treat!" is shouted	on Easter.

Student B: *Look here and cover the other chart.*

Handmade cards are given to Dad	on Mother's Day.
Cherry pie is eaten	on Thanksgiving.
Red and white carnations are worn by sons and daughters	on Halloween.
Romantic cards are chosen for sweethearts	on Father's Day.
New clothes are worn to church	after Labor Day.
Carols are sung	on New Year's Day.
A candle is lit each night	on St. Patrick's Day.
Cookouts and picnics are held	on Presidents' Day.
Green beer is sometimes drunk	during Hanukkah.
"April fool!" is shouted after jokes	on Valentine's Day.
Black-eyed peas are eaten in the South	on Independence Day.
Football games are shown on television	on April Fools' Day.
Pools are closed for the summer	on Christmas.
"Trick or treat!" is shouted	on Easter.

FACTS NOTE:

Cherry pie is associated with Presidents' Day because of a legend about George Washington. The legend says that when he was a boy, George Washington chopped down his father's cherry tree. When his father asked him about it, George said, "I cannot tell a lie. I chopped down your tree."

GRAMMAR NOTE:

Review the irregular past participles from this exercise.

give—given	eat—eaten	wear—worn
choose—chosen	sing—sung	light—lit
hold—held	show—shown	drink—drunk

Talk About This!

Countries often celebrate the same holiday but in a different way, with different traditions. The New Year's holiday is one shared by many countries around the world. Does your country celebrate a New Year's holiday? If so, when and how do you celebrate it?

In the chart below, you will see some of the characteristics of New Year's in the U.S.A. Use the space to write some notes about your country's New Year's traditions. Then talk with a partner and find out what is done in his/her country to welcome in the New Year. When your chart is complete, share what you learned with your classmates.

CHARACTERISTICS	THE UNITED STATES	YOUR COUNTRY	YOUR PARTNER'S COUNTRY
Season of the Year	winter		
Special Greetings	Happy New Year!		
Food and Drink	champagne at midnight on New Year's Eve; black-eyed peas on New Year's Day for good luck		
Special Clothes	ball gowns, tuxedos		
Other Traditions	make resolutions, sing "Auld Lang Syne"		

FOCUS ON CONTENT: HOLIDAY SYMBOLS AND GREETINGS

In this section you will learn about one very popular holiday tradition in the U.S.A.—sending greeting cards. On many holidays, cards are sent with "greetings," special wishes for a happy day. These cards are usually decorated with symbols that Americans associate with these holidays.

Matching

In this exercise you will work with a partner to form greeting cards. First write the names of the symbols under the correct greeting card. Then draw a line to match the holiday card with the greeting you would find inside. Note that some holiday greetings can be used with two different cards.

SYMBOLS		
a shamrock	champagne and confetti	a horn of plenty
a menorah	a heart-shaped candy box	an evergreen tree
painted eggs	a jack-o-lantern	a bunny
a turkey	wrapped presents	

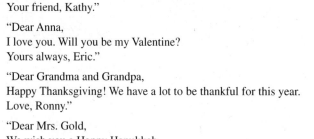

GREETINGS

"Dear Shawn,
Wishing you the luck of the Irish. Happy St. Patrick's Day.
Your friend, Kathy."

"Dear Anna,
I love you. Will you be my Valentine?
Yours always, Eric."

"Dear Grandma and Grandpa,
Happy Thanksgiving! We have a lot to be thankful for this year.
Love, Ronny."

"Dear Mrs. Gold,
We wish you a Happy Hanukkah.
Sincerely, Rob and Gloria."

"To the Adsons.
A very Merry Christmas to you and all your family.
Yours truly, Sue and Dave Bella."

"Dear Jenny,
Watch out for those ghosts and witches tonight. Hope you get lots of good candy. Have a Happy Halloween.
Love, Grandma."

"Hi there, Sis!
Have a fun and happy New Year.
Drink a gloss of champagne for me!
Take care, Greg."

"Dear Mom and Dad,
I hope you have a wonderful Easter. Wish I could be home.
Love, Lisa."

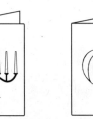

Speak, Listen, and Write

A *tag question* is a question that you add to the end of a statement. You can use the negative statement/affirmative tag pattern when you think the information is wrong but you want to make sure.

Usually, if your information is wrong, you will get a *no* answer and the correct information.

[–] STATEMENT	[+] TAG	[–] ANSWER
Americans *don't* celebrate Labor Day in May,	*do* they?	No, they *don't*.

NOTE: For practice with affirmative statements/negative tags, see page 92.

In this exercise you and a partner will ask and answer tag questions about American holiday symbols. Use the information in the charts below. Student A will first ask all (6) of his/her questions, and Student B will answer. Then Student B will ask all (6) of his/her questions, and Student A will answer. When you finish, check your answers by looking at your partner's chart.

Follow this example:

Student A asks: A shamrock isn't a symbol of Christmas, is it?
Student B responds: No, it isn't. It is a symbol of St. Patrick's Day.
Student A writes *St. Patrick's Day* in the CORRECT column.

Student A: *Look here and cover the chart on page 184.*

ASK	INCORRECT	CORRECT
1. A shamrock . . .	Christmas	*St. Patrick's Day*
2. A horn of plenty . . .	Halloween	
3. Champagne and confetti . . .	Easter	
4. A jack-o-lantern . . .	Valentine's Day	
5. Painted eggs . . .	Thanksgiving	
6. A heart . . .	St. Patrick's Day	

ANSWER	
7. a menorah	Hanukkah
8. an evergreen tree	Christmas
9. a turkey and a horn of plenty	Thanksgiving
10. a bunny	Easter
11. a candy box	Valentine's Day
12. wrapped presents	Christmas

Student B: *Look here and cover the chart on page 183.*

ANSWER		
1.	A shamrock	St. Patrick's Day
2.	A horn of plenty	Thanksgiving
3.	Champagne and confetti	New Year's Day
4.	A jack-o-lantern	Halloween
5.	Painted eggs	Easter
6.	A heart	Valentine's Day

ASK		INCORRECT	CORRECT
7.	A menorah . . .	New Year's Day	
8.	An evergreen tree . . .	Valentine's Day	
9.	A turkey and a horn of plenty . . .	Christmas	
10.	A bunny . . .	Hanukkah	
11.	A candy box . . .	Thanksgiving	
12.	Wrapped presents . . .	St. Patrick's Day	

Talk About This!

1. Think of some typical holiday symbols or greetings associated with holidays in your country and explain their meanings to your classmates. You can make notes here:

HOLIDAY	SYMBOL OR GREETING	MEANING

2. Are holiday greeting cards a tradition in your country? If so, choose one of your country's holidays, and make a card with some typical holiday symbols and greetings. (Provide an English translation.) Show your card to your classmates.

FOCUS ON CONTENT: HOLIDAY LEGENDS AND SUPERSTITIONS

Some American holidays have special legends, or superstitions, associated with them. For example, Groundhog Day, on February 2, is a day when American legend says that the actions of a small animal, the groundhog, can predict an early or late spring.

Matching

Work with your classmates to match the holiday in the box with the legend or superstition below.

Groundhog Day	Valentine's Day	Halloween
Christmas	St. Patrick's Day	Easter

1. A religious man drove all the snakes out of Ireland. _____

2. The birds find their mates on this day. _____

3. Santa Claus comes down the chimney at night to put presents under the tree for all good children. The children find them and open them in the morning. _____

4. An animal comes out of his hole in the ground near the end of a long winter. If he sees his shadow, he goes back in the hole, and there will be six more weeks of winter. If he doesn't see his shadow, there will be an early spring. _____

5. Ghosts, spirits, and witches come out at midnight to frighten people on this night. People put scary black and orange decorations on their houses to keep the evil spirits away. _____

6. A bunny comes at night to put colored eggs and candy in children's baskets in this springtime holiday. _____

Speak, Listen, and Decide

You can use the prepositions of time *at* and *in* to talk about holiday legends and superstitions.

Use *at* with a specific time.	at 12:00
Use *at* with some times of day.	at night, at midnight, at noon, at sunrise
Use *in* with a season.	in the winter, in the spring, in the summer, in the fall
Use *in* with some times of day.	in the morning, in the afternoon, in the evening

In this exercise you and a partner will practice prepositions of time by asking and answering questions about American holiday legends and superstitions. Listen to the question your partner asks. Circle the letter of the best answer, fill in the correct preposition, and answer with a short answer. Refer to the Matching exercise on pages 178 and 179 if you can't remember an answer. When you're finished, check your answers with your teacher.

Follow this example:

Student A asks first: When is St. Patrick remembered?
Student B responds: In March.
  and circles *b*, filling in *in*.

Student B then asks: On Halloween, when do evil spirits come out?
Student A responds: At midnight.
  and circles *b*, filling in *at*.

Student A: *Look here and cover the right side of the page.*

1. When is St. Patrick remembered?

2. a. _____ noon
   b. _____ midnight

3. When does Santa Claus come with presents?

4. a. _____ the winter
   b. _____ the fall

5. When do children find candy in their Easter baskets?

6. a. _____ January
   b. _____ Valentine's Day

7. When are houses decorated in black and orange colors?

8. a. _____ night
   b. _____ noon

9. When do ghosts and witches come out?

10. a. _____ the morning
    b. _____ noon

11. When do children dye eggs?

12. a. _____ December
    b. _____ Halloween

Student B: *Look here and cover the left side of the page.*

1. a. _____ the summer
   b. _____ March

2. On Halloween, when do evil spirits come out?

3. a. _____ night
   b. _____ the morning

4. When does the groundhog see his shadow?

5. a. _____ the morning
   b. _____ night

6. When do birds find their mates?

7. a. _____ February
   b. _____ Halloween

8. When does the Easter Bunny visit homes?

9. a. _____ the fall
   b. _____ the spring

10. When do most children open Christmas presents?

11. a. _____ the winter
    b. _____ the spring

12. When does Santa Claus come down the chimney?

Talk About This!

Are there some legends or superstitions associated with any holidays in your country? Write down one or two in the box below, and make a short presentation to your classmates about it.

HOLIDAY	LEGEND OR SUPERSTITION

ong

A very popular Christmas tradition in the United States is the singing of carols, which are special Christmas songs. Some carols are religious and celebrate the birth of Jesus Christ. Other carols are not religious, and they sing of winter fun and holiday happiness. Groups of people singing these songs are called *carolers*. They walk around a neighborhood at night, stopping in front of houses to sing a carol. Carolers may also visit people in their offices at work, or people in hospitals. Carols are also sung at shopping malls, in concert halls, and at family Christmas parties.

Listen and Write

Listen to a few verses from these popular Christmas carols and fill in the missing words below.

"Silent Night" (religious)
Silent night, _____ night.
All is _____, all is bright
'Round yon virgin _____ and child,
Holy _____ so tender and mild.
Sleep in heavenly _____,
Sleep in heavenly _____.

"Jingle Bells" (not religious)
1. Dashing through the _____
   On a one-horse _____ sleigh,
   O'er the fields we _____,
   Laughing all the _____.
3. Jingle bells, jingle bells,
   Jingle all the _____.
   Oh, what fun it is to _____
   In a one-horse open _____. (*Repeat*)

2. Bells on bobtails _____,
   Making spirits _____.
   What fun it is to ride and _____
   A sleighing song _____!

Talk About the Songs

1. Study the vocabulary from "Silent Night."

Find a word that means	and write it here:
sacred, blessed by God	_____
the one over there (short for "yonder")	_____
baby	_____
calm, gentle	_____

2. Study the vocabulary from "Jingle Bells."

Find a word in	that means	and write it here:
Verse 1	riding very fast	_____
	form of transportation	_____
Verse 2	horse with a short tail	_____
Verse 3	the sound a bell makes	_____

3. Do you sing either of these two songs in your country? If you do, sing them in your language for your classmates.
4. Tell your classmates about other songs associated with holidays in your country. Sing a verse from a holiday song from your country for your classmates.

PUT IT TOGETHER

Twenty Questions

WHO AM I? WHAT AM I?

1. You teacher will have a stack of cards with vocabulary words from the chapter related to who, what, and how holidays are celebrated in the U.S.A. They may include people honored, holiday symbols and legends, special food or clothing, and so on.

2. Your teacher will divide the class into two teams. A student from Team A will go up to the front of the class. The teacher will show the rest of the class a card with a word. The student must try to find out *who* or *what* he/she is by asking the class questions. However, they must be *yes–no* questions. The student may ask up to 20 questions. If the student guesses correctly, Team A gets a point. If the student doesn't guess correctly, the class tells him/her the answer, and Team B gets a point.

3. Teams take turns sending students up to the front.

VARIATION: After 10 questions, the opposite team may give a clue.
A correct guess without a clue gets 2 points.
A correct guess with a clue gets 1 point.

Passive Voice Sentence Combinations

Work with your classmates to combine the following into sentences in the passive voice about the information in this chapter. How many sentences can you make? Change all of the verbs to past participles and use *is* or *are*.

Example: Cards are exchanged on Christmas and Valentine's Day.

"April Fool!"		
Carols		
Green		
Candles		
Turkey		
Gifts		during Hanukkah.
Football games	drink	on St. Patrick's Day.
Orange and black	shout	at Christmastime.
Hot dogs and hamburgers	use	on Easter.
"Trick or treat !"	eat	on April Fools' Day.
Red and green	exchange	on Columbus Day.
New clothes	hold	on Halloween.
Cards	give	on Valentine's Day.
Formal clothes	hear	on Presidents' Day.
Parades	see	on Thanksgiving.
Cherry pie	wear	on Independence Day.
Candy	light	on New Year's Eve.
Cookouts and picnics		on Christmas.
Champagne		
Fireworks		
Green beer		
Decorated trees		

Jumble

Do you remember the irregular past participles of these verbs? Some letters are written in to give you hints.

send	fight	sing	eat	light
choose	wear	hide	make	drink

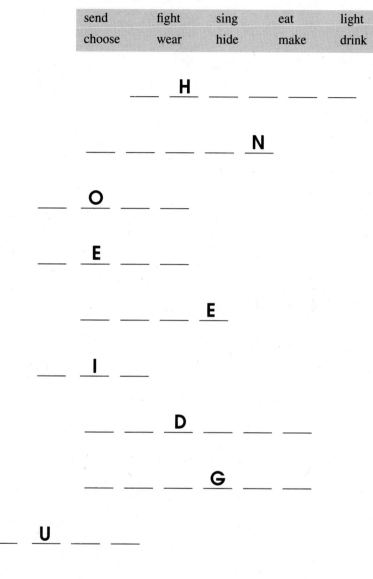

___ **H** ___ ___ ___ ___

___ ___ ___ ___ **N**

___ **O** ___ ___

___ **E** ___ ___

___ ___ ___ **E**

___ **I** ___

___ ___ **D** ___ ___ ___

___ ___ ___ **G** ___ ___

___ ___ **U** ___ ___

___ ___ ___ **G**

CHAPTER EIGHTEEN

· A TASTE OF THANKSGIVING

Of all American holidays, Thanksgiving is the most typically American and, for many, one of the most loved. In this chapter you will learn about the history and traditions of Thanksgiving and take a closer look at the special foods that are part of this holiday celebration.

SHOW WHAT YOU KNOW

1. What do you already know about Thanksgiving? Write down two things.

    a. _____

    b. _____

2. What would you like to find out about Thanksgiving? Look at the title of this chapter and the introduction above. Write down three questions about Thanksgiving that you think you might learn the answers to in this chapter.

    a. _____ ?

    b. _____ ?

    c. _____ ?

3. As a class, try to answer some of the questions you've written.

FOCUS ON CONTENT: THANKSGIVING HISTORY AND TRADITIONS

In this section you will listen to a lecture about Thanksgiving. You will learn a little about the history of the holiday and some typical American Thanksgiving traditions.

Vocabulary 🔲

The following words are important in the lecture. Listen to the cassette and fill in the sentences with words from the box.

charity	pilgrim	struggle	starvation
crops	harvest	hunt	volunteer

1. The _____ was not very successful because the man did not catch any deer.

2. Now that the vegetables and wheat are all grown, it is time for the _____.

3. They went without food for days and were beginning to suffer from _____.

4. There are not enough nurses to care for all the patients in the hospital, so many young people _____ to help.

5. A _____ is a person who travels for religious reasons.

6. The farmer plants a variety of _____, such as corn, wheat, and vegetables.

7. It was a _____ to complete all my papers and exams by the end of the semester, but I did it.

8. Christmas is a holiday when many people give time and money to their favorite _____.

Listen and Write 🔲

The first part of the lecture tells about the history of Thanksgiving, and the second part tells about Thanksgiving traditions. Listen to the lecture as many times as necessary in order to fill in the missing information in the chart below. Now look at the list of traditions below, and put a check mark next to the traditions that you heard in the lecture. When you complete this page, look at the questions that you and your classmates wrote on page 190. Which questions were answered in the lecture? Which were not?

THANKSGIVING HISTORY	
Dates	**What Happened?**
	The Pilgrims left England.
November 1620	
winter, 1620 – 1621	
spring and summer, 1621	
	The Pilgrims had a great harvest.
after the harvest, 1621	
1941	

Thanksgiving Traditions

✔   Most people travel home.

_____   People buy presents for one another.

_____   People buy and wear special new clothes.

_____   Families eat a traditional meal with turkey and stuffing.

_____   Some families go to church to give thanks.

_____   People watch parades on the street or on TV.

_____   Sports fans watch football games on TV.

_____   Families decorate a tree with lights and toys.

_____   People decorate their houses in orange and black.

_____   Children paint and eat eggs.

_____   People volunteer to work with the poor and needy.

Listen and Choose 🔲

Listen to the questions on the cassette and circle the letter of the best answer.

1. a. for health reasons
   b. for religious reasons
   c. for economic reasons

2. a. in England
   b. in Mayflower
   c. in Massachusetts

3. a. corn
   b. rice
   c. turkey

4. a. They taught them to hunt.
   b. They taught them to sail.
   c. They taught them to pray.

5. a. the parades
   b. the football games
   c. the meal

6. a. in New York
   b. in Massachusetts
   c. in Washington, D.C.

7. a. in schools
   b. in stores
   c. in soup kitchens

8. a. over 100 years
   b. over 200 years
   c. over 300 years

Read and Decide

Read each statement and decide if it is true or false. Write T *or* F *on the line. If a statement is false, change it to make it true. Listen to the lecture again if you can't remember all the information.*

1. _____ The first Thanksgiving was celebrated in 1641.

2. _____ The *Mayflower* was the ship that the Pilgrims sailed on to reach the new land.

3. _____ Massachusetts Rock is the name of the place where the Pilgrims' ship landed in 1620.

4. _____ The first year in the new land was an easy one for the Pilgrims.

5. _____ In the winter of 1620, the Native Americans experienced sickness and starvation.

6. _____ The harvest of 1621 was a bad one.

7. _____ In 1931, President Roosevelt declared the last Thursday in November to be a national Thanksgiving holiday.

8. _____ Thanksgiving has more traditions shared by all Americans than any other holiday.

9. _____ Thanksgiving Day itself, the last Thursday in November, is the busiest travel day of the year.

10. _____ Cookies and ice cream are traditional Thanksgiving Day desserts.

Speak, Listen, and Write

A *tag question* is a question that you add to the end of a statement. You can use the negative statement/affirmative tag pattern when you think the information is wrong but you want to make sure.

Usually, if your information is wrong, you will get a *no* answer and the correct information.

[–] STATEMENT	[+] TAG	[–] ANSWER
Americans *don't* celebrate Thanksgiving on Tuesday,	*do* they?	No, they *don't*.

NOTE: For practice with affirmative statements/negative tags, see page 92.

In this exercise you and a partner will ask and answer tag questions about Thanksgiving traditions. Use the information in the boxes below. Student A will first ask all (6) of his/her questions and Student B will answer. Then, Student B will ask all (6) of his/her questions and Student A will answer. When you finish, check your answers by looking at your partner's chart.

Follow this example:

Student A asks: Americans don't celebrate Thanksgiving on Tuesday, do they?
Student B responds: No, they don't. They celebrate Thanksgiving on Thursday.
Student A writes *Thursday* in the CORRECT column.

Student A: *Look here and cover the chart on page 194.*

ASK	INCORRECT	CORRECT
Americans don't . . .		
1. celebrate Thanksgiving . . .	Tuesday	*Thursday*
2. eat . . .	chicken	
3. play . . .	soccer	
4. drink . . .	eggnog	
5. give . . .	presents	
6. collect . . .	books for the needy	

ANSWER	
7. celebrate Thanksgiving	November
8. eat	pumpkin pie
9. watch	parades
10. send	nothing
11. celebrate	with families
12. volunteer	in soup kitchens

Student B: *Look here and cover the chart on page 193.*

ANSWER	
1. celebrate Thanksgiving	Thursday
2. eat	turkey
3. play	football
4. drink	apple cider
5. give	nothing
6. collect	food and presents

ASK	INCORRECT	CORRECT
Americans don't . . .		
7. celebrate Thanksgiving . . .	September	
8. eat . . .	blueberry pie	
9. watch . . .	game shows	
10. send . . .	greeting cards	
11. celebrate . . .	with classmates	
12. volunteer . . .	in schools	

Talk About This!

Is there a holiday in your country that has something in common with the American Thanksgiving? Think about the following questions and, in a short presentation to your class, compare a holiday tradition in your country to one that is part of the American Thanksgiving celebration.

1. Is there a day when you remember your country's ancestors?
2. Do you have a holiday on which you give thanks?
3. Is there a time when you make a special effort to help the needy?
4. Do you have a holiday on which you celebrate by eating certain traditional foods?

FOCUS ON SKILLS: TALKING ABOUT THANKSGIVING DINNER

In this section you will learn about the Thanksgiving meal while you practice the names of foods and measure words, such as containers and portions.

Matching

On Thanksgiving Day you may see almost the same meal on every table in the U.S.A. Of course, every family has its own specialties, but the list below gives you some examples of the food you might find.

1. With a partner, first match the food names in the box below with the correct picture. Write the names on the lines.

2. Then match the food items with the correct part of the Thanksgiving meal, putting the food names in the box under the category to which it belongs. When you're finished, compare your answers with those of your classmates.

FOOD NAMES				
peas	pumpkin pie	fruit and nuts	turkey	rolls
wine	salad	homemade bread	gravy	corn
stuffing	apple pie	cranberry sauce	potatoes	apple cider

peas

_____   _____   _____   _____   _____

_____   _____   _____   _____   _____

_____   _____   _____   _____   _____

PARTS OF THE THANKSGIVING MEAL				
Appetizers	Main Dish	Side Dishes	Desserts	Beverages
		peas		

Matching

In this exercise you and a partner will study some measure words used with food. Then you will match them with the traditional Thanksgiving foods and drinks from the previous Matching exercise.

Use **measure words** with **food** to make non-count nouns countable or to give a set quantity to plural nouns that are too numerous to count individually.				
a	*piece*	of	pie	(non-count)
a	*bowl*	of	nuts	(plural)
a/an	MEASURE WORD	*of*	NOUN	

Some measure words used for food are *containers* and *portions*. Study the measure words in the box below.

CONTAINERS			PORTIONS		
a bowl	a glass	a basket	a slice	a piece	a bit
a dish	a bottle	a spoonful	a spoonful		

1. Write the measure words next to the pictures below.
2. Look at the kinds of food on page 195 that Americans eat on Thanksgiving. Match the food names with measure words you could use for that food. Write the food names on the lines below. Some foods may have more than one possibility. Compare your answers with those of your class.

    Follow the example below.

Picture Difference

It's true that on Thanksgiving you may find that the dinner tables of many Americans look very similar. But no two families' meals are *exactly* the same. In this exercise you and a partner will find the differences in your Thanksgiving tables. Take turns asking and answering some questions using some of the **food names** and **measure words** you learned. Write down the 6 differences you find.

Follow this example:

Student A asks:	My table has a bowl of applesauce. Does yours?
Student B answers:	Yes, it does.
Student B then asks:	My table has a turkey. Does yours?
Student A answers:	Yes, it does.

Student A: *Look here and cover the other illustration.*

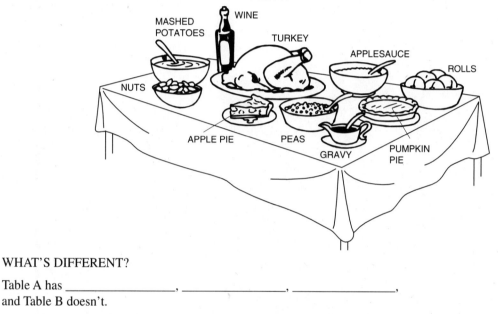

WHAT'S DIFFERENT?

Table A has _____, _____, _____,
and Table B doesn't.

Table B has _____, _____, _____,
and Table A doesn't.

Student B: *Look here and cover the other illustration.*

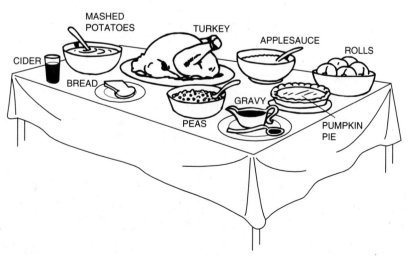

Talk About This!

Imagine a typical holiday meal in your country. Draw a simple picture of what your family's holiday table would look like.

1. Describe that table to a partner using some of the measure words you've learned.

2. Then look at your partner's picture to learn a little about a holiday meal from his/her country.

PUT IT TOGETHER

Hangman

Play a game of Hangman with these and any other vocabulary words from the Thanksgiving chapter. Refer to the instructions on page 18 in Chapter Two.

Word Search Puzzle

Find the traditional Thanksgiving dishes. There are 15 food names in the puzzle below. They may be horizontal (←—→), vertical (↕), or diagonal (↙↗).

```
p  e  l  z  r  u  n  h  o  t  t  c  r  d  a
m  d  o  h  l  d  p  o  t  a  t  o  e  s  f
w  n  w  e  g  i  t  m  q  p  i  n  o  t  m
k  i  j  a  p  p  l  e  c  i  d  e  r  u  e
y  s  n  o  u  n  d  m  e  f  g  v  o  f  i
i  b  f  e  m  f  e  a  m  z  o  u  s  f  p
r  c  k  a  p  r  s  d  e  a  n  y  a  i  l
o  m  p  r  k  o  w  e  y  p  u  p  s  n  o
l  o  f  t  i  c  e  b  x  n  t  r  a  g  h
l  c  r  a  n  b  e  r  r  y  s  a  u  c  e
s  h  u  o  p  d  l  e  h  m  r  a  v  r  b
a  n  i  p  i  w  n  a  i  g  o  m  l  t  h
q  o  t  z  e  b  m  d  f  l  r  h  g  a  o
e  d  g  v  i  a  w  j  b  p  e  l  a  o  d
t  u  r  k  e  y  s  a  v  g  o  c  o  r  n
```

Cloze 🔲

Read the following information about Thanksgiving. Try to fill in the blanks with the correct words. After you have filled in as much as you can, listen to the lecture on the cassette again as many times as necessary to fill in the blanks.

Thanksgiving is the oldest and perhaps the most loved American holiday. It is a day _____ by Americans of all religions and backgrounds, a day for _____ to get together and give thanks.

The story of the _____ Thanksgiving, celebrated in 1621, has become such a _____ that it is hard to say how much is _____ and how much fiction. But it is this _____ that is the basis of the American Thanksgiving _____ today. In September, 1620, the Pilgrims of Plymouth, England, set _____ on a ship called the *Mayflower* in search of a _____ where they could practice their religion freely. By _____, they arrived at the shore of Massachusetts, at a _____ they named Plymouth Rock. The first year was a struggle. A difficult _____ caused sickness and starvation. But in the _____ and summer of that year, Native Americans helped the Pilgrims to _____ and grow crops, such as corn, to catch fish, _____, and learn to live in the new land. With much _____ work, they made it through the year. In the fall of _____, there was a great harvest, and the Pilgrims wanted to give _____ to God for their safety. After the harvest, they planned a big _____ of local foods and invited their Indian neighbors to _____ with them.

Thanksgiving has been celebrated in the _____ _____ since the time of the Pilgrims. But it wasn't until _____, under the presidency of Franklin D. Roosevelt, that it became a _____ holiday to be celebrated every year on the last Thursday of _____.

All holidays have their traditions, but Thanksgiving seems to _____ the most traditions shared by *all* Americans, and not just *one* _____ or ethnic group. Thanksgiving is a rather _____ holiday. People don't shop for gifts or special _____. They go home, wherever that may be. So many Americans want to be with their _____ on Thanksgiving that the Wednesday before and the Sunday after are the _____ travel days of the entire year in the United States.

Once people arrive home, the holiday _____ becomes the center of the Thanksgiving celebration, a tradition Americans _____ they got from the Pilgrims. From the early morning _____, houses will be filled with delicious smells coming from the _____. Almost every holiday table will have the traditional turkey with _____, corn, potatoes, and lots of pies. It's important that there be _____ of food and variety, or it just wouldn't be Thanksgiving dinner!

_____ families also begin their Thanksgiving at church, where they _____ thanks to God for the good things in their lives. Others might go to a Thanksgiving Day _____ or watch New York City's famous Macy's parade on TV. For _____ lovers, Thanksgiving wouldn't be Thanksgiving without the traditional _____ games shown throughout the day on television. The holiday is also a _____ for charity. Many Americans volunteer to work in a _____ kitchen or collect food, clothing, and money for those in _____.

ON YOUR OWN CELEBRATING HOLIDAYS IN THE U.S.A.

Here are some activities related to holidays for you to do on your own, with a small group, or with your whole class.

1. Plan a Thanksgiving dinner with your class. Divide the class into groups, with each group responsible for a part of the meal. Get recipes from your teacher or from cookbooks in the library. Make a grocery list and go shopping. When you meet for the dinner, make sure to bring typed copies of the recipe for your classmates. Be prepared to explain how you made the food.

2. Plan an international Food Fest with your class. Bring to class a food typical of your country. Prepare a poster about the food and how you make it, and be ready to explain it to your classmates. Have copies of the recipe on hand to give out. You and your classmates will then go around and ask each other about the food, taste some samples, and take recipes home to try out.

3. Prepare a 5-minute demonstration speech describing a holiday tradition of your country. Examples might be a special game you play, cards or decorations you make, songs you sing. Be creative and use audio-visual aids to make it more interesting. Try to get the class to participate, if possible.

4. Present an American holiday (aside from Thanksgiving) to your class. Go to the library and read about it. Interview an American or two about how they view the holiday. Make a poster, an overhead, or a handout for the class. Discuss some of the background of the holiday and traditions of the holiday celebration.

5. Invite an American student to speak to your class about a holiday. Prepare questions for the student about the history of the holiday, how he/she celebrates it, and what special food, songs, or activities are a part of the celebration.

6. Organize a week of Secret Santas in your class, something Americans like to do in their offices or dorms during the Christmas holiday. Everyone chooses a name of a classmate and every day for a week brings in a small gift for that person. The idea is to give your person the present in secret, without telling him/her who you are. At the end of the week, have a little party, and let everyone know who his/her Secret Santa is.

7. Find out about the possibility of having a holiday dinner with an American family. Many universities and communities have groups that organize homestay visits for international students, especially around the Thanksgiving and Christmas holidays. Give your class information on how to sign up for such a visit. After a visit, report to your class on what you saw, ate, did, and so on.

8. Watch a popular holiday movie on your own or with your class. You can go to the library to borrow the classic Christmas movie, *It's a Wonderful Life*. Many Americans watch this film every year around Christmas.

9. With a group of classmates or your whole class, visit a local charity organization, such as a soup kitchen, homeless shelter, or home for the elderly. Call or write for information about what they do, and arrange a visit. Report to the class on what your group learned, or discuss in small groups what the whole class experienced.

Unit

On Vacation in the U.S.A.

CHAPTER NINETEEN

IN TOUCH WITH NATURE IN THE NATIONAL PARKS

Many people in the United States like to spend their vacation time in the mountains or near water. In this chapter you will learn about the natural lands in the United States that the government has designated as national parks. Then you will talk about recreation possibilities in the parks and listen to two songs that you might hear on a camping trip.

SHOW WHAT YOU KNOW

When the National Park Service designates land as a national park, development of the land is limited. Work with your classmates to list some reasons why governments create national parks:

_____

_____

_____

What are some things you might do in a national park?

_____

_____

_____

Have you visited a national park in the United States? Which one? What did you do there?

FOCUS ON CONTENT: THE NATIONAL PARKS

In this section you will listen to a lecture about some national parks. Then you will talk about the fifty-two national parks that are located throughout the United States. You will learn their names, where they are located, and when they were established.

Vocabulary 📼

The following words are important in the lecture. Listen to the cassette and complete the sentences with words from the box.

protect	preserve	scenic	established
created	balance	recreation	administers

1. The _____ area is very beautiful.
2. The National Park Service _____, or manages, many parks and monuments.
3. The Park Service was _____ to manage Yellowstone and other national parks.
4. We must _____ the beauty of the land so that it doesn't change.
5. Yellowstone National Park was _____ in 1872.
6. We must _____ the animals in the park so that no one can hurt them.
7. The Park Service must find a _____ between preservation and recreation.
8. You can swim, picnic, and play ball in the _____ area.

Listen and Write 🔲

Listen to the lecture on your cassette as many times as necessary in order to fill in the dates and numbers below.

DATES
Yellowstone National Park was established on March _____, _____.
Mt. Rainier National Park was established in _____.
Crater Lake National Park was established in _____.
The National Park Service was created in _____.

NUMBERS
There are _____ national parks in the United States.
The National Park Service administers more than _____ units.
National parks, monuments, seashores, etc., cover more than _____ acres.

Read and Decide

Read each statement and decide if it is true or false. Write T or F on the line. If a statement is false, change it to make it true.

1. _____ National parks protect the beauty of the land.
2. _____ They usually contain a variety of scenic features.
3. _____ National parks are closed to the public.
4. _____ National parks have billions of visitors each year.
5. _____ Yellowstone was the first national park.
6. _____ Yellowstone was established on March 1, 1972.
7. _____ The National Park Service was created in 1916.
8. _____ More parks have been established since the National Park Service was created.
9. _____ The National Park Service only administers national parks.
10. _____ The National Park Service administers more than 350 million acres of land.

Listen and Choose 🔲

Listen to the questions on the cassette and circle the letter of the best answer.

1. a. in the West
   b. in the East
   c. in many parts of the United States

2. a. to protect and preserve the beauty of the land
   b. to make recreation areas
   c. to use the land for farming

3. a. hotels and casinos
   b. streets and houses
   c. a variety of scenic features

4. a. only National Park Service employees
   b. only people who live near the parks
   c. everyone

5. a. millions of people
   b. thousands of people
   c. billions of people

6. a. to protect the beauty of the land
   b. to provide recreation areas
   c. to find a balance between preservation and recreation

7. a. 320
   b. 76
   c. 52

8. a. national monuments, national historic parks, national seashores, and so on
   b. amusement parks
   c. national forests

Listen and Write 🔲

Are all of the national parks in the West? Were all of the national parks created many years ago? Are they all large? In this exercise you will learn about the locations, ages, and sizes of some national parks. Listen to the information on the cassette and complete the chart, filling in the name of the state where the park is located, the year in which it was established, and the size in square miles.

NATIONAL PARK	STATE	YEAR ESTABLISHED	SQUARE MILES
Acadia	Maine	1919	60
Everglades		1947	2,188
Mesa Verde	Colorado		81
Olympic	Washington	1938	
Rocky Mountain		1915	414
Shenandoah	Virginia	1935	
Lake Clark			4,115
Sequoia			619

Speak, Listen, and Write

Practice the pronunciation of the names of these national parks. Repeat the names after your teacher and practice with your classmates.

Mt. Rainier	Glacier	Acadia	Mesa Verde
Shenandoah	Sequoia	Bryce	Carlsbad Caverns
Denali	Grand Teton	Yosemite	Yellowstone

In this exercise you and a partner will talk about twelve more national parks. Take turns describing the national parks in the charts on page 207. Work back and forth, speaking and writing, until your charts are complete. When you finish, check your answers by looking at your partner's chart.

Follow this example:

Student A says: Tell me about Bryce National Park.
Student B responds: Bryce National Park is in Utah. It was established in 1923. It is 56 square miles.
Student A writes *Utah, 1923,* and *56.*

Student B then says: Tell me about Crater Lake National Park.
Student A responds: Crater Lake National Park is in Oregon. It was established in 1902. It is 286 square miles.
Student B writes *Oregon, 1902,* and *286.*

Student A: *Look here and cover the other chart.*

NATIONAL PARK	STATE	YEAR EST.	SQUARE MILES
Bryce	*Utah*	*1923*	*56*
Crater Lake	Oregon	1902	286
Glacier			
Grand Canyon	Arizona	1919	1,009
Great Smoky Mountain			
Yellowstone	Wyoming	1872	3,472
Yosemite			
Carlsbad Caverns	New Mexico	1930	73
Denali			
Badlands	South Dakota	1939	379
Grand Teton			
Mt. Rainier	Washington	1899	378

Student B: *Look here and cover the other chart.*

NATIONAL PARK	STATE	YEAR EST.	SQUARE MILES
Bryce	Utah	1923	56
Crater Lake	*Oregon*	*1902*	*286*
Glacier	Montana	1910	1,583
Grand Canyon			
Great Smoky Mountain	N. Carolina & Tennessee	1934	800
Yellowstone			
Yosemite	California	1890	1,189
Carlsbad Caverns			
Denali	Alaska	1917	7,341
Badlands			
Grand Teton	Wyoming	1929	485
Mt. Rainier			

Speak, Listen, and Decide

You can compare two parks using the comparative.

Acadia National Park covers 60 square miles.
Mesa Verde National Park covers 81 square miles.

Mesa Verde	is	larger	than	Acadia.
	be	ADJ + -er	than	

Everglades National Park was established in 1947.
Rocky Mountain National Park was established in 1915.

Rocky Mountain	is	older	than	Everglades.
	be	ADJ + -er	than	

In this exercise you and a partner will take turns asking and answering questions about the parks described in the charts on pages 206 and 207. Refer to the charts when you make your answer. When you finish, check your answers with your teacher.

Follow this example:

Student A asks first: Which park is larger, Rocky Mountain or Shenandoah?
Student B responds: Rocky Mountain is larger than Shenandoah.
   and writes *Rocky Mountain*.

Student B then asks: Which park is larger, Olympic or Everglades?
Student A responds: Everglades is larger than Olympic.
   and writes *Everglades*.

Student A: *Look here and cover the right side of the page.*

WHICH PARK IS LARGER?
_____ is larger than _____

1. Rocky Mountain or Shenandoah?
2. _____
3. Bryce or Carlsbad Caverns?
4. _____
5. Grand Teton or Mt. Rainier?
6. _____
7. Glacier or Grand Canyon?
8. _____
9. Lake Clark or Everglades?
10. _____

WHICH PARK IS OLDER?
_____ is older than _____

1. Crater Lake or Yosemite?
2. _____
3. Great Smoky Mountain or Badlands?
4. _____
5. Yellowstone or Denali?
6. _____
7. Sequoia or Mesa Verde?
8. _____
9. Lake Clark or Everglades?
10. _____

Student B: *Look here and cover the left side of the page.*

WHICH PARK IS LARGER?
_____ is larger than _____

1. _____
2. Olympic or Everglades?
3. _____
4. Crater Lake or Badlands?
5. _____
6. Yellowstone or Denali?
7. _____
8. Yosemite or Great Smoky Mountain?
9. _____
10. Sequoia or Acadia?

WHICH PARK IS OLDER?
_____ is older than _____

1. _____
2. Bryce or Glacier?
3. _____
4. Grand Canyon or Grand Teton?
5. _____
6. Mt. Rainier or Carlsbad Caverns?
7. _____
8. Shenandoah or Olympic?
9. _____
10. Acadia or Shenandoah?

Talk About This!

Does your country have government-owned national or state parks? Fill in the following chart with information about parks in your country. Then share the information with your classmates.

NAME OF THE PARK	LOCATION	WHAT IS THERE?

FOCUS ON SKILLS: USING -ING WORDS FOR ACTIVITIES

In this section you will practice using *-ing* words for activities while you talk about recreation.

Matching

National parks offer a wide variety of recreation activities. Park guide books often use *icons*, or simple pictures, to represent the activities available in each park. Match the name of the activity with the picture (icon) in the box below. Write the name of the activity on the line under the icon.

skiing   swimming   hunting   boating   horseback riding

bicycling   fishing   hiking   mountain climbing

Read and Decide

Look at the icons listed after each park below. Which activities are available at these parks? Work with your classmates to name the activities.

Follow this example:

You see: Grand Canyon National Park

You say: At Grand Canyon National Park, you can go hiking, boating, bicycling, fishing, and horseback riding.

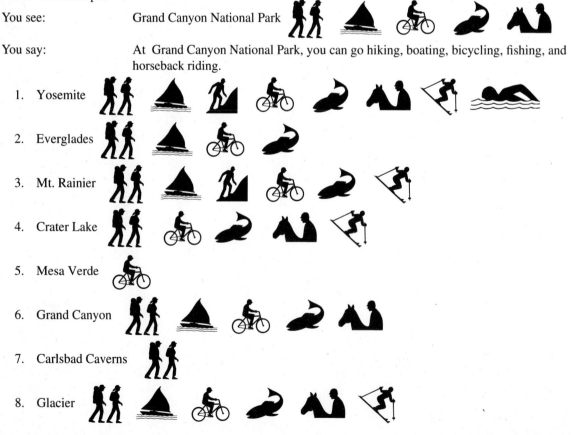

1. Yosemite

2. Everglades

3. Mt. Rainier

4. Crater Lake

5. Mesa Verde

6. Grand Canyon

7. Carlsbad Caverns

8. Glacier

Speak, Listen, and Check

In this exercise you and a partner will take turns describing the activities available at twelve national parks by looking at the icons at the top of each column. When you finish, check your answers by looking at your partner's grid.

Follow this example:

Student A says:	Tell me about Sequoia National Park.
Student B responds:	At Sequoia National Park, you can go hiking, mountain climbing, bicycling, fishing, horseback riding, and skiing.

Student A checks six activities.

Student B then says:	Tell me about Rocky Mountain National Park.
Student A responds:	At Rocky Mountain National Park, you can go hiking, mountain climbing, fishing, horseback riding, and skiing.

Student B checks five activities.

Student A: *Look here and cover the other chart.*

NATIONAL PARK	Hiking	Sailing	Climbing	Bicycling	Fishing	Horseback	Hunting	Skiing	Swimming
Sequoia	✓		✓	✓	✓	✓		✓	
Rocky Mountain	✓		✓		✓	✓		✓	
Acadia									
Bryce Canyon	✓					✓		✓	
Shenandoah									
Olympic	✓		✓		✓			✓	✓
Grand Teton									
Yellowstone	✓	✓		✓	✓	✓		✓	
Great Smoky Mountain									
Denali	✓	✓	✓		✓		✓	✓	
Lake Clark									
Badlands	✓					✓			

Student B: *Look here and cover the other chart.*

NATIONAL PARK	Hiking	Sailing	Climbing	Bicycling	Fishing	Horseback	Hunting	Skiing	Swimming
Sequoia	✓		✓	✓	✓	✓		✓	
Rocky Mountain	✓		✓		✓	✓		✓	
Acadia	✓	✓		✓	✓	✓		✓	✓
Bryce Canyon									
Shenandoah	✓				✓	✓			
Olympic									
Grand Teton		✓	✓	✓	✓	✓	✓		✓
Yellowstone									
Great Smoky Mountain	✓				✓	✓			
Denali									
Lake Clark	✓	✓	✓		✓		✓	✓	
Badlands									

Talk About This!

What are your favorite recreation activities? Review the activities and icons on page 210 and talk about the activities there that you enjoy. Then form small groups and work with your classmates to think of six more activities that you enjoy. Write them in the box below, and decide on an icon for each. Draw the icon and describe it. When you finish, share your group's icons with the class.

Example: I like shopping. The icon could be a person holding shopping bags in both hands.

ACTIVITY	ICON	DESCRIPTION
shopping		a person holding shopping bags in both hands

 # ong

"Red River Valley" and "Home on the Range"

Camping is a popular activity in national parks, and singing songs around a campfire is a popular camping activity. Two well-known songs that you might hear around a campfire are "Red River Valley" and "Home on the Range."

Listen and Write 📼

It was a cowboy's job to move frequently, following herds of cattle. In "Red River Valley," a girlfriend says goodbye. Listen to the songs and fill in the blanks below.

1. From this _____ they say you are going;
   We will miss your bright eyes and your _____,
   For they say you are _____ the sunshine,
   Which has brightened our pathway a _____.

Chorus: *Come and sit by my _____ if you love me,*
         Do not hasten to bid me adieu,
         But _____ the Red River Valley
         And the girl that has _____ you so true.

2. Won't you _____ of the valley you're leaving?
   Oh, how lonely, how _____ it will be,
   Oh think of the fond _____ you're breaking,
   _____ the grief you are causing me.

Chorus: *Come and _____ by my side if you love me,*
         Do not hasten to bid me adieu,
         But remember the Red _____ Valley
         And the _____ that has loved you so true.

Talk About the Song

1. Study the vocabulary.

Find a word in	that means	and write it here:
Verse 1	shining	_____
the Chorus	be quick	_____
the Chorus	say goodbye (2 words, one word is French)	_____
Verse 2	loving, affectionate	_____
Verse 2	sadness	_____
		_____

2. Find some words or phrases that show how happy the cowboy makes his girlfriend feel:

   _____

   _____

3. Find some words or phrases that show how sad the girlfriend will be when he leaves:

   _____

   _____

Listen and Write 📼

The range *refers to the large open areas of land where cowboys tend cattle. The song title "Home on the Range" tells of the cowboys' love of the open land. Listen to the song and fill in the blanks below.*

1. Oh, give me a _____ where the buffalo roam,
   Where the deer and the antelope _____;
   Where seldom is heard a discouraging _____,
   And the _____ are not cloudy all day.

Chorus: Home, home on the _____,
    Where the _____ and the antelope play;
    Where seldom is _____ a discouraging word,
    And the skies are not _____ all day.

2. Where the _____ is so pure, the zephyrs so free,
   The breezes so balmy and _____,
   That I would not exchange my _____ on the range
   For all the _____ so bright.

Chorus: Home, _____ on the range,
    Where the deer and the _____ play;
    Where _____ is heard a discouraging word,
    And the skies are not cloudy all _____.

Talk about the Song

1. Study the vocabulary.

Find a word in	that means	and write it here:
Verse 1	wander	_____
Verse 1	rarely	_____

2. In Verse 2, *zephyr* means "light wind." Find the other word in Verse 2 that means "light wind":

   _____

3. Find three animals in the song: _____

             _____

             _____

4. Find three reasons the cowboy likes living on the range:

   _____

   _____

   _____

PUT IT TOGETHER

Find Someone Who . . .

Use questions beginning with "Do you . . . ?" to find someone for each of the items on the left. BE CAREFUL. Sometimes you need a yes *answer and sometimes you need a* no. *When you hear the answer you need, write the person's name in the space. After you have asked all of the questions, share what you learned about your classmates with the rest of the class.*

Examples: *Do you* like boating?
            Do you like bicycling?

Find someone who . . .   **Write that person's name here:**

likes boating.   _____

likes bicycling.   _____

likes fishing.   _____

doesn't like hunting.   _____

doesn't like swimming.   _____

likes horseback riding.   _____

likes swimming.   _____

doesn't like hiking.   _____

doesn't like skiing.   _____

likes mountain climbing.   _____

Cloze

Read the following information about the national parks. Try to fill in the blanks with the correct words. After you have filled in as much as you can, listen to the lecture on the cassette again as many times as necessary to fill in all the blanks.

Our National Parks

In many parts of the United States, large _____ of land have been made into national _____ to protect and preserve the natural beauty of the _____. National parks usually contain a variety of _____ features such as mountains, _____, and unusual animals. They are all open to the public and have _____ of visitors each year.

Yellowstone National Park, in _____, was the first national park. It was _____ on March 1, 1872. In the following years, more parks were established, such as Mt. Rainier National Park, in Washington, in 1899; Crater _____ National Park, in Oregon, in 1902; and Glacier _____ Park, in Montana, in 1910. Then, in 1916, the National Park _____ was created to manage the parks. The job of the National Park Service is to find a _____ between preserving the land in the parks and providing _____ for the visitors. Many more parks have been added to the system since the _____ Park Service was created.

Today, there are _____ national parks in the United States. The National Park Service also administers national _____, national seashores, national lakeshores, national historical _____, national recreation areas, and more, for a _____ of more than 350 areas with more than 75 million acres.

CHAPTER TWENTY

FUN AND LEARNING AT AMUSEMENT PARKS

Amusement parks are favorite destinations for American families on vacation. In this chapter you will talk about a new Disney park and some favorite amusement parks.

SHOW WHAT YOU KNOW

The Walt Disney Company has amusement parks in the United States and in other countries. Can you list them all?

_____   _____

_____   _____

In the fall of 1993, Disney announced plans for a new amusement park. What have you heard about it?

FOCUS ON CONTENT: DISNEY AMERICA

In this section you will hear a lecture about a new amusement park that the Walt Disney Company plans to build.

Vocabulary 🔲

The following words are important in the lecture. Listen to the cassette and complete the sentences with words from the box.

theme parks	acres	golf course	purchased	hire
reenactment	greet	historical	exhibits	fantasy

1. We learned what the Civil War was like in the _____ of the Battle of Bull Run.
2. The Walt Disney Company _____ 3,000 acres of land.
3. There are 640 _____ in a square mile.
4. You can learn about the history of immigration by looking at the _____ in the Immigration Museum at Ellis Island.
5. _____ exhibits can teach you about what happened in the past.
6. Mickey Mouse will _____ you when you enter Walt Disney World.
7. People will be able to play golf on a 27-hole public _____ _____.
8. Disney will _____ about 3,000 people to work in the new park.
9. Disneyland and Walt Disney World are _____ _____.
10. Disneyland and Disney World have many _____ themes, many of which came from the imagination of Walt Disney.

Listen and Write 🔲

Listen to the lecture about Disney America as many times as necessary in order to fill in the numbers and dates below.

> Disney America will be _____ miles west of Washington, D.C.
>
> The first part of Disney America will be a _____ -acre theme park.
> There will also be a _____ -hole golf course.
>
> The park will be built on _____ acres of land.
>
> The park and golf course will open in _____.
>
> _____ people will be hired to build the park.
> _____ people will be hired to work there.
> _____ people will visit the park every day.
>
> Disney America will be the _____ Disney park in the United States.
> Disneyland opened in _____.
> Walt Disney World opened more than _____ years ago.

Read and Decide

1. *Read each statement and decide if it is true or false. Write T or F on the line. If a statement is false, change it to make it true. Listen to the lecture again if you can't remember all of the information.*

    1. _____ Disney America will be in Washington, D.C.
    2. _____ The first part of Disney America will include tennis courts.
    3. _____ Disney has recently purchased 3,000 acres of land.
    4. _____ Disney America will open in 1998.
    5. _____ It will cost hundreds of thousands of dollars to build.
    6. _____ 20,000 people will be hired to build the park.
    7. _____ Disney will hire 3,000 people to work at Disney America.
    8. _____ The state of Virginia will receive more than one and a half billion dollars in taxes over the next thirty years from Disney America.
    9. _____ Disney America will be the first Disney park in the United States.
    10. _____ Disney America will include fantasy themes.
    11. _____ You will see Mickey Mouse at Disney America.
    12. _____ You will see reenactments of historical events at Disney America.

2. *What happened first? What will happen when the park is built? Put the following events in the correct order.*

    _____ Walt Disney World opened in Orlando, Florida.

    _____ The Walt Disney Company purchased 3,000 acres in Virginia.

    _____ 2,000 people will be hired to build the park.

    ___1___ Disneyland opened in Anaheim, California.

    _____ The Walt Disney Company announced a new theme park.

    _____ 3,000 people will be hired to work in the park.

    _____ 30,000 people will visit the park every day.

Speak, Listen, and Choose

Since Disney America is planned for the future, you can talk about it using *will* and *won't*.

Use *will + base form* to talk about the future:

> Disney America *will* be in Virginia.
> 30,000 people *will* visit Disney America every day.

Use *will not* or *won't* for negatives:

> Disney America *will not* be like Disneyland.
> Disney America *won't* have fantasy themes.

Put *will* before the subject in questions:

> *Will* Disney America open in 1997?
> When *will* Disney America open?

In this exercise you and a partner will take turns asking and answering questions about the information in the lecture. Make questions with will *and the cues and circle and say the best answer. When you finish, check your answers with your teacher.*

Follow this example:

Student A asks first:	When will Disney America open?
Student B responds:	In 1998.
and circles *a*.	
Student B then asks:	How many people will visit Disney America?
Student A responds:	30,000 every day.
and circles *b*.	

Student A: *Look here and cover the right side of this page.*

1. When ___ Disney America open?

2. a. 30,000 every year
   (b.) 30,000 every day
3. Where ___ Disney America be located?

4. a. hundreds of thousands of dollars
   b. hundreds of millions of dollars
5. How many people ___ be hired to build Disney America?
6. a. 3,000
   b. 30,000
7. How much money ___ the state receive in taxes?

8. a. fantasy themes
   b. history themes
9. How many historical themes ___ there be?

10. a. U.S. history
    b. world history

Student B: *Look here and cover the left side of this page.*

1. (a.) in 1998
   b. in 1996
2. How many people ___ visit Disney America?

3. a. in Florida
   b. in Virginia
4. How much ___ Disney America cost?

5. a. 1,000
   b. 2,000
6. How many people ___ be hired to work at Disney America?
7. a. $1.5 billion
   b. $1.5 million
8. What themes ___ Disney America include?

9. a. 90
   b. 9
10. What ___ visitors to the park learn?

Speak, Listen, and Connect

There will be nine historical themes in Disney America. In this exercise you will learn the names of the theme areas and a little of what they will contain. You and a partner will work back and forth, describing the areas and drawing lines. When you finish, check your answers by looking at your partner's chart.

Follow this example:

Student A says: Tell me about Crossroads U.S.A.
Student B responds: That will be a Civil War town.
Student A draws a line.

Student A: *Look here and cover the other chart.*

Crossroads U.S.A.	explain some military history.
Presidents' Square	contain authentic Indian villages and art.
Native America	show the formation and history of the United States.
Civil War Fort	be a Civil War town.
We the People	have a barn dance and teach visitors to milk a cow.
Enterprise	show life in the United States in the Civil War and will reenact ship battles.
Victory Field	show the country's immigrant heritage, including food and music.
State Fair	include a ferris wheel and a tribute to baseball.
Family Farm	show the nation's inventions and industry and will include a roller coaster ride.

Student B: *Look here and cover the other chart.*

Crossroads U.S.A.	explain some military history.
Presidents' Square	contain authentic Indian villages and art.
Native America	show the formation and history of the United States.
Civil War Fort	be a Civil War town.
We the People	have a barn dance and teach visitors to milk a cow.
Enterprise	show life in the United States in the Civil War and will reenact ship battles.
Victory Field	show the country's immigrant heritage, including food and music.
State Fair	include a ferris wheel and a tribute to baseball.
Family Farm	show the nation's inventions and industry and will include a roller coaster ride.

Talk About This!

About 500 people live in Haymarket, Virginia, the town closest to the location of Disney America. Some of the people are *for* the park, and some are *against*. Read the following statements and write *for* or *against* it. If you lived in Haymarket, Virginia, would you be for or against Disney America? Why?

_____ The roads will be crowded with 10,000 extra cars every day.
_____ Air pollution will increase with the extra cars.
_____ The park will bring in a lot of extra tax money.
_____ People will find jobs.
_____ Disney will build and improve roads.
_____ Haymarket will lose its small-town feel.
_____ Large areas of open land will disappear.

Work with your classmates to list some more *for* and *against* statements in the box below.

FOR	AGAINST

FOCUS ON SKILLS: USING COMPARATIVES AND SUPERLATIVES

In this section you will practice making statements using comparatives and superlatives while you talk about six popular amusement parks located across the United States.

American amusement parks are often organized into theme areas, such as Tomorrowland and Fantasyland at Disneyland, World Showcase at Epcot Center, Pioneer Frontier at Hersheypark, and so on. Within these theme areas, there are rides such as roller coasters and train and boat rides, shows, exhibits, and restaurants. The information in this chart shows what six popular amusement parks have to offer.

PARK	PLACE	$				
Disneyland	Anaheim, California	$25	38	12	5	32
Dollywood	Pigeon Forge, Tennessee	$20	10	6	1	20
Epcot Center	Lake Buena Vista, Florida	$31	8	9	15	24
Hersheypark	Hershey, Pennsylvania	$21	42	7	0	55
Knotts Berry Farm	Buena Park, California	$19	30	14	6	30
Six Flags Over Texas	Arlington, Texas	$22	26	8	2	35

Speak, Listen, and Decide

You can talk about the differences between the parks using comparatives.

With adjectives of two or more syllables: Disneyland *is more expensive than* Knotts Berry Farm. (+ + +) Knotts Berry Farm *is less expensive than* Disneyland. (---)
With nouns: Knotts Berry Farm *has more shows than* Six Flags Over Texas. (+ + +) Six Flags Over Texas *has fewer shows than* Knotts Berry Farm. (---)

In this exercise you and a partner will talk about the information in the amusement park chart. Take turns asking and answering questions to compare two parks at a time. Make questions beginning with "Which park . . . ?" When you finish, check your answers with your teacher.

Follow this example:

Student A asks first: Which park is more expensive: Dollywood or Hersheypark?
Student B responds: Hersheypark is more expensive than Dollywood.
Student A writes *Hersheypark*.

Student B then asks: Which park has more shows: Knotts Berry Farm or Six Flags?
Student A answers: Knotts Berry Farm has more shows than Six Flags.
Student B writes *Knotts Berry Farm*.

Student A: *You ask the first question.*

1. More expensive: Dollywood or Hersheypark?

2. _____

3. More rides: Disneyland or Epcot?

4. _____

5. Fewer shows: Six Flags or Knotts Berry Farm?

6. _____

7. More exhibits: Epcot or Knotts Berry Farm?

8. _____

9. Fewer rides: Dollywood or Epcot?

10. _____

11. More shows: Disneyland or Hersheypark?

12. _____

13. More restaurants: Knotts Berry Farm or Epcot?

14. _____

Student B: *Listen to your partner's question, look at the chart, and decide on the best answer.*

1. _____

2. More shows: Knotts Berry Farm or Six Flags?

3. _____

4. Less expensive: Six Flags or Disneyland?

5. _____

6. More rides: Six Flags or Knotts Berry Farm?

7. _____

8. More restaurants: Disneyland or Hersheypark?

9. _____

10. More expensive: Knotts Berry Farm or Epcot?

11. _____

12. More exhibits: Disneyland or Six Flags?

13. _____

14. Fewer restaurants: Dollywood or Six Flags?

Speak, Listen, and Write

You can compare one park with all the others using superlatives

With adjectives of two or more syllables:		
	Epcot Center *is the most expensive than.* (+ + +)	
	Knotts Berry Farm *is the least expensive.* (---)	
With nouns:		
	Knotts Berry Farm *has the most shows.* (+ + +)	
	Dollywood *has the fewest shows.* (---)	

In this exercise you and a partner will talk about the amusement parks described in the chart on page 221. Take turns asking questions in the superlative and answering them until both charts on page 223 are complete. When you are finished, check your answers by looking at your partner's chart.

Follow this example:

Student A asks first: Which park has the most rides?
Student B answers: Hersheypark has the most rides.
Student A writes Hersheypark.

Student B then asks: Which park has the fewest rides?
Student A answers: Epcot Center has the fewest rides.
Student B writes Epcot.

Student A: *Look here and cover the other chart.*

CATEGORY	THE MOST	THE FEWEST
Rides		Epcot Center
Shows	Knotts Berry Farm	
Exhibits		Hersheypark
Restaurants	Hersheypark	

Student B: *Look here and cover the other chart.*

CATEGORY	THE MOST	THE FEWEST
Rides	Hersheypark	
Shows		Dollywood
Exhibits	Epcot Center	
Restaurants		Dollywood

Talk About This!

Review the information about the six amusement parks. Choose the one that you would most like to visit and think about why. Then break into groups, with all the people who chose the same amusement park together in one group. List your group's reasons for choosing that park. After you discuss your reasons, share what your group decided with the class.

Name of park: _____

Reasons: _____

_____

_____

_____

_____

_____

_____

PUT IT TOGETHER

Crossword

ACROSS

1. _____ is in Anaheim, California.
4. Walt Disney _____ is in Florida.
6. Disney America will be a _____ park.
9. Hersheypark and Dollywood are _____ parks.
10. The Walt _____ Company is building a new park.
14. Disney America will have _____ exhibits.
15. Hersheypark is in _____ (state).

DOWN

1. _____ is in Tennessee.
2. People like to watch ____ at amusement parks.
3. _____ Center is in Florida.
5. A _____ coaster is a popular ride.
7. _____, Virginia, is a town near Disney America.
8. _____ park is in Pennsylvania.
11. _____ Flags Over Texas
12. Walt Disney World is in _____.
13. Knotts _____ Farm

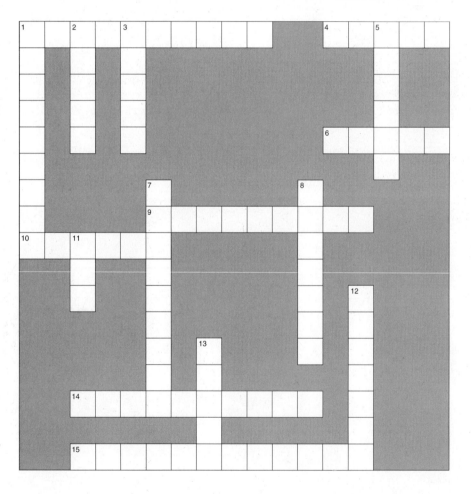

Cloze 📼

Read the following announcement about Disney America. Try and fill in the blanks with the correct word. After you have filled in as much as you can, listen to the lecture on your cassette again as many times as necessary to fill in all the blanks.

The Walt Disney Company made an _____ announcement in the fall of 1993. The company announced that it will open a new amusement _____ near the nation's capital. It will be called Disney _____, and it will be located in Prince William County, _____, about 30 miles west of Washington, D.C.

The first part of _____ America will be a 100-acre _____ park and a 27-hole public _____ course. They will be built on 3,000 acres of land that Disney _____ just before making the announcement. The park and golf course will open in 1998 and will cost hundreds of millions of _____ to build. Two thousand people will be hired to _____ the park, and three thousand people will be hired to _____ there after it opens. About 30,000 people will visit Disney America every day, and the _____ of Virginia will receive more than one and a half billion dollars in _____ over the next thirty years.

Disney America will be the _____ Disney park in the United States. The Walt Disney Company opened its first park, _____, in California in 1955. Walt Disney World, in Florida, opened more than 20 years ago. Disney America will not be like the _____ Disney parks. Disney America will be a theme park, but it won't include _____ themes. Mickey _____ and Donald Duck won't greet visitors. Instead, Disney America will have nine _____ themes, including exhibits on the Civil War and American Indian life, and reenactments of historical _____. Visitors will enjoy themselves while they learn about U.S. history.

CHAPTER TWENTY-ONE

SIGHTS TO SEE: NATIONAL MONUMENTS AND LANDMARKS

National monuments and landmarks are important tourist destinations for people from the United States as well as foreign visitors. In this chapter you will learn about ten monuments and landmarks, and you will hear about how one of them was built.

SHOW WHAT YOU KNOW

Many landmarks are easy to recognize. Look quickly at the pictures on this page. Which monuments and landmarks do you recognize? Which ones have you visited?

FOCUS ON CONTENT: NATIONAL MONUMENTS AND LANDMARKS

In this section you will learn about ten national monuments and landmarks that are located across the United States.

Matching

Work with your classmates to match the following, drawing a line between the name and the picture.

The Empire State Building
The Gateway Arch
The Golden Gate Bridge
The Lincoln Memorial
Mount Rushmore
The Statue of Liberty
The Sears Tower
The Space Needle
The Washington Monument
The World Trade Center

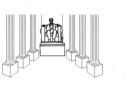

Speak, Listen, and Connect

In this exercise you will learn the locations of the ten monuments and landmarks that you saw in the previous exercise.

You and a partner will take turns asking and answering questions. Start each question with "Where is . . . ?" and connect the site with the city or state. When you finish, check your answers by looking at your partner's box.

Follow this example:

Student A asks first: Where is the Empire State Building?
Student B responds: It's in New York.
Student A draws a line.

Student B then asks: Where is the Gateway Arch?
Student A responds: It's in St. Louis.
Student B draws a line.

GRAMMAR NOTE:
Use *in* with cities and states.

Student A: *Look here and cover the other box.*

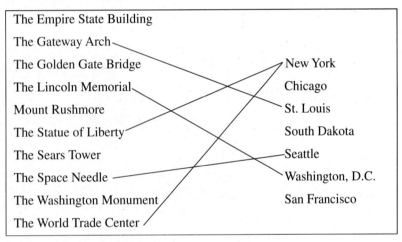

The Empire State Building
The Gateway Arch
The Golden Gate Bridge
The Lincoln Memorial
Mount Rushmore
The Statue of Liberty
The Sears Tower
The Space Needle
The Washington Monument
The World Trade Center

New York
Chicago
St. Louis
South Dakota
Seattle
Washington, D.C.
San Francisco

Student B: *Look here and cover the other box.*

The Empire State Building
The Gateway Arch
The Golden Gate Bridge
The Lincoln Memorial
Mount Rushmore
The Statue of Liberty
The Sears Tower
The Space Needle
The Washington Monument
The World Trade Center

New York
Chicago
St. Louis
South Dakota
Seattle
Washington, D.C.
San Francisco

Concentration

Play Concentration to help you memorize the locations of the monuments. Make six pairs of cards. Write a monument on one card and the location on the other. Follow the directions for Concentration on page 24.

Matching

Do you remember the locations of the cities and states that you have talked about so far in this chapter? Review the locations of the cities and states by looking at Chapters Two and Three.

Look below at the map of the United States. There is a circle on the map for each landmark and monument in this chapter. Work with your classmates to put the number of the monument in the correct circle.

1. The Empire State Building
2. The Gateway Arch
3. The Golden Gate Bridge
4. The Lincoln Memorial
5. Mount Rushmore
6. The Statue of Liberty
7. The Sears Tower
8. The Space Needle
9. The Washington Monument
10. The World Trade Center

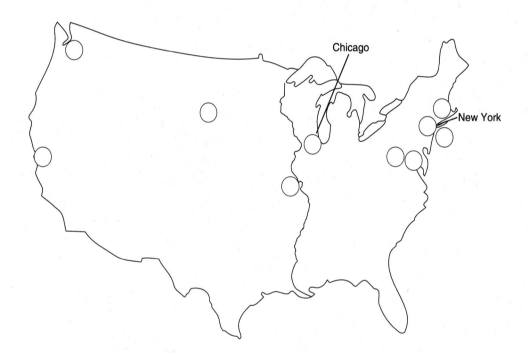

Read and Decide

Here are some short descriptions of the landmarks and monuments shown in the illustrations on page 226. Work with your classmates to write the name of the landmark or monument to the left of each description.

_____ Part of the Jefferson National Expansion Memorial, this monument on the Mississippi River symbolizes the gateway to the western part of the United States.

_____ This huge sculpture on a mountainside in South Dakota honors four presidents: Washington, Jefferson, Lincoln, and Teddy Roosevelt.

_____ This large statue sits on a small island in New York Harbor, facing down the harbor toward arriving ships. It is a symbol of freedom and opportunity in the U.S.A.

_____ This landmark was built for the 1962 "Century 21" Exposition in Seattle, which had "Man in Space" for a theme. The 600-foot tower has a restaurant on the top.

_____ The tallest building in the world until 1970, this landmark has a popular observation deck on the 86th floor and is often used as a symbol of New York.

_____ This white marble obelisk in the nation's capital is a monument to the first president of the United States.

_____ This bright orange bridge is the second longest suspension bridge in the world, connecting San Francisco with the suburbs to the north.

_____ These twin 110-story towers are located in the financial center of the world: lower Manhattan. The observation deck on the 107th floor offers a panoramic view of New York.

_____ This Chicago skyscraper is the tallest building in the world.

_____ This monument, located in Washington, D.C., honors the president of the United States who was in office during the Civil War.

Vocabulary

Are there any words you don't know in the descriptions above? Write them here and ask a classmate or your teacher to explain.

Word	**Explanation, Synonym, or Example**
_____	_____
_____	_____
_____	_____
_____	_____

Listen and Write 🔲

In this exercise you will hear some statements on the cassette about the national monuments and landmarks that you have talked about in this chapter. Listen and fill in the blanks. Then study the information in the sentences for later exercises.

Fill in the numbers you hear.

1. The Washington Monument is _____ feet tall. Visitors can ride the elevator to the top.
2. The Golden Gate Bridge is _____ feet long and has a main span of _____ feet.
3. The World Trade Center has _____ windows.
4. The _____-foot Space Needle is located near a convention center in Seattle.
5. Visitors can ride gondolas to the top of the _____-foot, stainless steel Gateway Arch.
6. Mount Rushmore is _____ feet high. The faces of the presidents carved into the mountain are _____ feet from chin to forehead.
7. The Statue of Liberty weighs _____ tons and is _____ feet tall.
8. The Sears Tower is _____ feet tall, and the Empire State Building is _____ feet tall.
9. There are _____ columns around the perimeter of the Lincoln Memorial. They are _____ feet high.

Now fill in the dates you hear.

10. The Seattle Space Needle was built for the _____ World's Fair.
11. The Empire State Building was opened for occupancy on _____, at the start of the Great Depression.
12. Construction of the Washington Monument started in _____ but soon stopped due to lack of money. Construction resumed in _____, and the monument was opened in _____.
13. The twin towers of the World Trade Center were the tallest in the world until _____, when the Sears Tower opened in Chicago.
14. The Golden Gate Bridge was opened in _____.
15. The Jefferson National Expansion Memorial, location of the Gateway Arch, was established in _____.
16. Mount Rushmore was established as a national memorial on _____.
17. The Statue of Liberty was given to the United States by the people of France in _____.
18. The Lincoln Memorial was dedicated on Memorial Day, _____.

Speak, Listen, and Decide

In this exercise you and a partner will take turns reading statements about monuments and landmarks and deciding if they are true or false. Look at the information earlier in this chapter if you can't remember an answer. When you finish, check your answers with your teacher.

Follow this example:

Student A reads: The Empire State Building is in Chicago.
Student B responds: That's false.
and circles FALSE.

Student B then reads: The Gateway Arch is in St. Louis.
Student A responds: That's true.
and circles TRUE.

Student A: *Look here and cover the right side of the page.*

1. The Empire State Building is in Chicago.

2. TRUE   FALSE

3. The Golden Gate Bridge is in San Francisco.

4. TRUE   FALSE

5. The Gateway Arch is on the Mississippi River.

6. TRUE   FALSE

7. Mount Rushmore honors six presidents.

8. TRUE   FALSE

9. The Statue of Liberty is on an island in a lake.

10. TRUE   FALSE

11. There is a restaurant on the top of the Space Needle.

12. TRUE   FALSE

13. You can't go to the top of the Gateway Arch.

14. TRUE   FALSE

Student B: *Look here and cover the left side of the page.*

1. TRUE   FALSE

2. The Gateway Arch is in St. Louis.

3. TRUE   FALSE

4. The Sears Tower is the tallest building in New York.

5. TRUE   FALSE

6. Lincoln was president during the Civil War.

7. TRUE   FALSE

8. The World Trade Center is made up of three towers.

9. TRUE   FALSE

10. The Golden Gate Bridge is painted bright green.

11. TRUE   FALSE

12. George Washington was the first president of the United States.

13. TRUE   FALSE

14. If you want to go to the top of the Washington Monument, you must walk.

Speak, Listen, and Choose

You can use indirect questions to ask about sights when you are a tourist. Indirect questions sound more polite than direct questions.

QUESTION	INDIRECT QUESTION
Where is the Gateway Arch?	Can you tell me where the Gateway Arch is?
Wh + *be* + SUBJ	*Can you tell me* + *wh* + SUBJ + *be*

Use statement word order. Put *is* at the end of the indirect question.

Begin with: Excuse me,   can you tell me . . . ?

                                             could you tell me . . . ?

                                             do you know . . . ?

In this exercise you and your partner will review the information in this section. Take turns changing the questions to indirect questions. Circle and say the best answer. Look back for the information if you don't remember an answer. When you finish, check your answers with your teacher.

Follow this example:

Student A asks first: Excuse me, could you tell me where the Gateway Arch is?
Student B responds: Yes. It's on the Mississippi River.
  and circles *b*.
Student B then asks: Excuse me, could you tell me how tall the Washington Monument is?
Student A responds: Yes. It's 555 feet tall.
  and circles *a*.

Student A: *Look here and cover the right side of the page.*

1. Where is the Gateway Arch?

2. a.   555 feet
    b.   100 feet

3. Where is the Statue of Liberty?

4. a.   on the top.
    b.   at the base.

5. Where is the observation deck in the Empire State Building?

6. a.   between San Francisco and the northern suburbs
    b.   between San Francisco and Oakland

7. Where is the world's tallest building?

8. a.   on the 110th floor
    b.   on the 107th floor

Student B: *Look here and cover the left side of the page*

1. a.   on Lake Michigan
    b.   on the Mississippi River

2. How tall is the Washington Monument?

3. a.   in the Atlantic Ocean.
    b.   in New York Harbor.

4. Where is the restaurant in the Space Needle?

5. a.   on the 86th floor
    b.   on the 186th floor

6. Where is the Golden Gate Bridge?

7. a.   in Chicago
    b.   in New York

8. Where is the observation deck in the World Trade Center?

(continued on next page)   *(continued on next page)*

9. How long is the Golden Gate Bridge?

9. a. 8,982 feet
    b. 89,081 feet

10. a. 600 feet
    b. 6,000 feet

10. How tall is the Space Needle?

11. How old is the Washington Monument?

11. a. more than 100 years
    b. more than 200 years

12. a. 225 tons
    b. 225 pounds

12. How heavy is the Statue of Liberty?

Talk About This!

New York has the Statue of Liberty. Paris has the Eiffel Tower. What famous landmarks or national monuments does your country have? Choose one and write about it here. Follow the example. Then share the information you wrote with your classmates. Ask at least four classmates about landmarks or monuments in their countries and fill in the rest of the chart below.

Monument/Landmark	Country	Description
The Statue of Liberty	The U.S.A. (your country)	A statue in New York Harbor. The statue welcomes immigrants to New York.

FOCUS ON CONTENT: THE STORY BEHIND THE WASHINGTON MONUMENT

The Washington Monument is one of the country's most important national monuments. It took more than 36 years and a combination of public and private money to build it. In this section you will hear a lecture to learn more about the construction of the Washington Monument.

Vocabulary 🔊

The following words are important in the lecture. Listen to the cassette and complete the sentences below with words from the box.

mourned	expenditure	private	obelisk
funds	construction	centennial	capstone

1. It took six months to build the house. _____ began in June and ended in December.
2. The family _____ the death of their relative. They felt very sad.
3. The _____ is the top stone of the monument.
4. One hundred years after independence, the United States celebrated its _____.
5. An _____ is a tall, four-sided tower made of stone.
6. Some people decided to build a monument with _____ , not public, money.
7. They ran out of _____. They did not have enough money.
8. Congress approved the _____. They decided to spend the money.

Listen and Write 🔊

Listen to the lecture as many times as necessary in order to fill in the blanks below.

Fill in the years.

George Washington was president from _____ to _____.
He died in _____.
The Washington National Monument Society was organized in _____.
Construction started on July 4, _____.
Construction stopped in the middle of the _____s.
Congress voted to complete the monument in _____.
The capstone was set on December 6, _____.
The Washington Monument was dedicated on February 21, _____.

Fill in the amounts of money.

After Washington died, the House of Representatives voted to spend $_____ on a monument.
The Washington National Monument Society raised $ _____ in private funds for the monument.
Finally, Congress voted to spend $ _____ to complete the monument.

Speak, Listen, and Decide

Use what you learned about the pronunciation of past tense verbs on page 138 to talk about the Washington Monument.

[t]	[d]	[id]
finished	returned	voted
stopped	raised	dedicated

In this exercise you and a partner will take turns reading statements and decide if they are true or false. Be sure to pronounce the past verbs correctly. Circle TRUE *or* FALSE. *When you finish, check your answers with your teacher.*

Follow this example:

Student A reads first: George Washington served as the second president of the U.S.A.
Student B responds: That's false.
  and circles FALSE.

Student B then reads: Washington returned to his home, Mount Vernon, on the Mississippi River.
Student A responds: That's false.
  and circles FALSE.

Student A: *Look here and cover the right side of the page.*

Student B: *Look here and cover the left side of the page.*

1. George Washington served [d] as the second president of the U.S.A.

1. TRUE   FALSE

2. TRUE   FALSE

2. Washington returned [d] to his home, Mount Vernon, on the Mississippi River.

3. Washington died [d] in 1700.

3. TRUE   FALSE

4. TRUE   FALSE

4. The House of Representatives voted [id] to spend $200,000 to build a monument to Washington.

5. The Washington National Monument Society raised [d] all the money needed to build the monument.

5. TRUE   FALSE

6. TRUE   FALSE

6. Construction on the monument stopped [t] in the 1850s.

7. Congress voted [id] to spend $200,000 to complete the monument in 1876.

7. TRUE   FALSE

8. TRUE   FALSE

8. The Army Corps of Engineers finished [t] the monument in 1888.

9. The monument was dedicated [id] in 1876.

9. TRUE   FALSE

10. TRUE   FALSE

10. The Washington Monument opened [d] to the public the same year it was finished.

PUT IT TOGETHER

Present Tense Sentence Combinations

Work with your classmates to combine the following into sentences about the monuments and landmarks you learned about in this chapter. How many sentences can you make? All of the verbs are present tense.

		in Chicago.
The Gateway Arch		four presidents.
		an observation deck.
The Empire State Building		freedom and opportunity.
	are	in Seattle.
The Golden Gate Bridge		New York.
		"Man in Space"
The Lincoln Memorial	is	The gateway to the West.
		two towers.
Mount Rushmore		bright orange.
	symbolizes	in New York Harbor.
The Sears Tower		a suspension bridge.
		Abraham Lincoln.
The Space Needle	honors	a restaurant on top.
		in South Dakota.
The Washington Monument	has	in New York.
		the first president of the United States.
The World Trade Center		between San Francisco and Marin County.
	have	in Washington, D.C.
The Statue of Liberty		The tallest building in the world.
		in St. Louis.

Tic Tac Toe

Play Tic Tac Toe with the names of the monuments and landmarks. Your teacher will make a tic-tac-toe grid on the blackboard and fill in the names of 9 of the places in this chapter. Choose a place and make a good sentence to receive the X or O. Follow the directions on page 37.

Cloze 🔲

Read the following information about the Washington Monument. Try to fill in the blanks with the correct word. After you have filled in as much as you can, listen to the lecture on the cassette again as many times as necessary to fill in all the blanks.

The Story Behind the Washington Monument

George Washington _____ as the first president of the United States from 1789 to 1797. After that, he returned to his _____ on the Potomac River, Mount Vernon, _____ he died two years later. The whole _____ mourned his death, and the _____ of Representatives quickly voted to spend $200,000 to _____ a monument to Washington in the capital _____. But the Senate did not _____ the expenditure, and interest in building a _____ died for 33 years. Then, in 1833, the Washington National Monument Society was _____ to build a monument with private money. By 1847, $87,000 had been raised, and _____ started on July 4, 1848. Construction stopped when funds ran out in the _____ of the 1850s, and it was _____ to continue construction during the Civil War. Then, with the _____ of the country's centennial in 1876, Congress voted to _____ $200,000 to complete the monument. The Army Corps of Engineers _____ building the monument, and on December 6, 1884, the capstone was set, completing the 555-foot tall _____ obelisk. It was dedicated on February 21, 1885, and opened to the _____ three years later. _____ can travel to the top of the monument by elevator, where they have an impressive view of Washington, D.C. from the monument's eight _____ .

ON YOUR OWN ON VACATION IN THE U.S.A.

Here are some activities related to vacation and leisure activities for you to do on your own, with a small group, or with your whole class.

1. Plan and give a 5-minute presentation on one or more National Parks to your classmates. Find information in the library, call or write the National Park Service, or ask a travel agent for information. Bring pictures, maps, and other visual aids to class to make your presentation more interesting.

2. If there is an office or unit of the National Park Service near you, invite a Park Ranger to come and speak to your class.

3. Plan a trip to a local park. Find out if it is part of the National Park system, a state park, or a city park. When you return to class, discuss the recreation activities and other programs available at the park.

4. Investigate camping opportunities near you. Does your college or university have an outdoors club? Find out if they have a camping or hiking trip planned. Invite a representative from the club to speak to your class on opportunities for outdoor recreation.

5. Have a sing-along of campfire songs. Check out a songbook from the library, and find someone who can play the guitar. Copy the words for everyone; the melodies are easy to learn. If the weather (and local laws!) permit, build a campfire and roast marshmallows while you sing.

6. Find out about a nearby amusement park. Look in a newspaper for advertisements and visit a local tourist information center for a brochure. Find out information such as prices, open hours, location, and number and type of rides, shows, and exhibits. Share the information with your classmates. Plan a trip to the amusement park, when you return to class, discuss what you saw.

7. Prepare and give a 5-minute presentation on the life and work of Walt Disney or on Disneyland or Walt Disney World. Find information in the library or in the travel section of a bookstore. Use visual aids such as pictures, or prepare a poster, overhead, or handout to help your classmates understand your presentation.

8. If you are living close to one of the landmarks or monuments in Chapter 21, plan a visit. Share what you learned when you return to class.

9. If you cannot visit one of the landmarks in Chapter 21, find out about the most important monuments or landmarks in the city or town where you are studying. What or who does it honor or symbolize? What is the history behind it? Work with your classmates to write a letter to the authors of this textbook stating why the monument or landmark should be included in future editions of this book.

10. Chapter 21 contains a description of the Washington Monument. Choose one of the other nine monuments or landmarks in the chapter, and prepare a similar description of it. You can find information in the library, using the encyclopedia or other reference materials. Also, the children's and young adult's section of the library often has easy-to-understand materials. Share what you learn with your classmates in a 5-minute presentation. Be sure to bring visual aids to your presentation to make it more interesting.

Notes:

Notes:

Notes:

Notes:

Notes:

Notes:

Notes:

Notes:

Notes:

Notes:

Notes: